LENDER LIABILITY

ENVIRONMENTAL RISK AND DEBT

by John Jarvis QC and Michael Fordham

Published by CAMERON MAY
in association with
The United Kingdom
Environmental Law Association

First published 1993

Cameron May Ltd.
4 Rita Road
London SW8 1JU

ISBN 1 874698 05 8

Printed by Island Press Ltd. 0323 490222 UK.
3 Cradle Hill Industrial Estate,
Seaford, East Sussex BN25 3JE

Contents

PART III: LENDER LIABILITY

PART IV: LENDER SELF-PROTECTION

FOREWORD

Environmental responsibility is a major issue for us all as we confront the historical legacies of earlier generations for whom the environment was a free resource just waiting to be tapped. Those days are now behind us and together we must develop new strategies which solve our past difficulties and prevent repetition of similar scenarios in the future.

As providers of the nation's capital, the financial services industry has a key role to play in bringing about such change by encouraging its customers to strive towards environmental best practice.

This book has been written not simply for environmental lawyers but also for banking and insolvency practitioners. The sheer volume of environmental legislation at the local, national and international levels is daunting, as is the potential for liability to affect existing security. In order to avoid falling from the legal tightrope which links environmental due diligence and shadow directorships, lenders must develop sound, responsible practices which allow them effectively to manage the direct and indirect risks associated with environmental issues, of which contingent liability is one of the most crucial.

At the same time, we must also allow our economy to prosper if we are to pay for the improvements we seek. A clear, unambiguous and long-term legal framework will be an integral part of this success, but is still some way away from development. In the interregnum, this book should help members of the financial services industry and their clients through the maze of current legislation. In so doing it will enable responsible and prudent decision-making.

Lord Alexander of Weedon QC
Chairman
National Westminster Bank Plc

TABLE OF CASES

TABLE OF STATUTES

TABLE OF STATUTORY INSTRUMENTS

PART I

OVERVIEW

CHAPTER 1

INTRODUCTION

"Lender liability" for environmental harm is a concept unknown to English law. There is no domestic statutory provision which states, or reported case which decides, that a bank is liable for pollution. But, as will be shown, there is sufficient to justify the existence of this book. The ingredients, as it were, are available. To pursue the metaphor, the question is whether environmental advocates can produce a recipe sufficiently appetising for domestic courts to stomach.

The initial reaction of a banker may be that this is scaremongering and that the development of 'lender liability' is not imminent, though it is interesting that major banks are already opening "Environmental Management Units". What will be considered in this book are the risks for lenders, and opportunities for environmentalists. We will also discuss the ways in which lenders can guard against environmental liability. Of course one irony is that if lenders take the risks seriously, and take adequate steps to avoid them, 'lender liability' may not develop.

Why should 'lender liability' develop? Banks do not pollute rivers. Why should they be responsible for the activities of their borrowers ? If someone buys a car and kills a pedestrian the bank which provided the loan is not held responsible.

Should it be enough, then, that the lender could have prevented the pollution, by refusing to lend or by supervising the activities of its borrower ? What if the lender knew about the polluting process, or act? What if its loan officer was a member of the borrower's board, or the loan terms allowed it to authorise the borrower's dealings or to collect his debts ?

The lender may have provided the funds to allow the activity to continue, and may have made considerable profits from that activity itself. Some lenders are in a position of great control: factoring companies for instance, and mortgagees in possession. Banks are in an excellent position to assess the nature of the activities of those with whom they deal. The concept of 'lender liability' encourages them to insist on strict environmental assessment, and proof of compliance with legal requirements. The paradox is that attaching direct liability to lenders may be seen either to encourage, or discourage, such scrutiny.

In the discussion which follows the terms 'lender' and 'liability' are intended to convey a broad definition. This book addresses much more than the question whether a bank may be fined for its borrower's pollution or made to pay the clean-up costs which result.

The risks which we will discuss concern two main phases: lending and debt-collecting. By "lender" we therefore mean a person concerned with either of these. We include, then, any person involved with monitoring the status of debtors, deciding whether and when to enforce security and recoup debts, and conducting the process for doing so. The role of receivers is particularly significant. First, because they are involved in debt-collection and security-enforcement. Secondly, because a bank-appointed receiver's liabilities may have to be paid by the bank, if (or unless) there is the appropriate indemnity.

This is, then, a book intended not only for those who are or who advise bankers, but also for mortgagees, debenture-holders, receivers and administrators. Accordingly we frequently use the generic term "lender" to include the 'non-money supplier'.

As for "liability", we mean more than simply any risk on the part of the lender of direct criminal or civil responsibility at law: the prospect of a lender being fined, or made liable for clean-up costs, compensatory damages, a contribution to assets, and so on. We include the indirect but commercially vital concerns of increased exposure or vulnerability through environmental harm: for example, the risks of lending to a company likely to go out of business because of its own environmental liability or its inability to secure a relevant licence; the risks of taking security over land which becomes worthless because of its inclusion on the register of contaminated land; the risks of ranking in priority behind the borrower's massive clean-up debt owed to a regulatory authority; the risks of taking an appointment as receiver over a polluter.

At its widest, lender "liability" should embrace factors such as the following: environmental risks and the test for 'insolvency'; the prospect of insurance for environmental damage; the impact of pollution on property valuation; its impact on planning permission; and the effect of bad publicity on the polluter's business and assets.

As will be shown, lender liability is firmly established in both the United States and Canada. Moreover, there are cases in English Law in which the Courts have discussed the concept of 'lender liability' in various contexts. Here are some of the examples that will be discussed later:

- *Maguire v Leigh-on-Sea UDC* (1906) 95 LT 319: whether a mortgagee in possession of land was the appropriate person in the context of liability to pay expenses for works performed by a Local Authority under the Private Streets Act 1892.

- *Meigh v Wickenden* [1942] 2 KB 160: whether a receiver was liable for breach of statutory duty to provide a guard for machinery in a factory.

- *Solomons v Gertzenstein* [1954] 2 QB 243: whether a Law of Property Act receiver who handled rent monies was liable for breach of statutory duty to provide and maintain a fire-escape.

- *Midland Bank v Conway* [1965] 1 WLR 1165: whether a bank which handled rent monies was liable to comply with a statutory nuisance abatement notice.

- *Westminster City Council v Haymarket* [1981] 1 WLR 677: whether a mortgagee not in possession could be liable to pay a rating surcharge.

- *Standard Chartered Bank v Walker* [1982] 1 WLR 1410: whether a bank's acts in giving instructions to a receiver could be sufficient to render it liable for the receiver's acts.

- *Ratford v North Avon DC* [1987] QB 357: whether a receiver appointed under a debenture was liable for rating purposes.

- *re a Company ex parte Copp* [1989] BCLC 13; 4 BCC 424: whether a bank could be in a relationship with its borrower such as to render it liable for wrongful trading.

- *Lord Advocate v Aero Technologies* [1991] SLT 134: whether a receiver appointed under a debenture should be ordered to take steps to secure an explosives factory.

Clearly, most of these cases were decided in non-'environmental' contexts. Moreover, they consider potential 'lender liabilities' owed to a range of different people including guarantors, visitors, local authorities. However, some of them may assume a new significance in the sphere of environmental protection.

As will be shown, it is the impact of the environmental statutory regimes which make it quite conceivable that "lender liability" could arise in situations such as the following:

- A mortgagee-bank has taken possession of land which is a disused landfill site. The waste regulation authority demands entry and conducts an inspection. It finds that, unknown to anyone (least of all the bank), certain chemical reactions have taken place underground producing a large accumulation of "noxious gases". The bank is then informed that the authority has carried out extensive operations which it says were designed to avoid pollution of the environment or harm to human health, and the bank is sent a bill for the costs of the operations. Those costs far exceed the value of the land, which has by now been registered as "contaminated" and cannot be marketed. The bank is duly pursued for the clean-up costs and is found liable, as owner "for the time being" of the land. Unfortunately for the bank, it discovers that it would have had a complete defence if it had gone into possession only after ensuring that the surrender of an old waste disposal licence for the site had been formally accepted by the authority.

- A debenture-holding bank appoints a receiver over the assets of a paper-manufacturing company whose plant is on the banks of a river. Both debenture and appointment state that the receiver is agent of the company, and there is no indemnity from the bank to the receiver of any liability he incurs. The receiver allows the company's business to continue, for the time being at least, visiting from time to time but leaving operational matters to the company's employees. The bank writes to the receiver regularly and makes some suggestions about how the business should continue to operate. Unfortunately, just before the visit of the NRA inspector, the autumn leaves block up a pump and pollution pours out of a settling tank into the river. The NRA prosecutes the receiver for causing the pollution, and the bank (on the basis that it interfered with the receivership) is held liable for the receiver's acts notwithstanding the terms of the debenture and appointment.

- A factoring company lends to a metal production company. The factoring agreement enables the lender to collect the company's debts, and requires its approval of contracts and prices. The metal company is found to have no authorization from HMIP. To its surprise the factoring company finds itself prosecuted for "carrying on" the process. It is convicted by a jury and finds itself faced by a sentencing judge with an unlimited power to fine it.

- A receiver is appointed over a company which used to operate a coke-plant but which has ceased operations. He discovers that one part of the company's difficulties was that the Local Authority had served the company with a nuisance abatement notice in respect of smoke. The notice was ignored and the local authority had decided to move in to stop the problem itself. At the time of the receiver's appointment, clean-up operations were well under-way. When those operations have been completed, the receiver is sued for the costs incurred in conducting them. The Court holds that the receiver is liable as the owner "for the time being" of the land.

- A Building Society holds a Legal Charge over a residential property. It decides to go into possession when it discovers that its customer has abandoned the house and gone off (apparently sailing round the world), defaulting on his repayments. In the garden is a shed, containing leaking petrol drums and infested by rats. The neighbours complain and the Building Society is served with an abatement notice. After taking legal advice, the Building Society realises that since the "person responsible cannot be found" it is liable for the nuisance, and fearing both prosecution and liability for clean-up costs incurred by the Local Authority, complies with the notice.

- A receiver is appointed over the assets of a waste management company, whose business continues pending a sale. Recognising that there are potential liabilities, the receiver ensures that the relevant waste management licence is held, and communicates directly with the waste regulation authority who seem happy. However, an environmental pressure group brings a civil action against the receiver for damaging the environment. The receiver argues that the pressure group has neither standing nor a cause of action, but the group persuades the Court that both these matters are questions for EC law. On a reference to the European Court of Justice under Article 177 of the EC Treaty, the European Court holds that the

Environmental Protection Act is to be "interpreted in accordance with EC law", even though neither the receiver nor the company are state bodies. This means that the Act is "interpreted" as containing a completely different scheme, one contained in an EC Waste Directive which allows for a civil law action against a "deemed producer" (for damage to and impairment of the environment irrespective of fault) and grants standing to public interest groups. The case goes back to the English Court which awards damages against the receiver.

- One of the customers of a reputable bank is a large chemical company. The bank decides that in order to avoid any possibility of liability itself, it will distance itself completely from the company's management and operations. The NRA becomes both exasperated and emboldened, having discovered that the company has persistently ignored its repeated warnings about river pollution from the plant. The authority gathers together compelling information which shows that the company has deliberately decided to continue the process at the plant, taking the attitude that it will be able to pay any fine and still make massive profits. Completely out of the blue, the bank finds itself served with a 'criminal Mareva order', freezing all of the company's assets. There is no term in the order providing for payment of the bank's reasonable expenses of compliance. The bank succeeds in applying to vary the order in one respect, namely to allow it to combine the company's accounts (using the credit balance on some to reduce the indebtedness on others). The company is later committed by magistrates, convicted by a jury and sentenced by the Crown Court to a large fine. Most importantly, the judge is outraged by the company's conduct and makes a confiscation order requiring that the entire profits from the chemical process which caused the pollution be seized. In subsequent litigation the Court holds that the confiscation order has priority over the bank's position as unsecured creditor. The company goes into liquidation and the bank's debts go largely unpaid. In the press the bank is branded as having supported the business of an "ecological vandal".

- A receiver is about to be appointed under a bank's debenture. The company's business involves the disposal of waste and the receiver, prior to taking the appointment, sensibly ensures that the appropriate waste management licence is held. The company continues to trade and the waste disposal operations remain in the hands of the company's site foreman. When the waste regulation authority carries out a spot-check it discovers that oil waste is being deposited at the site without being covered with overburden, as required by one of the terms of the licence. The authority serves a waste removal notice on the receiver. The costs of compliance will be enormous and the receiver applies to have the notice quashed on the grounds that he did not "deposit, knowingly cause or knowingly permit" the illegal deposit. The Court refuses to grant the application, concluding that the receiver was responsible for the operation of the plant, had the power to ensure compliance with the conditions, and that it is sufficient that the receiver knew that the deposit of waste was taking place: he need not have known that the deposit was in breach of the licence.

- A petro-chemical company has gone into liquidation. Its secured creditors include a bank. During the liquidation it transpires that the NRA has obtained a Court order against the company for clean-up costs relating to pollution by the company of a nearby estuary. The question of priority is litigated and the bank is postponed after the authority, on the basis that the clean-up liability is not to be viewed as a debt but a "public duty".

Although these examples may appear distant and over-imaginative, they are all examples of "lender liabilities" which it would be open for an English court to recognise.

This book is not intended to be a definitive analysis of the substantive law. Moreover in many instances it will be necessary to anticipate future trends in this area of the law. The aim is to describe the aspects of environmental law of which practitioners should be aware. That means bringing together several things, including illustrations of lender liability from North America, a summary of the significance and content of EC environmental law, and a description of the themes of the domestic common law and statutory regimes.

We will then look in more detail at the 'trigger terms' of the most important parts of the statutory framework, notably the Environmental Protection Act 1990 (EPA) and the Water Resources Act 1991 (WRA). These include terms such as "carrying on", "causing", "permitting", "owner", "occupier". We consider them not just to ask whether and when lenders may be at risk of themselves becoming liable for environmental harm, but also to give a flavour of the jurisprudence and themes of environmental protection. After all, whether the Courts will countenance direct lender liability will depend not just on opportunities presented by construction arguments, but also on the strength of judicial policy motivation, and in particular, the extent to which judges are prepared to indulge in 'the hunt for the deeper pocket'.

The 'trigger terms' discussion may be branded speculative. Those able to wait for the benefit of hindsight will be in the best position of course to assess the force of what we say. Lenders are not among them. The perspective of banks in particular is necessarily long-term: lending money is necessarily a prospective exercise. Prudent bankers need to know the nature of the risks now. Of course, the risks may not crystallise. Indeed, this may be precisely because of precautionary steps taken by lenders.

To urge this 'new faith' on lenders, that they should be aware of the principles and machinery of environmental liability, may be said then to be based upon a certain amount of speculation. Speculative it may be. Sensible it certainly is. It is true that there is no express lender liability provision in the EPA or the WRA. But as will be seen, that is what American lenders said to themselves about CERCLA. They were in for a shock.

Finally, we will suggest some practical ways in which lenders can protect themselves against liability for environmental damage. In this respect we follow on from some of the general articles on the subject (see eg. Bryce, *Environmental Liability: Practical Issues for Lenders* 1992 4 Journal of International Banking Law 131; Beringer & Thomas, *Lenders & Environmental Liability* Practical Law for Companies, November 1991 p.3), to whose authors we are grateful.

CHAPTER 2

A TRANS-ATLANTIC GLANCE

(1) The US : Superfund and *Fleet Factors*

It may be asked why UK lenders, and those who advise them, should take any notice of developments in the United States. Is it a matter of relevance only to UK lenders whose clients are involved in American industry ?

In the first place there is the obvious relevance to those whose commercial activities have an international flavour. Many a Lloyds name must wish he or his syndicate had been more aware of the risks involved in reinsuring American pollution liabilities. The international banking community will have taken note of the experiences of the international insurance market.

But secondly and more importantly, the United States provides the furthest-developed illustration of primary lender liability. American lenders have found themselves responsible for clean-up costs arising from the polluting activities of their borrowers. The US has therefore become a forum for vigorous argument as to lender liability issues and the balancing of the policy questions arising. The irony is that it all came from a statutory scheme which imposed no specific obligation on lenders, and indeed provided a specific defence for them. The US experience is an illustration of what can happen as a result of a judicial resolve based on notions of policy commitment and practical necessity. We will tell the story so far, in outline form.

Superfund

The framework of environmental protection in the US is found in a series of individual enactments and, significantly, one comprehensive clean-up scheme. That scheme (known as "Superfund") was enacted in 1980 in the form of the Comprehensive Environmental Response, Compensation and Liability Act 1980 (CERCLA) and amended by the Superfund Amendments and Reauthorisation Act 1986 (SARA).

As its name suggests, the scheme centres around an enormous environmental trust fund (of some $8.5 billion). The United States Environmental Protection Agency (USEPA) is empowered by

CERCLA to move into a contaminated site and conduct clean-up operations using monies from the fund. The choice of means and needs is in the discretion of USEPA (see eg. *United States v Northeastern Pharmaceutical* 810 F.2d 726 (8th Cir. 1986)).

The clean-up costs are then recoverable from "potentially responsible parties" (CERCLA § 9601). Clean-up costs include the following: all costs of removal and remedial action incurred by USEPA; "any other necessary costs"; compensation for injury, loss or destruction to natural resources; and cost of health assessments (§ 9607(a)).

The American experience is instructive because of the sheer size of the stakes. It is said that USEPA's average clean-up costs are around $25 million. Moreover, those costs frequently far exceed the extent of any debts and the market value of the land concerned.

Liability under CERCLA is strict, requiring no proof of fault. It is also retroactive, applying to pollution which occurred prior to its enactment. It attaches to a person who is "owner or operator" of contaminated land or a contaminating facility or who arranges for the disposal or treatment of hazardous substances (CERCLA § 9607(a)).

The CERCLA net is wide. There is a prohibition on attempts to contract out of liability, including by way of an indemnity (§ 9607(e)(1)). Liability can rest at the door of more than one person, including present and past owners or operators; stockholders; officers; managers; etc. The liability is joint and several.

There is a defence for the "innocent landowner" who can show that the pollution was caused by a third party or previous owner/occupier (§ 9607(b)(3)). However, built into the defence is a rigorous "due diligence" requirement, that the landowner "did not know or had no reason to know" the site was (being) contaminated. Accordingly, an 'innocent purchaser' is one who has taken adequate (that is, thorough, and expensive) steps to conduct an environmental assessment of the land.

The 'deeper pocket' opportunities of CERCLA are obvious. The question was and is to what extent those opportunities could extend to dipping into what is often the deepest pocket: the polluter's banker, or a mortgagee/receiver of the contaminated land.

It is significant that when CERCLA was adopted in 1980 it was not heralded as introducing lender liability. CERCLA was widely received with a self-confidence on the part of lenders that 'it cannot mean us'. It could, and did. Whether the impact of CERCLA as it has been applied by the US Courts is a justified shock to complacent lenders, or the product of an over-enthusiastic search for the 'deeper pocket', may not matter. It is enough to say that CERCLA as it has been interpreted has provoked a dramatic surge of lobbying activity from increasingly anxious American lenders.

The secured creditor exemption

Perhaps the main reason for the self-assurance of lenders in the face of CERCLA was that the Act contained a provision designed specifically to protect creditors holding security over contaminated land. The 'secured creditor exemption' (CERCLA § 9601(20)(a)) provides that a person is not an "owner or operator" who:

> "without participating in the management of [the] facility, holds indicia of ownership primarily to protect his security interest in the ... facility".

This appeared to be a 'green light' for a lender enforcing its security. And if security-enforcement was protected, then it would seem to follow that general monitoring of the creditor, designed to facilitate the decision of whether or when to enforce security would be protected too. Of course, it all depended on what was meant by "participating in the management".

The Mirabile test

In this respect, some degree of comfort for lenders came in the early judicial interpretation of that key phrase, in *United States v Mirabile* 15 ELR 20994 (E.D. Pa 1985). There, a clean-up costs' application was brought against three creditors. The Court held that the secured creditor exemption protected two of them but that there was a triable issue as to the third:

- Creditor 1 was a foreclosing mortgagee who was exempt on the basis that its activities were characterised as 'routine and prudent steps to secure the mortgaged property against further depreciation'. Those activities had included securing the property against vandalism; making enquiries as to the costs of disposing of drums of toxins; monitoring cash collateral accounts; and ensuring receivables went to the proper accounts.

- Creditor 2, who was also exempt, had provided management assistance: monitoring the company's liquidation, requiring approval prior to the execution of contracts for management consultancy services, and restricting certain business dealings.

- Creditor 3, whose involvement was held to raise a triable issue, was a bank who had been represented on the borrower's advisory board and (more importantly) whose loan officer was said to have had "post-bankruptcy oversight of the company". To lenders, an example of every silver lining having its cloud.

The vital distinction drawn in *Mirabile* was between "participation in purely financial aspects of operations" and "participation in operational, production or waste disposal activities". Only the latter voided the secured creditor exemption.

This distinction was applied to the further comfort of lenders in *Guidice v BFG Electroplating & Manufacturing Co.* 732 F Supp 556 (W.D. Pa 1989) where the Court held a bank exempt in respect of its pre-foreclosure activities. Those activities had included the following: having representatives attend meetings where they were informed of the presence of raw materials; communicating with local officials as to wastewater discharge compliance; inspecting the property after operations had stopped; making attempts at restructuring the lending; and communicating with a proposed purchaser regarding waste dumping approval. All these matters were held to be steps directed at protecting the security interest rather than controlling the operation, production of waste disposal activities of the facility. However, the bank was not held exempt in respect of the post-foreclosure period, it having purchased the site at the 'foreclosure sale'.

Significantly, the Court in *Mirabile* had rejected "mere financial ability to control waste disposal practices" as a trigger to liability, resisting the temptations presented by policy considerations including the 'deeper pocket', and stating (at 20996):

> "Obviously, imposition of liability on secured creditors or lending institutions would enhance the government's chances of recovering its cleanup costs, given the fact that owners and occupiers of hazardous waste dumpsites are often elusive, defunct or otherwise judgment proof. It may well be that the

> imposition of such liability would help to ensure more responsible management of such sites. The consideration of such policy matters, and the decision as to the imposition of such liability, however, lies with Congress. In enacting CERCLA Congress singled out secured creditors for protection from liability under certain circumstances."

The first real suggestion that *Mirabile* might be too favourable to lenders had come in *United States v Maryland Bank & Trust* 632 F. Supp. 573 (D. Md. 1986). On the face of it that case was concerned simply with acquisition following foreclosure (and so is perfectly consistent with *Guidice*). The Court found that at the time of the clean-up the creditor bank's interest in the land had ripened into title, its acquisition of the site at the foreclosure sale being a step taken "not to protect its security interest but to protect its investment".

It was the policy-basis of *US v Maryland Bank* which was more revealing, and capable of deployment beyond its foreclosure context. Problems as to the wording of CERCLA were sidestepped as concerning "grammar" in the context of a "hastily conceived compromise statute". The Court considered its stance as a refusal to "carve a judicially-created loophole in the statutory structure" (by putting a mortgagee in a better position than a purchaser), and designed to encourage 'prudent lending' (at 580):

> "At the foreclosure sale, the mortgagee could acquire the property cheaply. All other prospective purchasers would be faced with potential CERCLA liability, and would shy away from the sale. Yet once the property has been cleared at the taxpayers' expense and becomes marketable, the mortgagee-turned-owner would be in a position to sell the site at a profit. In essence, the defendant's position would convert CERCLA into an insurance scheme for financial institutions, protecting them against possible losses due to the security of loans with polluted properties. Mortgagees, however, already have the means to protect themselves, by making prudent loans. Financial institutions are in a position to investigate and discover potential problems in their secured properties. For many lending institutions, such research is routine. CERCLA will not absolve them from responsibility for their mistakes of judgment."

The seriousness of CERCLA for lenders was becoming obvious. Ironically perhaps, on the one hand even the *Mirabile* test attracted criticism and concern. It was seen as providing inadequate protection for banks generally (see eg. Tom, *Interpreting the Meaning of Lender Management Under Section 101(20(A) of CERCLA*, 98 Yale LJ 925 (1989), advocating a test of "total domination" for "participating in management"). And special concern was voiced in respect of lenders under schemes entitling them to share the borrower's profits (see eg. Malloy, *Equity Participations and Lender Liability Under CERCLA*, Columbia Journal of Environmental Law Vol. 15 p.63 (1990)).

On the other hand, and more worrying to the lender, was the prospect of a shift from *Mirabile*. Whether or not hinted at in *US v Maryland Bank*, it was a shift executed in the landmark decision of *United States v Fleet Factors Corporation* 901 F 2d 1550 (11th Cir. 1990).

US v Fleet Factors

Fleet Factors was a 'strike-out' action by a defendant lender in respect of USEPA proceedings for clean-up costs of some $400,000. The 11th Circuit Court of Appeals held that the claim disclosed a good cause of action, rejecting the *Mirabile* test, and holding that a lender is liable for clean-up costs where its participation in a facility's financial management reveals "a capacity to influence" the borrower's treatment of waste (at 1557-8):

> "It is not necessary for the secured creditor actually to involve itself in the day-to-day operations of the facility in order to be liable although such conduct will certainly lead to the loss of the protection of the statutory exemption. Nor is it necessary for the secured creditor to participate in management decisions relating to hazardous waste. Rather, a secured creditor will be liable if its involvement with the management of the facility is sufficiently broad to support the inference that it could affect hazardous waste disposal decisions if it so chose."

The defendant in *US v Fleet Factors*, as is obvious from the name, was a lender under a factoring agreement. Its security included an assignment of future profits enabling it to collect the borrower's receivables. Its "participation" under the agreement had included the following: approval of goods shipped; price setting; control of access to the facility and supervising of office administration, tax forms, and redundancy. The Court held that all this was enough to render Fleet Factors the "owner" or "operator" of the site and, vitally, to take it outside the secured creditor exemption. Fleet's argument based upon the *Mirabile* interpretation was rejected as too permissive an approach.

The Court in *Fleet Factors* did seek to comfort lenders in two respects. First, it had rejected as too narrow the interpretation suggested by USEPA, that any manner of "participation" would suffice to preclude exemption. The Court acknowledged that this interpretation (at 1556):

> "would largely eviscerate the exemption Congress intended to afford to secured creditors. Secured lenders frequently have some involvement in the financial affairs of their debtors in order to insure that their interests are being adequately protected. To adopt the government's interpretation of the secured creditor exemption could expose all such lenders to CERCLA liability for engaging in their normal course of business."

Secondly, the Court stated that lender liability would not be triggered by a secured creditor's conduct in "monitoring any aspect of a debtor's business" or becoming "involved in occasional and discrete financial decisions relating to the protection of its security" or giving "specific, management advice" to the debtor.

Nevertheless, the Court showed itself as primarily concerned with the "overwhelmingly remedial" goal of CERCLA and the desire to promote green lending. It wanted to "encourage potential creditors to investigate thoroughly the waste treatment systems and policies of potential debtors" and "to monitor the hazardous waste treatment systems and policies of their debtors and insist upon compliance with acceptable treatment standards as a prerequisite to continued and future financial support".

The CERCLA dilemma

As will be obvious, *US v Fleet Factors* presents a dilemma for lenders, and in turn illustrates a dilemma for the Courts. From the lender's point-of-view, it wants both to closely monitor its borrower, and distance itself from his activities. It needs to know when to support, or bring to an end, the borrower's activities, though primarily for commercial rather than environmental reasons. On the other hand, it wants to keep as detached from those activities as possible, for fear of being made liable for massive clean-up costs.

From the Court's point of view the dilemma is that it wants to both encourage participatory lending, and penalise it. The more involved and knowledgeable the lender is, the more likely it is to stop the pollution, again for commercial reasons. But the more involved it is, the more 'culpable' it is if it does not stop the pollution. Rich lenders' pockets may be the most convenient source for putting matters right. The trouble is that attaching liability to the "involved" lender may not lead to the desired result, indeed to its reverse. Instead of producing lenders who "scrutinize" and "supervise" their borrowers, refusing to lend to polluters, it could produce lenders who deliberately avoid "scrutiny" or "supervision", but lend the money that allows the pollution to continue nevertheless.

The Fleet Factors aftermath

There has been some subsequent judicial uneasiness with *Fleet Factors*. Notably *re Bergsoe Metal Corporation* 910 F. 2d 668 (9th Cir. 1990), where the capacity test was rejected: "what is critical is not what rights the [secured creditor] had, but what it did". There the lender was a government body which had investigated the borrower prior to the loan and retained the right to re-enter and foreclose on default. The Court held that these were steps essential to any loan practice which if interpreted as "participating in management" would render the secured creditor exemption meaningless. However, the US Supreme Court is seen to have endorsed *US v Fleet Factors*, by allowing it to stand without comment (111 S. Ct. 752 (1991)).

The American lending community, in the meantime, was sent into something of a panic, with immediate lobbying resulting in the sponsoring of several Bills designed to alleviate the effect of *Fleet Factors* and to seek to resolve the CERCLA dilemma, including:

- Senate Proposal: Asset Conservation and Deposit Insurance Protection Act of 1991 S.543 102d Cong. 1st Sess. § 1001 (1991) ("Title X"), proposing that lenders' liability be limited to the actual benefit conferred on the lender by removal of hazardous substances from the property, up to the fair market value, but imposing 'due diligence' requirements on a lender (essentially a pre-lending environmental audit);

- House Bill 1450 H.R. 1450 102d Cong. 1st Sess. (1991), proposing an amendment to "owner or operator" to clarify the need for actual participation in the management of the facility;

- Senate Bill 651 S.651 102d Cong. 1st Sess (1991) proposing an amendment to Federal Banking Laws to limit environmental liability of financial institutions who are not themselves responsible for the contamination.

Most importantly perhaps, the response to *US v Fleet Factors* was such that USEPA felt moved to draft its own "Rule" regarding the interpretation of the secured creditor exemption.

USEPA's Lender Liability Rule

USEPA's Rule, then, is its own attempt to resolve the CERCLA dilemma and pacify anxious lenders, together with those who 'underwrote' their liabilities (notably the Resolution Trust Corporation and Federal Deposit Insurance Corporation). It was published in April 1992 (57 Fed Reg 18,344 (1992)).

The Rule has three purposes: first to make clear that all bona fide security interests fall within the secured creditor exemption; second to urge pre-lending environmental assessment for all loans secured on commercial or industrial properties; and third to list instances when a creditor is taken to "participate" (or not) in the management of a facility. Crucially, it is stated not to be sufficient that the lender has "the mere capacity, or ability to influence, or the unexercised right to control facility operations".

That central statement makes the Rule appear to represent a deliberate antidote to the *Fleet Factors* decision. Of course the very fact that the US Supreme Court has (silently) endorsed *US v Fleet Factors*, would support those who question the legal status of USEPA's Rule. The confusion is perhaps compounded by USEPA's insistence that the Rule is "consistent with principles expressed in the caselaw" and is not "an attempt to administratively overrule" *Fleet Factors*. Interestingly, the *Fleet Factors* litigation, stayed pending the formulation of the Rule, seems set to recommence with USEPA asserting lender liability.

In terms of principle, USEPA's Rule contrasts the lender which has "the mere capacity, or ability to influence, or the unexercised right to control facility operations" (exempt) with two other kinds of lender (not exempt). The first non-exempt lender is one who "exercises decision-making control over the borrower's environmental compliance" (that is, "responsibility for the borrower's hazardous substance handling or disposal practices"). The second is one who "exercises control at a level comparable to that of manager of the borrower's enterprise" (that is, so as to have "assumed or manifested responsibility for the overall management of the enterprise encompassing ... day-to-day decision-making") regarding either "environmental compliance or ... all or substantially all of the operational (as opposed to financial or administrative) aspects of the enterprise".

Finally, there are the specific examples given in the Rule as to when lenders can expect to retain the exemption. It is worth outlining some of these, if for no other reason than because they reveal an approach to lender liability which it would be open for domestic law to adopt. They relate loosely to 3 different chronological stages.

First, prior to the making of a loan the lender is free to take any steps without fear of liability. Specifically, it can:

- undertake or require an environmental inspection of property (it being made clear that the lender need not conduct such an exercise in order to qualify for exemption); and

- require the borrower to clean up the facility or comply with environmental regulation.

Second, during the term of the loan the lender can:

- inspect the facility;

- monitor the borrower's business and financial position;

- require the borrower to comply with environmental regulations, including any clean-up obligation;

- provide financial advice;

- take steps to prevent the effects of a default by the borrower; and

- prevent a diminution in value of the property.

Third, when enforcing security, the lender can:

- take title to or possession of the facility, if taken primarily to protect the security interest, and providing the lender then takes "commercially reasonable means" to "divest itself of the property in a reasonably expeditious manner" (the Rule provides certain conditions in this respect, including advertising the property and a duty to accept a bona fide offer);

- maintain business activities at a facility after foreclosure (if directed towards protecting the security interest); and

- take steps to prepare the property for sale.

(2) Canada: *Northern Badger*

We pluck from Canadian law one excellent illustration of lender liability in its broadest sense, which is of particular concern to receivers and secured creditors. It is the decision of the Alberta Court of Appeal in *Panamericana De Bienes Y Servicos v Northern Badger Oil & Gas Ltd* (1991) 81 DLR (4th) 280.

Two points of introduction should be made. First, English Courts will readily take account of Canadian authorities. Second, even were the *Northern Badger* decision confined, as turning on the workings of the Canadian statutory regime for corporate insolvency, the approach and policy considerations underpinning it could well appear in domestic litigation.

The case concerned a Receiver of a facility which included seven oil wells. The Receiver had been Court-appointed, but on an application by a debenture-holding lender. He had collected some C$226,000 and was applying to the Court for a discharge, to enable him to use the money to pay off secured creditors and his own fees, with the residual balance being passed on to the trustee in bankruptcy.

The dispute arose because the Canadian Energy Resources Conservation Board (ERCB) had obtained an Order in Council requiring the Receiver to take steps to protect the environment: essentially a shutting-down and cleaning-up operation (known as "abandonment") in respect of the seven oil wells. Compliance with the Order in Council would exceed C$200,000 in cost, leaving very little for the secured creditors and the Receiver fees.

This was very clearly 'environmental law meets insolvency law'. The secured creditors and Receiver were potentially extremely exposed, the crux of the case being the question of 'priority' between them and the ERCB's clean-up order.

At first instance ((1989) 75 Alta LR (2d) 185), the lender won. MacPherson J held that the ERCB was "a creditor seeking to have its claim preferred to the claim of the secured creditor", and that such a "preference" was contrary to the insolvency legislation. The ERCB's claim was characterised simply as "a claim provable in bankruptcy". There was no reason to require the Receiver to carry out the clean-up: the ERCB was entitled to do so itself and seek to recover the debt from the Company, but would rank as unsecured creditor. The Receiver was discharged and directed to pay off the secured creditor notwithstanding the Order In Council.

The lender's relief was short-lived. The ERCB's appeal succeeded, and if 'insolvency law' had won at first instance, then 'environmental law' certainly won on appeal. The Court of Appeal held that the Receiver was obliged to use the moneys held to comply with the Order in Council.

The Court of Appeal characterised the issue not as whether the ERCB was avoiding the statutory priority scheme, but whether the Receiver was under a duty to shut-down and clean-up the oil wells in accordance with "the general law". The Court emphasized the significance of the clean-up duty, "enacted to protect the environment and for the health and safety of all citizens"; "owed as a public duty by all the citizens of the community to their fellow citizens".

The ERCB in turn was characterised not as a creditor with a debt provable in the insolvency, but "a public authority given the duty of enforcing a public law". There being no "creditor", there was no question of "subverting" the insolvency scheme. In this regard, there was a hint that things would have been different had the ERCB been seeking to enforce an order for clean-up costs which it had itself already incurred, rather than an order that the Receiver carry out the clean-up operations. We will return to this point in Chapter 7.

Strong policy considerations led the Court to an approach the gist of which was a notion of 'taking the rough with the smooth' akin to the approach in *US v Maryland Bank* in the US (above). Here the idea was that a Receiver (like a lender) who 'moves in' on a site cannot "pick and choose": taking the benefit of property while leaving the (environmental) liabilities for the public to bear.

Laycraft C.J.A., who delivered the judgment of the Court of Appeal, stated (at 297-8) that:

"The Receiver has had complete control of the wells and has operated them since May 1987, when it was appointed Receiver and Manager of them. It has carried on for more than three years activities with respect to the wells which only a licensee is authorised to do under the provisions of the Oil and Gas Conservation Act. In that position, it cannot pick and choose whether an operation is profitable or not in deciding whether to carry it out. If one of the wells of which the Receiver has chosen to take control should blow out of control or catch fire, for example, it would be a remarkable rule of law which would permit him to walk away from the disaster saying simply that remedial action would diminish distribution to secured creditors."

This direct "operation" of the facility by the Receiver clearly made the decision easier to justify, and may be an attempt to resolve a CERCLA-type dilemma through a notion of 'culpability' akin to its US counterpart "participation in the management of the facility" (above).

However, as is pointed out in Patrick Fettig's note on *Panamericana v Northern Badger* (see (1991) 11 JIBL 476), the presence or absence of such "operation" by the Receiver would not seem to affect the 'priority' issue (between secured creditors and the ERCB's Order), since the ERCB could have obtained an Order whether or not the Receiver had operated the facility. Nor, on one view, would it affect the principle of 'taking the rough with the smooth', since the facility could (and would) have had environmental liabilities whether or not the Receiver had operated the facility after his appointment.

It may well be that the true spirit of *Panamericana v Northern Badger* is that a 'lender liability' attaches where a receiver accepts an appointment over a polluting facility. The argument would be that the appointment itself presents the receiver "complete control" and that it is not necessary that he has "operated" the facility thereafter. Clearly, this would be a *US v Fleet Factors*-type approach, based on the capacity to control.

Such an interpretation of the case draws some support from the following passage (found at 298):

"While the Receiver was in control of the wells, there was no other entity with whom the board could deal. An order addressed to Northern Badger would have been fruitless. That is so because, by order of the court, upon the application of the debenture-holder, neither Northern Badger nor its trustee in bankruptcy had any right even to enter the well sites or to undertake any operation with respect to them. Moreover, under the regulatory scheme for Alberta oil wells, only a licensee is entitled to produce oil and gas. The Receiver cannot be heard to say that, while functioning as a licensee to produce the wells and to profit from them, it assumed none of a licensee's obligations ..."

The idea here, that environmental responsibility attaches where the lender had the ability to control the site and was the appropriate person with whom the policing authority could deal, may emerge as a general theme of lender liability. It was an approach fortified in *Panamericana v Northern Badger* by the evidence: there had been various letters from the ERCB to the Receiver, from which the Court concluded (at 294) that:

"it is clear that almost from the commencement of the receivership, the Receiver was aware of the obligation in law, of Northern Badger to see the oil and gas wells properly abandoned ..."

We think it would be a grave mistake to conclude that the lesson to be learned from *Panamericana v Northern Badger* is that Canadian Court-appointed receivers should think hard before continuing to operate a potentially polluting facility. The lesson may be of a more general nature, and may start at the earlier stage: that all receivers should think hard before accepting an appointment over a potentially polluting facility, and should insist first on a full environmental audit and an adequate indemnity.

CHAPTER 3

A CROSS-CHANNEL GLANCE

(1) The relevance of EC Law

European Community Law is no longer seen as 'something for the future' or 'something for the specialists'. It is part of the mainstream. It features in mainstream advice, pleading and advocacy.

Every legal development in the EC is relevant for one of three reasons. First, that it might become part of domestic law: having a status a little like a Law Commission Report or Government Green Paper. Second, that it must become part of domestic law: for example, EC legislation which is to be implemented by the Member States and will take effect when it has. Third, and most importantly, that it has become part of domestic law: either because of implementation or because of the self-promoting jurisprudence of the European Court of Justice (ECJ).

The EC is an 'initiator' of what become domestic law concepts. Thus, several domestic environmental law concepts were EC-driven, notably BATNEEC (see below), environmental impact assessments, and public registers of environmental information. However, it would be quite wrong to adopt the attitude of 'waiting for the domestic legislation'. EC Law can be applicable in its own right, irrespective of domestic enactment. And in any case, lenders more than most need to keep abreast of proposed developments and future trends. As we have said, lending is by its very nature a prospective enterprise. A prudent lender will want to know what EC regulation is imminent which is likely to affect its borrower's business, and its own loan recovery.

That said, the primary focus is undoubtedly the domestic legislation which implements EC regulation. But there are three powerful principles which have evolved in the ECJ to encourage or achieve implementation, including by supplementing and even nullifying domestic legislative sources. And, at least as long as the European Communities Act 1972 is on the statute-book, those principles are capable of affecting lenders in the UK.

direct effect

The first of the three principles is the doctrine of 'direct effect'. This operates to give certain EC sources the status of domestic legislation and to enable those sources to be relied upon in domestic Courts. The relevant sources are EC Treaty provisions, Regulations, Decisions and Directives. As to the last of these, the Directive must be sufficiently "clear, precise and unconditional" and its time limit for implementation (if any) must have expired (see eg. *Van Duyn v Home Office* [1975] Ch 358).

There is one important restriction as to directly effective Directives: they are said to have 'vertical' and not 'horizontal' effect. This means that they can be relied upon only as against an "emanation of the state", though this concept was interpreted widely in *Foster v British Gas* [1991] 2 AC 306, so as to include (per Lord Templeman, at 313):

> "a body whatever its legal form, which has been made responsible, pursuant to a measure adopted by the state, for providing a public service under the control of the state and has for that purpose special powers beyond those which result from the normal rules applicable in relations between individuals"

Thus a directly effective provision might found a defence to a criminal prosecution, an action for damages for 'breach of EC statutory duty' (like *Garden Cottage Foods v Milk Marketing Board* [1984] AC 130), or an application for judicial review for failure to implement the provision (as in the *Factortame* case, see [1991] 1 AC 603 & [1992] 3 WLR 288).

interpretation theory

This principle is an extension of direct effect, achieved through the notion that domestic law is to be 'interpreted in the light of' EC law. The idea was developed first in the context of a clash between express domestic and EC provisions, in which the latter won the day (*Simmenthal* [1978] ECR 629), was extended to the situation where the policy of a domestic statute conflicted with that of EC legislation (*Murphy* [1988] 2 CMLR 753), and has been further developed in two recent cases.

In *Litster v Forth Dry Dock Engineering* [1990] 1 AC 546 the House of Lords stated that it would read extra words into a domestic statute which was intended to implement an EC Directive but did not do so completely. And in *Marleasing v La Comercial Internacional de Alimentacion SA* [1990] ECR 4135, the ECJ suggested that the same principle might apply to pre-existing domestic law which conflicts with a directly effective EC Directive.

Accordingly, the wording of a domestic statute is by no means conclusive and may be supplemented and arguably ignored in favour of that of an EC Directive. It is even arguable that the *Marleasing* principle could apply to domestic common law.

damages for non-implementation

The third principle supplements direct effect, and seeks to reduce the effect of that doctrine's "clear, precise and unconditional" and "emanation of the state" limitations. It derives from the celebrated *Francovich* case (Times 20th November 1991; [1992] IRLR 84; cited in *Kirklees BC v Wickes* [1992] 3 WLR 170): see eg. Lasok, *State Liability for Breach of Community Law* in [1992] ICLR 186.

In *Francovich* the ECJ held that a private person was entitled to compensatory damages against a Member State where the latter's failure to implement an EC Directive had caused loss to the person. This was so notwithstanding that the Directive in question was not directly effective. It was enough that the Directive disclosed an identifiable content and identifiable beneficiaries. The Court's reasoning was, as ever, policy-based and EC-promoting: to deny compensation would weaken the force of EC Law.

So, an individual wanting to rely upon a Directive which has not been implemented, either against a person who is not an "emanation of the state" or where the Directive is not directly effective, may seek to bring a *Francovich* action against the Member State for compensation.

(2) The development of EC environmental law

At its outset, the view was that the institutions of an "economic" community had nothing to say about the environment, and there was no reference to the environment at all in the 1957 Treaty of Rome. This attitude has changed drastically, corresponding perhaps to the dropping of the EEC's middle-E in Euro-speech. There have been well over 300 environmental Directives alone, including regimes covering water, air, noise, chemicals and waste. We shall return to the most recent example relating to the last of these.

It is worth describing in outline some of the highlights in the rise (and rise) of environmental policy in EC Law:

- The first of four declarations of intent called the 'EC Action Programmes on the Environment', drafted in 1973 (O.J. 1973 C 112/1). Since then there have been three others (O.J. 1977 C 391; O.J. 1983 C 46/1 and O.J. 1987 C 328/1), and a fifth is imminent.

- The enactment of environmental legislation, notwithstanding the absence of any specific Treaty power, by use of the general provisions of Articles 100 and 235 of the EC Treaty.

- The 1975 Recommendation on the "Polluter Pays Principle" (O.J. 1975 L.194).

- The Single European Act (SEA), which came into force in July 1987 and amended the EC Treaty to add Articles 100A(3) (under which environmental protection is to attract as base a "high level of protection") and Articles 130r, s & t, which set out the EC's environmental objectives. (See generally Kramer, *EEC Treaty and Environmental Protection* (1990)). The central provisions of Article 130r as amended by the SEA state that:

  "1. Action by the Community relating to the environment shall have the following objectives:

  (i) to preserve, protect and improve the quality of the environment ...

  2. Action by the Community relating to the environment shall be based on the principles that preventive action should be taken, that environmental damage should as a priority be rectified at source, and that the polluter should pay. Environmental protection requirements shall be a component of the Community's other policies ..."

- The December 1989 Report of a Task Force on the Environment and the Internal Market, which acknowledged the principles of prevention and 'polluter pays' and redefined economic efficiency as embracing the "choice of appropriate economic incentives to secure the achievement of existing environmental protection goals with the lowest possible costs for the economy ... and which also offer permanent incentives to further economic improvements".

- In May 1990, Council Regulation 1210/90/EEC (O.J. 1990 L 120/1) on the establishment of the European Environment Agency and the European environmental information and observation network.

- The Maastricht Summit, in December 1991, which signalled a stronger commitment to environmental protection and amended the provisions of Article 130r, s & t, including by adding to the notion of prevention of environmental damage those of 'precaution' and 'protection'.

- The Commission Green Paper on Environmental Liability, intended to go beyond the context of waste, publication of which was awaited at the time of writing.

(3) The approach of the ECJ

The ECJ, unsurprisingly, has been active in the development of EC environmental law. Again, we set out some highlights:

- In *Handelskwekerij GJ Bier v Mines de Potasses d'Alsace* [1976] ECR 1735, the Court was concerned with Article 5(3) of the Brussels Convention, which grants jurisdiction in tort matters to the Courts "where the harmful event occurred". It was held that the Plaintiff had "an option to commence proceedings either at the place where the damage occurred or the place of the event giving rise to it".

- *Commission v Italian Republic* [1980] ECR 1099 & 1115 where the Court endorsed the use of Articles 100 and 235 for secondary legislation on the environment (see above).

- In *Procureur de la République v Association de Défense des Brûleurs d'Huiles Usagées* [1985] ECR 531 it was held that the protection of the environment is "one of the Community's essential objectives" which could justify restrictions on the free movement of goods.

- *Commission v Denmark* ("The Danish Bottles Case") [1989] 1 CMLR 619, is the celebrated example applying the *Procureur de la République* principle. The EC Commission challenged a green Danish Law requiring drinks containers to be returnable, alleging that this breached Article 30 of the EC Treaty (free movement of goods). The Court rejected this challenge (while upholding a similar challenge to a Danish law requiring containers to be approved by a domestic environmental agency), characterising "the protection of the environment [as] a mandatory requirement" of the EC.

- In the *Vessosso & Zanetti* cases (Cases 206-207/88 & 359/88) the Court widened the definition of "waste" under the waste Directive of 1975, holding that this was "not to be understood as excluding substances and objects which are capable of re-utilization".

(4) The EC regulatory framework

We can see little utility in trying to describe, less still in simply listing, the environmental Directives of the EC. However, it is useful to make some observations and give some examples regarding the framework and machinery of EC environmental regulation:

- It is possible to identify the common themes of the Directive regime, which can be described as follows: liability which is strict, unlimited, joint and several, but not retroactive; recoverability of clean-up costs; prohibition on contracting out of duties; facilitation of action by 'common interest groups'; and long limitation periods.

- The principles of environmental protection have begun to appear in some slightly unusual places. For example, the 1989 Broadcasting Directive (89/552/EEC; O.J. 1989 L 298/23) provides that TV advertising shall not "encourage behaviour prejudicial to the protection of the environment".

- A useful illustration of an imminent Directive of great environmental significance is the Amended Draft Directive on Civil Liability Caused by Waste (91/C 192/04), whose regime includes new causes of action and new remedies in respect of waste. Under the Directive a "producer" or "deemed producer" is liable under civil law for damage to and impairment of the environment, irrespective of fault. The "deemed producer" is defined as the person who had "actual control of the waste when the incident giving rise to the damage or impairment of the environment occurred, if he is not able within a reasonable period to identify the producer". There is a defence for a person who can prove no fault on his part and that the damage or impairment was intentionally caused by a third party, or due to force majeure.

- An emerging notion, capable of revolutionising EC environmental law is that of the "single environment". This is really only an extension of the *Handelskwekerij GJ Bier* case (above). The gist of the idea is that any pollution is harm to the EC environment, and that any citizen of the EC can sue the polluter anywhere in the EC. The potential implications of this for forum-shopping are obvious.

- One feature of the Euro scene which should not be underestimated is the power of the 'green lobby', which can be illustrated with reference to the Waste Directive (above). The original draft contained a burden of proof of "overwhelming probability", but the final version provides that the burden of proof "shall be no higher than the standard burden of proof in civil law". Similarly, the original draft contained no guarantee of standing for 'common interest' groups, but the final version expressly provides that such groups have the right to commence or join in proceedings.

(5) The impact for lenders

What does it all mean for banks and receivers ? In the first place, it is wrong to characterise EC regulation as adding simply to the anxiety of lenders, having been concerned solely with liability for environmental harm and the setting of environmental 'trigger' standards for such liability. The EC has also provided the initiative for machinery which can serve to protect lenders, including environmental assessment, public access to records, and environmental auditing.

That said, the lender's main lesson is that there may be far more to potential environmental liability, whether its borrower's or its own, than is indicated by domestic regulation. And it is no longer a case of worrying only if lending to an "emanation of the state". If domestic legislation is flawed, or implementation of some of its provisions delayed, EC sources may be used to 'fill the gaps' (see eg. Wheeler, *The EC piece of the contaminated land jigsaw* Solicitors Journal 12th June 1992 p.580).

The draft Waste Directive again provides an example. Its requirement of strict civil liability is clearly not met by the criminal regime of the EPA Part II and arguably not by *Rylands v Fletcher* either (as to both see below). Thus, a *Marleasing* argument might succeed in invoking the Directive and attaching to a borrower or lender a civil liability which is not in the EPA, and doing so notwithstanding that the defendant is not an "emanation of the state".

And what of the prospect of direct lender liability? It is true that there is as yet no express reference to 'lender liability' in the EC framework. But there is no express 'lender protection' either. The principle is that the "polluter" should pay, but who is to be included within "polluter"? And what if the primary "polluter" is impecunious?

Once again, the position is well illustrated by the Waste Directive. The "deemed producer" definition turns on "control" and has something of a *Panamericana v Northern Badger* or even *US v Fleet Factors* ring to it. There is clearly some potential for a lender to become the "polluter". It may be argued that the lender need only fear if he is a mortgagee in possession (see eg. Bryce in [1992] 4 JIBL 131 at 133), though the issues are the same as those which we discuss in connection with a 'relationship with the activity' in Chapter 8 below. What is notable is that the EC Commission declined to include any lender liability exemption in the Directive, even of a CERCLA type, and this notwithstanding intensive lobbying from the lending community.

What should perhaps give most cause for concern to lenders is the prospect of the combination of the malleable wording of EC environmental legislation and the well-known policy-based flexi-jurisprudence of the ECJ. One can imagine the Court simply being unable to resist a lender's 'deeper pocket', especially when reminded that it is an "essential objective" of the EC to protect the environment and rectify environmental damage.

PART II

DOMESTIC ENVIRONMENTAL LIABILITY

CHAPTER 4

CIVIL LIABILITY

It is obvious that in order to address the question of lender liability for environmental harm in the UK one must start with a grasp of the parameters and principles of domestic environmental liability. The emergence of statutory regimes such as the Environmental Protection Act 1990 (EPA) and the Water Resources Act 1991 (WRA), under which liability is primarily (but not completely) criminal, means it is easy to think of environmental liability as simply statutory, and criminal. In fact it is neither.

We start then with an overview of the five main areas which make up the civil law back-cloth, namely private nuisance, public nuisance, *Rylands v Fletcher*, negligence and breach of statutory duty. The second of these is actionable both as crime and a civil suit. The first four are all matters of common law, whereas the fifth is concerned with civil law implications of statutory duties.

We will offer a synopsis of each, to set out the general principles of liability: who is liable ?, when ?, and for what ?

(1) Private nuisance

Liability for private nuisance arises where an activity on the Defendant's land represents an unlawful interference with the Plaintiff's use or enjoyment of his own land or of some right over or in connection with that land. The activity complained of must be on-going, not isolated or temporary.

The Defendant is a person who has caused the nuisance, and need not be in occupation of the land where it has occurred. However, an occupier of land will be liable for continuing or adopting a nuisance taking place there, if he knows or ought to know of its existence and is in a position where it would be possible for him to take effective steps to prevent it: *Sedleigh-Denfield v O'Callaghan* [1940] AC 880.

In order to succeed in a private nuisance claim the Plaintiff must himself have an interest in land. He must also prove that he has suffered either physical damage or personal discomfort. The former requires material physical injury to his person, premises or chattels. The latter requires material interference with his ordinary physical comfort.

Nuisance is perhaps inherently 'environmental' and there are several examples of successful private nuisance actions which relate to 'pollution', including:

Walter v Selfe (1852) 19 LTOS 308: smoke from brick-burning operations;

Sturges v Bridgman (1879) 11 Ch D 852 (the famous pestle and mortar case): noise from a confectioner;

West v Bristol Tramways [1908] 2 KB 14: creosote fumes from blocks belonging to a tram company;

Pwllbach Colliery v Woodman [1915] AC 634: dust from a coal-stocking depot;

Halsey v Esso Petroleum [1961] 1 WLR 683: noxious smells and smuts from an oil distribution depot.

In nuisance actions the Courts are confronted with a direct clash of competing claims as to land-use, whether it be a factory's claim to be entitled to produce steel, or an individual's claim to be entitled to restful sleep. The test of nuisance itself requires an overt balancing of interests, with notions of "reasonableness" governing either side of the equation and presenting a malleable concept well-suited to accommodating policy considerations.

One question is whether fault is a necessary component of private nuisance. It was not according to Lord Symonds in *Read v Lyons* [1947] AC 156, though the question is not a settled one. The *Cambridge Water* case (see note below) was decided by the Court of Appeal on the basis of no-fault nuisance.

Then there is the 'locality' factor. In relation to a 'personal discomfort' claim at least, the Courts will take into account the nature and characteristics of the area in which the activity takes place. Thus in *St Helen's Smelting v Tipping* (1865) 11 HLC 642 it was a material factor that the Plaintiff lived in a locality which was the centre of the offensive industry complained of. And in *Sturges v Bridgman*, Thesiger L.J. felt able to say that a resident of Belgrave Square should be entitled to an easier time than his counterpart in Bermondsey. There is something rather self-serving for the Defendant in this, since his very activity itself may dictate the nature of the locality. This was precisely the case in *Gillingham BC v CV Medway (Chatham) Dock* [1992] 3 WLR 449, where the development of the Defendant's dock was held to have changed the nature of the 'locality' (though the true ratio of the case may be that a Local Authority cannot both grant planning permission for an operation and then seek to restrain it by suing in nuisance).

There is a certain tension between the 'locality' factor and another recognised principle, that it is no answer for the Defendant to say that the Plaintiff "came to the nuisance". The fact that I decide to move to a house next to a cricket ground (*Miller v Jackson* [1977] QB 966) or speed-boat lake (*Kennaway v Thompson* [1981] QB 88) does not prevent me from then suing in nuisance.

Defences which are available include: right acquired by prescription (broadly 20 years continuous use); right acquired by grant; and statutory authority. The last of these was applied in the pollution context in *Allen v Gulf Oil* [1981] AC 1001 where statutory authority was held to embrace both express and implied permission. One question arising is whether a relevant licence under the EPA or WRA (below) would suffice to trigger this defence to a private nuisance action.

Turning to remedies, the Plaintiff can recover compensatory damages for physical damage (eg. *St Helen's Smelting*) and presumably personal injury, though it is an issue for debate whether the latter would need proof of negligence. It is also a moot point whether the current resistance to recovery for economic loss in negligence (*Caparo v Dickman* [1990] 2 AC 605; *Murphy v Brentwood* [1991] 1 AC 398) is transferable to the nuisance context. Recovery of lost profits may depend on whether they can be characterised as resulting directly from physical damage. There are examples of awards of damages for personal discomfort, though these have tended to be modest (*Halsey v Esso Petroleum; Bone v Seale* [1975] 1 WLR 797).

The Courts have even been prepared to countenance the possibility of a claim for exemplary damages in private (but not public) nuisance: *Gibbons v South West Water* The Times 26th November 1992.

Finally, the Courts have shown themselves perfectly willing to grant injunctions, including against large-scale industrial activities: in *Halsey v Esso Petroleum* the Plaintiff was awarded an injunction in respect of noise from Esso's boilers, plant and vehicles, and smoke/smut from its chimneys.

(2) Public nuisance

Public nuisance is something of a hybrid. It is a common law liability, having developed through caselaw. But primarily it is a crime, prosecuted by the Attorney-General or a Local Authority (under s.222 of the Local Government Act 1972) on behalf of "the public", as for example in *AG v PYA Quarries* [1957] 2 QB 169. Its conceptual proximity to the criminal 'statutory nuisance' under the EPA and discussed in the next chapter will become clear.

However, it can found (or supplement) a private tort action, if brought by a private citizen who can show he has suffered "particular damage", as for example in *Halsey v Esso Petroleum* (above) and *Tate & Lyle v GLC* [1983] 2 AC 509. Unlike a private nuisance claim however, here the Plaintiff need not show an interest in land.

It is clear that there are notions here of 'standing' and the dilemma of recognising the 'public interest'. These are ideas with which administrative lawyers are familiar: in administrative law the standing rules are criticised for failing to accommodate the public interest (see eg. Justice-All Souls, *Administrative Justice: Some Necessary Reforms* 1988 chapter 8). Indeed, the role of the Attorney General (which makes him something of an environmental policing authority) can be used here to justify a hostility to public interest claims, just as it is in administrative law (see *Gouriet v Union of Post Office Workers* [1978] AC 435).

The test for public nuisance liability is whether the Defendant has committed an actionable wrong which has materially affected 'the public', that is a sufficiently large class of people. The first part, actionable wrong, overlaps substantially with private nuisance: factors such as locality and defences such as statutory authority (see eg. *Tate & Lyle v GLC*) will operate in a similar way.

The second part, class of people, was in issue in *AG v PYA Quarries*. There the Attorney-General had successfully prosecuted the Defendant and obtained injunctions in respect of quarrying and blasting activities, so as to stop the dust and vibration which were upsetting those who lived locally. The Court of Appeal held that it was sufficient that the activities affected a class of people sufficiently wide to be characterised as 'the local community' or 'the neighbourhood'.

As for remedies, although by a criminal route, a successful prosecution by the Attorney-General or a Local Authority can secure an injunction. A private tort action based on public nuisance can result in both an injunction and damages to compensate for 'particular damage' (again illustrated by *Halsey v Esso Petroleum* and *Tate & Lyle v GLC*). Further, unlike private nuisance where the position is unclear, it is said to be settled (by cases whose age can be said either to add to, or detract from, their force) that in 'public nuisance' damages can be awarded in respect of personal injury and pure economic loss (see *Castle v St Augustines Links* [1922] 38 TLR 615 and *Harper v Haden* [1933] 1 Ch D 298, respectively).

(3) The rule in *Rylands v Fletcher*

It is trite law that under the rule in *Rylands v Fletcher* (1868) LR 3 HL 330 a person has strict liability for damage caused by the escape of hazardous substances held on his land. One begins though with the observation that whereas *Rylands v Fletcher* has since been treated as a case about a substance "of an unusual nature, which was essentially dangerous in itself" (*Leakey v National Trust*, below) it was actually about damage caused by water.

The component parts of potential *Rylands v Fletcher* liability are as follows: that the person brings the substance onto land, that he collects and keeps it there, that he is the controller of the substance (he need not be the owner or occupier of the land), that the substance is likely to do mischief if it escapes, and that the use of the land is 'non-natural'. The rule is said to have the advantage over negligence (and arguably nuisance) of requiring proof of neither fault nor foreseeability.

The striking feature of the *Rylands v Fletcher* caselaw is how little of it there is. The courts have tended to restrict rather than deploy what would have seemed a readily available avenue for recourse for environmental damage, even to the extent of a suggestion in *Read v Lyons* that *Rylands v Fletcher* liability requires fault.

The most actively emphasized inhibitor in the restriction of *Rylands v Fletcher* has been the 'non-natural user' component, a notion developed as a gloss to the rule in cases such as *Rickards v Lothian* [1913] AC 263 and *British Celanese v Hunt* [1969] 1 WLR 959, and recognised at first instance in *Cambridge Water v Eastern Counties*

Leather The Times 23rd October 1991 (Note: this decision had been successfully appealed, but not reported, at the time of writing. The Court of Appeal side-stepped "fundamental" questions as to the scope of *Rylands v Fletcher*, preferring to characterise the case as representing strict nuisance liability: The Times 29th December 1992). The Court of Appeal in *Leakey v National Trust* [1980] QB 485 expressed disquiet at this restriction, but was there able to frame liability in terms of ordinary private nuisance.

Compounding this inhibition on the development of *Rylands v Fletcher* has been the relaxed interpretation of what land uses are 'natural'. Here the Courts have used a principle of public interest to characterise as 'natural' land uses which are seen to have a 'public benefit' (considered in eg. *North West Utilities v London Guarantee & Accident* [1936] AC 108). Again the most recent example is the *Cambridge Water* case, which concerned the storage of drums of chlorinated solvent used in the tanning industry. This was held at first instance (see note above) to be a 'natural user' in reliance on the 'public benefit' and upon something akin to the 'locality' factor common in nuisance cases. However, a Canadian court has held that a landfill site used for the disposal of waste could be a 'non-natural' use of land: *Gersten v Municipality of MC* [1974] 41 DLR (3rd) 646. On the facts, the Ontario High Court found that a waste disposal landfill site in a heavily populated urban area was a 'non-natural' user of land.

The defence of statutory authority is probably available here too, as in nuisance. As for *Rylands v Fletcher* remedies, they would include an injunction and damages, though apparently not damages for personal injuries (*Read v Lyons*).

(4) Negligence

Negligence can readily be treated as an avenue for civil liability supplemental to nuisance and *Rylands v Fletcher*, best described by comparison to those areas. However, it is worth recognising that as a common law device for imposing liability, negligence may well take the lead in the environmental field as elsewhere, especially given the waning judicial popularity of *Rylands v Fletcher* and to a lesser extent nuisance. The relative impact of the 'landmark' cases *Donoghue v Stevenson* and *Rylands v Fletcher* is startling.

Unlike nuisance, a negligence claim does not require an on-going complaint, nor a complainant holding an interest in land. The vital principle is not who the Plaintiff or Defendant are, but the relationship between them, and the flexible 'duty of care' concept allows policy considerations to be very much to the fore (which may not be so unusual) and acknowledged to be so (which certainly is).

Negligence differs from the others in that it will not found an injunction (*Miller v Jackson* [1977] QB 966). It allows damages, including those for personal injury, but there are strict limitations on the recovery of pure economic loss. Negligence does of course require both foreseeability and fault, though the latter may be assisted by the evidentiary doctrine 'res ipsa loquitur'. That doctrine places the burden of disproving fault on the Defendant, if the damage has been caused by something under his management or control which would not cause damage in the ordinary course of events if he exercised proper care (see *Scott v London & St Katherine Docks* (1865) 3 H & C 596). It is a doctrine whose potential compliments that of *Rylands v Fletcher* and says much for the judicial mood of the 1860s.

One can gain a feel for green negligence caselaw from just a few examples: in *Barnes v Irwell Valley Water Board* [1939] 1 KB 21 (and in *Scott-Whitehead v National Coal Board* (1987) 53 P & CR 263) liability in negligence arose from a failure to warn consumers of substances known to be present in the water supply. *Tutton v Walter* [1986] QB 61 is a memorable case in which the Defendant farmer who had sprayed his crop with insecticide was liable for killing the Plaintiff's trespassing bees. And in *Eckersley v Binnie* (Construction Law Reports Vol 18 p.1), liability arose from a tunnel construction scheme which struck methane gas resulting in an explosion and 16 deaths.

(5) Breach of statutory duty

Like public nuisance this is a hybrid, though of a rather different kind. It concerns liability arising from duties contained in various environmental statutes, in which respect it is like the liabilities discussed in the next chapter. However, unlike them it is enforced not by way of criminal prosecution, but by actions for damages brought by private persons in the civil Courts. Moreover, its existence requires reliance on case-law in that, whilst statutes sometimes expressly provide for their civil law implications (eg. the nature of civil liability, the existence of defences), often they do not.

Caselaw, then, may be deployed to answer such questions as these:

- Does civil liability arise as a result of the statutory obligation?

Here, the absence of some other sanction will be a compelling feature in favour of recognising civil liability, whilst its presence is not conclusive the other way (*Cutler v Wandsworth Stadium* [1949] AC 398).

- To whom is the duty intended to be owed, and the ability to sue intended to be given ? (see eg. *Knapp v Railway Executive* [1949] 2 All ER 508).

- What kind of harm does the statute intend to prevent: what harm is actionable ? (*Gorris v Scott* (1874) LR 9 Ex 125)

An illustration in the environmental field of the question of civil liability for breach of statutory duty is provided by *Merlin v British Nuclear Fuels* [1990] 2 QB 557. That case concerned the Nuclear Installations Act 1965. In one respect the Act was clear: section 12 provided that an injury sustained as a result of a breach of a duty contained in the Act would sound in compensatory damages. A second question was far from clear, namely the nature of the heads and measure of damages which were recoverable. The Court held that the owners of a contaminated house were not entitled to recover the diminution in value caused to that property.

Accordingly, the question of civil liability for breach of statutory duty compliments the 'big four' statutory regimes discussed in the next chapter: namely air pollution, water pollution, waste on land and statutory nuisance. Three examples are helpful.

- First, the regime in respect of water pollution is found in the WRA Part III. However, section 100 states expressly that breach of the duties contained in that part is not capable of resulting in civil damages. This is in contrast to the duty of the National Rivers Authority under section 39 of that Act (a duty in granting water abstraction rights not to derogate from existing protected rights of third parties), which by virtue of section 60 expressly does sound in compensatory civil damages.

- Secondly, the regime for waste on land is Part II of the EPA. Section 73(6) expressly provides that activity characterised as criminal by sections 33(1) or 63(2) will also sound in civil damages. The section goes on to provide for '100% contributory negligence' and 'volenti' defences (no liability if "the damage (a) was due wholly to the fault of the person who suffered it; or (b) was suffered by a person who voluntarily accepted the risk of the damage being caused"); and expressly provides that compensatory damage includes death and personal injury. There is no requirement in the section that the offender need have been convicted, or indeed prosecuted, for the offence, just that he has committed it.

- Third, whilst section 73 of the EPA makes clear that the section 33 liability can found a civil action (above), it does not say the same of the section 34 'duty of care'. On the other hand, nowhere is civil liability excluded in relation to that section. Moreover, it may well be that EC law is capable of providing a civil liability, with section 34 being 'interpreted' on *Marleasing* grounds in accordance with the imminent EC Waste Directive (see Chapter 3, above).

CHAPTER 5

CRIMINAL LIABILITY

(1) Introduction

Our emphasis here is on criminal liability as provided for under various statutory regimes relating to the environment. This is nearly the same as simply discussing the statutory framework. But not quite: it is important to acknowledge at the outset that the statutory framework can have a significant civil law impact.

Three examples are helpful to show the civil law implications of environmental protection statutes whose regimes are apparently criminal. First, and most obvious, there is the civil liability which we have just discussed: damages for breach of statutory duty. Second, there is the principle, well known in the sphere of traffic accidents, which enables a successful criminal conviction to be evidence in a civil claim. Third, criminal sanctions may be enforceable in civil courts: thus, under sections 24 and 81(5) of the EPA crimes relating to air pollution and breach of a nuisance abatement order (respectively) may be enforced through the High Court; as are criminal restraint orders (see Chapter 6 below). And liability for clean-up costs (discussed in this Chapter) is seemingly capable of constituting an action in debt.

There is also, we should point out, an overlap the other way: civil principles may be helpful in criminal cases. This is illustrated by *National Coal Board v Thorne* [1976] 1 WLR 543 (use of common law nuisance in a statutory nuisance prosecution) and *Southern Water Authority v Pegrum* [1990] JP 581 (use of *Rylands v Fletcher* in a water pollution prosecution), both of which are discussed below.

One statutory perspective which is not a matter of criminal law, nor indeed of civil liability, but which is of particular interest to lenders is that of planning legislation. Lenders are already well-versed in the importance of planning consent or the prospect of it on the prospects of their borrowers and the value of their security. What they need to add to this knowledge is an awareness of regimes like that contained in the Planning (Hazardous Substances) Act 1990, whose significance and operation is akin to that of the licensing and registration schemes which we discuss below.

Turning to the criminal statutes, the response of Parliament to environmental liability has been piecemeal. There is a daunting array of primary and delegated legislation, much of which is extremely specific. A survey of the field of primary environmental legislation leads to provisions as activity-specific as the Petroleum and Submarine Pipelines Act 1975 and the stubble-burning and abandoned-supermarket-trolley provisions of the EPA (ss.152 and 99 respectively). Likewise in relation to secondary legislation there are schemes such as the Aerosol Dispensers (EEC Requirements) & the Cosmetic Products (Amendment) Regulations 1985 and the Arsenic in Food Regulations 1959.

We do not intend to attempt here a comprehensive survey of the legislative map. Nor do we offer any apology in that regard. We consider it wholly unnecessary that a lender should, and inherently improbable that it would, seek to become acquainted with the intricacies of the entire regulatory framework. We are not averse though to stating the obvious: a prudent lender faced with a borrower whose dealings constitute a specific 'hazard' would be well-advised to consider the relevant part of the statutory framework. For example, before lending to a company owning a large combustion plant in Scotland, any consideration of its viability and future would do well to include the question of compliance with the Large Combustion Plant (Control of Emissions) (Scotland) Regulations 1991.

We do consider it helpful however to give a feel for the regulatory map, and list here some examples of subjects and (primary) sources of regulation, as to which we then intend to say no more:

- trade effluent discharges: Water Industry Act 1991;
- pollution at sea: Food & Environment Protection Act 1985 Part II; EPA s.146;
- radioactive substances: Radioactive Substances Act 1960; EPA Part V;
- storage of hazardous substances: Planning (Hazardous Substances) Act 1990;
- pesticides: Food & Environment Protection Act 1985 Part III
- genetically modified organisms: EPA Part VI;
- contamination of food: Food & Environment Protection Act 1985 Part I; Food Safety Act 1990;

- noise and vibration: Control of Pollution Act 1974 (COPA);
- abstraction of water: WRA Part II Chapter II;
- litter: EPA Part IV;
- carriers of waste: Control of Pollution (Amendment) Act 1989.

Nor would we pretend that any but the keenest, or most far-sighted lender would want to wade through the many official but non-statutory sources which indicate important policy directions. Such sources would include the Committee reports from both House of Commons (eg. on contaminated land) and House of Lords (eg. on hazardous waste disposal); Royal Commission reports (eg. on waste management) and the Government White Paper, 'This Common Inheritance'. The latter contrasts markedly with the provisions of the EPA and WRA, which could mean several things: that we can expect tougher domestic legislation in the near future, that there is the prospect of EC gap-filling, or that this is an illustration of the gulf between actions and words.

Of more practical use than policy-documents are the official guidelines contained in sources like the draft British standard EPC/50 on Environment Management Systems; the Department of the Environment's "Integrated Pollution Control, a Practical Guide", its "Process Management Notes" and the "Codes of Practice" issued under the various Acts.

In our view, it is vital that a lender has a basic knowledge of the themes of environmental regulation and the structure of the regimes governing the 'big four': the four areas of most general interest. These provide something by way of an integrated and settled legislative scheme. And whilst some of the provisions and machinery are not yet in force, we consider it most sensible to focus on what is soon to come rather than what is soon to become obsolete. We do mention specifically though that lenders should be aware that there are transitional provisions, and an old COPA waste licence for example will continue to be effective under section 77 of EPA until its expiry date.

The 'big four' are:

(a) Air pollution: EPA Part I;

(b) Water pollution: WRA Part III;

(c) Waste on land: EPA Part II;

(d) Statutory nuisance: EPA Part III.

(2) The emerging pattern

The 'big four' regimes, then, appear among the pages of the recent codifying statutes, the EPA and the WRA (extracts from which are reproduced in the Appendices at the end of this book). Disparate and unconnected they may seem, but on examination there emerges in respect of these regimes a pattern of common characteristics which can be labelled as follows:

1) The criminal activity

2) The policeman

3) The licence

4) Supervision

5) Clean-up

6) The register

7) Third party liability

We acknowledge at the outset that this is not a perfect analysis. Each regime has its particularities, and in the case of one of the regimes (nuisance) two of the characteristics (the licence and the register) are absent altogether. However, it is a convenient analysis, by which to introduce criminal environmental liability. We will take each element in turn:

1) The criminal activity

Under each of the regimes the 'polluter' commits a criminal offence. Broadly speaking, he is liable to be fined £20,000 maximum in a Magistrates' court and an unlimited sum in a Crown Court. However, it is not quite that simple. For example, statutory nuisance offences are summary only, and the level of fine is dependent upon whether the nuisance relates to land other than trade or business premises (s.80 EPA). And the level of fine in a Magistrates' Court for the waste 'duty of care' is different.

Under each regime the 'primary' offences are broadly the polluting activities themselves with additional offences of non-compliance with notices served by the relevant policing authority (see "Supervision", below). In the case of statutory nuisance though there is no separate polluting offence, and the sole primary offence is with an abatement notice.

There is also the question of liability for clean-up costs, which we consider separately below. We pause here simply to note that such liability does not always depend upon a notice having been served, and that in the case of statutory nuisance and "noxious gas" producing waste the person liable need not be a 'polluter': he may have acquired the property since the 'polluting act' began.

There are also what we will term various 'secondary' offences. These relate to such matters as obstructing the policing authority, failing to provide required information, and so on.

A common theme is that of the enviro-acronym 'BATNEEC' ("best available techniques not entailing excessive cost"), which means quite simply "best practical means". This is widely seen as an EC-concept, but it corresponds to notions from the Public Health Act 1936 (PHA) and COPA s.71, together with cases like *Wivenhoe Port v Colchester Borough Council* [1985] JPL 175 which are suggestive of quite a stiff test.

It is worthy of note that there is express provision in the EPA (s.156) for regulations enabling the statutory framework to "give effect" to EC obligations and "related rights". Failing such steps, the *Marleasing* doctrine may allow obligations contained in EC Directives (notably the draft Waste Directive) to be grafted into the EPA, as we suggested in Chapter 3, above.

We return to the 'primary' offences. These can be summarised as follows:

(a) Air pollution. The offences (EPA s.23) relate to "carrying on" (ss.6(1); 13(1); 14(1)) one of the activities designated a "prescribed process" (s.2).

The list of "prescribed processes" is contained in secondary legislation, currently the Environmental Protection (Prescribed Processes and Substances) Regulations 1991 (SI 1991 No. 472, as amended by SI 1991 No. 836). An idea of its contents can be gained from a glance at headings of the process groups: production of fuel and power; metal production; mineral industries; the chemical industry; waste disposal; other industries.

Two things about the air pollution regime are noteworthy. First, there is an extra enforcement option: a person who fails to comply with an enforcement notice (see "Supervision", below) may be pursued through the High Court "if the enforcing authority is of the opinion that [criminal] proceedings ... would afford an ineffectual remedy" (EPA s.24). Second, where the offence is failure to comply with the BATNEEC implied condition of an authorization (see below), the burden of proof is placed on the Defendant (s.25(1)).

(b) Water pollution. Here the offender is a person who "causes or knowingly permits" poisonous, noxious or polluting matter, solid waste, trade or sewage effluent etc. to enter "controlled waters" (WRA s.85(1)). "Controlled waters" are territorial, coastal, inland and ground waters (s.104).

(c) Waste on land. The criminal conduct is to "knowingly cause or knowingly permit" the deposit of "controlled waste" on land, or to treat, keep or dispose of it there (EPA s.33(1)). The latter offences are excused by a waste management licence (below), except for the separate offence of treating, keeping or disposing of controlled waste "in a manner likely to cause pollution of the environment or harm to human health" (s.33(1)(c)). There is a general defence for a person who can show "that he took all reasonable precautions and exercised all due diligence to avoid the commission of the offence" (s.33(7)(a)).

Curious though it may sound, there is also a crime of breaching a statutory "duty of care". The duty is owed by any person who imports, produces, carries, keeps or disposes of controlled waste or "as a broker, has control of such waste", and is a duty "to take all such measures applicable to him in that capacity as are reasonable in the circumstances" to prevent contravention of s.33 or an escape of waste (s.34(1)).

As we will see below, the clean-up costs' liability in respect of "noxious gas"-type waste does not require that the Defendant himself was a 'polluter', and as to other clean-up costs the onus is on him to prove he was not such a person.

(d) Statutory nuisance. Parliament has provided a (non-exhaustive) list of activities amounting to a "statutory nuisance". The common theme is of an activity (eg. smoke, fumes, dust, noise, state of premises) which is "prejudicial to health or a nuisance" (EPA s.79(1)). These do not represent offences per se: criminality depends upon having been served with an abatement notice (s.80).

There is a BATNEEC-type defence for some of the statutory nuisance offences, where "best practicable means" have been deployed (ss.80(7) & (8), 82(9)(10)). Accordingly, for these types of nuisance, statutory nuisance is less strict than its civil, common law equivalent, discussed in the last chapter. In other senses the common law meaning of 'nuisance' will be relevant, as under the earlier 'statutory nuisance' regimes (see *National Coal Board v Thorne* [1976] 1 WLR 543 applying common law principles to statutory nuisance under the PHA s.92).

2) The policeman

Each scheme entrusts supervision power to a policing authority, whose functions are far greater than that of prosecutor (cf. the Attorney-General's role in public nuisance). These functions include ensuring compliance by investigating, monitoring, granting licences, and compiling information. It is the existence of these authorities which provides the backbone of the environmental regulation, and their efficiency and resolve which provide its teeth. Indeed, the crucial factors in environmental law can be identified not as legal matters at all, but matters of 'command and control', such as the resources, staffing, policy and morale of the policing authorities.

It is worth pointing out that in the background is the government. It is not simply a matter of funding and staffing. The powers of the authorities are supplemented and circumscribed by regulations or objectives to be formulated from the Secretary of State in a manner familiar to any administrative lawyer. An example is the role of setting "quality objectives" regarding air and water pollution (EPA s.3 and WRA ss.82-3). There are also provisions providing for "directions" or "guidance" from the Secretary of State. From the point of view of the authority this presents the classic dilemma: ignoring the "guidance" will present the risk of ultra vires, whereas following it too keenly will draw the challenge of a fettered discretion (see cases like *Laker Airways v Department of Trade* [1977] QB 643).

The relevant policing authorities are:

(a) Air pollution. What is provided is a two-tiered system of centrally and locally controlled processes (EPA s.4). The former scheme is known as "Integrated Pollution Control" ('IPC') and policed by Her Majesty's Inspectorate of Pollution ('HMIP'). The latter, termed "Local Authority Air Pollution Control" ('LAAPC'), is policed by Local Authorities.

(b) Water pollution. The relevant body is the National Rivers Association ('NRA') (WRA s.221(1)).

(c) Waste on land. The bodies given the task of policing the regime are the "waste regulation authorities" referred to in EPA s.30(1), which are broadly the same as the old "waste disposal authorities" under COPA.

(d) Statutory nuisance. The statutory scheme is primarily policed by local authorities (EPA ss.80-81). Also there is a supplemental provision for citizen self-help, the environmental equivalent perhaps to the citizen's arrest: EPA s.82 allows direct action by any "person aggrieved" by means of complaint to a Magistrates' court. The Court can respond by imposing a fine or making an abatement or prohibition order against the wrongdoer.

3) The licence

With the exception of statutory nuisance, the schemes provide for the grant by the relevant policing authority of a permission, licence or authorization. Securing this licence is of such fundamental importance that filling out a form can acquire the flavour of written advocacy.

Licences are to be issued on appropriate conditions, for example as to means to be used, regular supply of information, and so on. Broadly speaking, conduct covered by a licence, providing there is compliance with its conditions, is immune from prosecution. This is achieved in one of two ways, either as a statutory defence of acting in accordance with a licence, or characterisation of the crime as exceeding a licence or breaching its conditions.

In the context of waste disposal, licensing conditions are nothing new. The pre-EPA regime was found in COPA, as to which the Courts have taken a somewhat restrictive view as to the power of imposing conditions (see eg. *AG's Reference No.2 of 1988* [1990] 1 QB 77) and of enforcement (see eg. *Leigh Land v Walsall* The Times 2nd November 1990, but see now *ex p. London Waste* The Times 14th January 1993).

The licence schemes are operated by the relevant policing authority. Each regime provides for the nature of the application, the relevant information to be supplied and the criteria to be applied. Typically, the applicant must furnish details of processes, plans and techniques sufficient to satisfy the policing authority of it its 'environmental-friendliness'. There are also provisions as to the transfer and, vitally, the surrender of licences. A summary is as follows:

(a) Air pollution. A person wishing to carry on a (new or substantially different) prescribed process will need to apply for an "authorization" (EPA ss.6-12). This will involve providing certain specified information as provided for by the Secretary of State in the Environmental Protection (Applications Appeals and Registers) Regulations 1991 (SI 1991 No. 507), enacted under EPA Schedule 1.

The information which the law-abiding air polluter must have provided includes details of the intended process and a written assurance as to techniques to be used to ensure the minimisation of pollution. The key is again BATNEEC ("best available techniques not entailing excessive cost") for preventing / reducing the release of polluting substances. BATNEEC is both expressly recognised in the Act (eg. EPA ss.7(2)(a) and 7(10)) and discussed in Department of the Environment Guidance issued under it (ie. under s.7(11)). In essence, the applicant must demonstrate a BATNEEC commitment for preventing pollution.

If granted, the authorization is to include conditions as considered appropriate by HMIP or the Local Authority, and again BATNEEC anti-pollution is a central feature. If not expressly imposed there is automatically a statutorily implied condition that BATNEEC steps will be used (s.7(4)).

(b) Water pollution. A 'water polluter' can apply to the NRA for a "discharge consent" on providing appropriate information and granted on appropriate conditions (WRA s.88; Schedule 10). Here though there is the alternative of relying upon some other licence, including an authorization (above) or a waste management licence (below) insofar as that permission covers the activity in question.

(c) Waste on land. A person in occupation of land may be granted a "waste management licence" authorising the treatment, keeping or disposal of waste on the land, again upon appropriate conditions (EPA ss.35-41). The applicant must be a "fit and proper person" (s.36(3)) which includes demonstrating "financial provision adequate to discharge the obligations arising from the licence" (s.74(3)(c)). There is an express recognition of after-care conditions: duties "after the activities which the licence authorises have ceased" (s.35(3)).

As has already been noted, there is a separate and absolute offence of treating, keeping or disposing of controlled waste "in a manner likely to cause pollution of the environment or harm to human health", which is not excused by any licence (s.33(1)(c)).

A waste management licence can only be surrendered when the authority is satisfied that the site is "unlikely to cause pollution to the environment or harm to human health" (s.39(6)). Upon accepting a surrender the authority will issue a "certificate of completion" (s.39(9). The authority is given the ultimate incentive for taking it all seriously: after accepting a surrender it is then itself liable for section 61 'clean-up' costs (s.61(9)).

(d) Statutory nuisance. As we have said, there is no licensing scheme here.

4) Supervision

It is a further function of the policing authority to carry out investigations and inspections, so as to ensure compliance with and enforcement of the schemes.

This function carries with it wide powers, including a general power under all four schemes to enter premises in order to investigate whether an offence is being or has been committed (EPA ss.17; WRA ss.169-173; EPA s.69; EPA Sch. 3 para 2). Any person who obstructs such entry, whether or not themselves a potential polluter, risks liability under a 'secondary' crime. The lesson for mortgagees in possession, receivers and the like is obvious.

Enforcement is largely via the service of various compliance notices, breach of which is an offence. The notices will also be relevant to the question of clean-up liability (below), though two of the waste clean-up provisions (ss.59(7) & s.61) do not require notices. The notices are broadly as follows:

(a) Air pollution. An "enforcement notice", specifying certain steps to be taken to comply with the terms of an authorization (EPA s.13), or a "prohibition notice", specifying certain steps to be taken to remove "an imminent risk of serious pollution of the environment" (s.14).

(b) Water pollution. Here the scheme provides for "prohibition notices" banning the making or continuing of certain discharges (WRA s.86) and notices requiring certain steps against pollution (s.92(2)(a)(ii), the latter under regulations by the Secretary of State.

(c) Waste on land. The "occupier" of the land may be served with a "waste removal notice", specifying steps required to deal with the waste and/or its consequences (EPA s.59). The recipient of the notice may apply to have it quashed and will succeed on showing that he did not deposit the waste or knowingly cause or knowingly permit its deposit (s.59(3)). It is also a defence to show that there was a "reasonable excuse" for not complying with the notice.

(d) Statutory nuisance. Under EPA s.80(2) an "abatement notice" requiring specified steps to abate or restrict the nuisance, can be served on (a) the "person responsible" for the nuisance (that is, "the person to whose act, default or sufferance the nuisance is attributable": s.79(7)); (b) in relation to a structural defect the "owner" of the premises; and (c) where the person responsible cannot be found or the nuisance has not yet occurred on the "owner or occupier" of the premises.

Three characteristics of the statutory nuisance supervision

scheme are significant. First, BATNEEC features here as a defence to proceedings for breach of an abatement notice (s.80(7)). Second, as with waste there is a "reasonable excuse" defence. Third, as in respect of the air pollution primary offences, the scheme allows High Court proceedings for breach of an abatement notice where criminal proceedings would in the authority's opinion "afford an inadequate remedy" (s.81(5)).

5) Clean-up

It is a common component of each of the statutory schemes that the policing authority has power to take steps itself to remedy harm caused by a pollution crime, and recover the expenses of so doing from the 'polluter'. This is then the domestic equivalent of the American "Superfund" (above). It should be remembered that clean-up has been part of UK environmental law since 1936 (PHA s.96).

To summarize, again:

(a) Air pollution. Here the power is to take "reasonable steps" towards remedying harm caused by a primary or secondary offence: that is, carrying on a prescribed process without an authorization, or breaching an authorization, enforcement notice or prohibition notice. The cost of such steps can be recovered from "any person convicted of that offence" (EPA s.27(1)).

(b) Water pollution. Under the WRA s.161, the NRA is empowered to do works and operations to: (i) prevent polluting matter likely to enter controlled waters from doing so; (ii) remove or dispose of matter which appears to be or is present in controlled waters; (iii) remedy or mitigate pollution caused by it; and (iv) so far as reasonably practicable, restore the waters including flora and fauna, to their state immediately prior to the presence of the matter. Recovery of the expenses reasonably incurred is from the person who caused or knowingly permitted the matter to be present in the waters or where it was likely to enter the waters.

(c) Waste on land. Here there are three different kinds of clean-up costs. The first kind is found in section 59(6) of the EPA. It arises where the waste regulation authority has served a waste removal notice on the occupier, who has neither complied with it nor had it quashed by satisfying a Court that he did not deposit, knowingly cause or knowingly permit the waste.

The second kind arises under section 59(8) and is similar. It applies where no notice has been served because the authority considered that emergency steps were necessary, there was no occupier, or the occupier had not made or knowingly permitted the deposit of waste. The costs are recoverable either from the person who deposited, knowingly caused or knowingly permitted the waste, or (in the case of emergency steps) the occupier unless he can prove he was not such a person.

Third, there is a special clean-up power under section 61. That section applies to any land where an accumulation of waste has resulted in the concentration, accumulation or discharge of noxious gases or liquids. There the authority has a general power to do works or take steps, on the land or on "adjacent land", reasonable to avoid pollution of the environment or harm to human health. The cost or part of it is recoverable from "the person who is for the time being the owner of the land" (presumably the 'polluting land' rather than the "adjacent land"). There are three exceptions: where the costs were incurred unreasonably; where that recovery would cause "hardship" to the owner; and where the authority accepted the surrender of the relevant waste management licence. The first two can operate to allow recoverable costs to be reduced, the third is all or nothing.

(d) Statutory nuisance. Where an abatement notice has not been complied with, and whether or not criminal proceedings have been commenced, the authority has a power to abate or prevent the recurrence of the nuisance and recover "any expenses reasonably incurred" from "the person by whose act or default the nuisance was caused". Importantly, if "that person is the owner of the premises" then the costs can be recovered "from any person who is for the time being the owner thereof" (EPA s.81).

6) The register

Except for statutory nuisance, each scheme requires that the policing authority maintain a public register (EPA s.20; WRA s.190; EPA s.64) containing information such as:

- applications for licences;
- licences granted;
- compliance notices served;
- revocations of licences;
- appeals;
- information provided under licence conditions;
- information acquired during supervision;
- convictions for offences.

In the context of water pollution, public registers are nothing new. Part II of COPA contained a similar regime, though it is worth noting that it took 11 years after the Act for the registers to be opened.

In addition to the requirements of a register specific to each scheme, there is a general provision in section 143 of the EPA which is of great significance, as it enables a 'contaminated land register' to be created. The section enables the Secretary of State to enact regulations requiring Local Authorities to maintain public registers of land put to "contaminative uses". The potential impact of this provision is demonstrated by the outcry at the effects of labelling land 'contaminated', doing so on the basis of a "contaminative use" rather than actual contamination having occurred, and the prospect that once entered on the register land may not be able to be removed from it. All of which has resulted in the planned implementation of the register being postponed.

The emergence of the public register as a common feature in relation to the environment is something which, unlike some of its companion features, could serve to comfort lenders rather than alarm them. Any responsible lender will have a well-developed mechanism for checking the value of the borrower's principal assets and of any security (which will often be the same property). Searches of the relevant public registers are already a central part of such mechanism.

The contaminated land register is readily added into any such process. An entry on that register can readily be seen as 'an encumbrance'. An entry on one of the other registers is more like a 'caution': on investigation it may prove harmless. Indeed some entries can reassure the lender, for instance confirming that the a relevant, current licence is held. But the lesson for lenders is clear: consult the relevant register(s) and investigate the significance of any entry found.

Clearly, surveyors will need to take into account actual or potential registration when assessing the value of land. And of course, lenders' solicitors will no doubt find themselves under additional duties in this regard, a matter which lenders would do well to articulate expressly when framing instructions.

7) Third Party Liability

Each of the schemes contains provision for 'third party liability', swept up in the general provisions of s.157-8 of the EPA and mirrored by the WRA s.217. Under these sections, third party liability arises where a pollution offence was:

- with the "consent or connivance of, or .. attributable to any neglect on the part of, any director, manager, secretary or other similar officer" of a corporate polluter, or "a person who was purporting to act in any such capacity", or where the company's affairs "are managed by its members ... the acts or defaults of a member in connection with his functions of management as if he were a director"; or

- (except for statutory nuisance) "due to the act or default of some other person".

CHAPTER 6

SEIZED PROFITS

The growth in the criminalisation of polluting activities and the vigour of its enforcement has knock-on effects which may go far beyond the specific environmental statutory schemes. The possibility of profit seizing is one example.

What we say in this chapter is simple, speculative but potentially dramatic. Its worth may only be capable of assessment when accompanied by hindsight. However, what we suggest here is we think perfectly feasible. It has the further advantage that it is premised not upon how the law might develop, but how it has done. The only speculation is that the environmental policing authorities and Courts may prove bold enough to make what is really a simple link between two contemporary statutory schemes.

(1) The profit-seizing regime

Seizure of the profits of crime is, like environmental law itself, the subject of fairly recent legislative activity. Criminal bankruptcy was one of the first legislative attempts to take the profit out of crime (s39 Powers of Criminal Courts Act 1973). To make such an order, there had to be an identifiable victim. Then came the Drug Trafficking Offences Act 1986 (DTOA) which allowed the pre-trial freezing and post-trial confiscation of drug traffickers' profits. This was expanded by the provisions of Part VI of the Criminal Justice Act 1988 (CJA) which introduced a more general power allowing orders for the seizure of profits of crime "in addition to dealing with an offender in any other way" (s.71(1)).

Under the CJA, the powers of magistrates to make profit-seizing orders are restricted to offences relating to such things as pornography and pirate videos (s.71(3) and Schedule 4), though the list can be added to by the Secretary of State. However, the Crown Court faces no such restriction. Section 71 gives to a Crown Court which finds that a person convicted of an indictable offence has enjoyed from the offence a benefit or pecuniary advantage of at least £10,000 a general power to order that person to pay a sum exceeding £10,000 but not exceeding the "realisable benefit".

As with the DTOA, the pre-trial position can be secured by the obtaining of a 'criminal Mareva', a restraint order prohibiting dealings with any realisable property (CJA ss.76-77). The prosecutor can apply ex parte to a Judge in Chambers to freeze assets believed to be the proceeds of crime (RSC Order 115). That order is enforceable by (civil) contempt proceedings (*re H* The Times 1st April 1988) and is according to Lord Donaldson MR in *re Peters* [1988] QB 871 (at 874):

> "designed to prevent an accused rendering a confiscation order inappropriate or nugatory by disposing of his assets between the time when an information is about to be laid against him and the making of a confiscation order in the event of conviction"

Moreover, the new powers are accompanied by an apparent judicial readiness to identify assets as the proceeds of crime. There is appears to be something of a presumption in favour of such identification: *R v Dickens* [1990] 2 QB 102; *R v Chrastny (No.2)* [1991] 1 WLR 1385. Further, there is a strong statutory statement of purpose in section 82(2) of the CJA, which provides that:

> "the powers shall be exercised with a view to making available for satisfying ... any confiscation order ... the value for the time being of realisable property".

(2) Why profit-seizing might apply to pollution

It is in our view perfectly conceivable that, in addition to the fines and clean-up costs provided for by the specific environmental schemes, polluters may fall foul of the profit-seizing provisions of the CJA. This would exclude statutory nuisance, where the appropriate offences are summary only (s.80).

One starts, of course, with a common sense observation. Parliament deliberately made the profit-seizing provisions of the CJA of general application. In principle, there is no reason to exclude pollution offences.

It is noteworthy that a similar link has already been endorsed between environmental offences and compensation orders, on the basis that s.35 of the Criminal Courts Act 1973 is of general application: see *Herbert v Lambeth London Borough Council* The Times 27th November 1991. Precisely the same link could be made with the CJA, and for precisely the same reason.

Indeed, there may be a special attraction to profit-seizing in the environmental sphere. The expanded framework of environmental liability is, after all, sufficiently recent to be seen as being without any settled conceptual home. Even the EC "polluter pays" catch-phrase begs an obvious question: polluter pays what? Compensation for damage? Premium for the right to pollute? Penalty for infringing regulations? Why not profits from flouting the law?

The arguments in favour of profit-seizing in the environmental context are quite powerful. We summarize them here. One could begin with the inadequacies of the common law approach. The negligence and nuisance models rest upon identifying a victim, harm, and causation. This may be seen as adequate to serve, say, a neighbouring land-owners situation, where competing property rights are balanced: A is only restricted in how he can use his land because of the way in which B wishes to use his (remember Hohfeld's symmetry of legal rights?).

But these models do not adequately confront a typical pollution problem. Emissions into the air, or discharges into water, are likely to cause damage as to which the victims and causal link are impossible to identify let alone prove. And mere damage to the environment will not suffice, there being no one to assert the necessary proprietory right and/or injury to enable them to sue. The situation is exacerbated in a jurisdiction where even public law is hostile to public interest claims (see eg. *R v Secretary of State for the Environment ex parte Rose Theatre Trust Co* [1990] 1 QB 504).

Moreover, there may be a built-in conservatism in the common law nuisance framework. One example may be the principle that damages must be an inadequate remedy before the grant of an injunction (eg. *Pride of Derby* [1953] Ch 149). A second may be the 'discount' principle illustrated by cases like *Andreae v Selfridge* [1938] Ch 1: that even if the plaintiff proves a nuisance, he is only entitled to such damages which flow from the activities which 'crossed the line' of legality. Accordingly in *Andreae* the Court acknowledged that a lesser degree of dust and noise would not have been actionable and Lord Greene MR awarded a 'discount', stating (at 11) that:

> "one must be careful not to penalise the defendant company by throwing into the scales against it the loss ... caused by operations which it was legitimately entitled to carry out. It can be made liable only in respect of matters, in which it has

crossed the permissible line ..."

Such a 'discount' principle makes sense. But the problem with it, (as for example with the 'green pencil' test in public law), is that it may encourage a wrongdoer to take a risk knowing that at worst his conduct will be penalised only insofar as it represents an excess.

One can state the issue in a different way. To the economist the neighbouring land-owner situation is a convenient analytical tool to demonstrate the underlying aim of the law, encouraging the most "efficient" use of resources. Each neighbour has a 'price' upon his wishes, so the theory goes, and absent 'transaction' costs they will naturally negotiate the most efficient solution. The more 'valuable' land-use will win the day, through being able to compensate the less 'valuable' one. Factory A continues its night-shift, and simply 'pays off' neighbour B who is distressed at the noise. Everyone is happy, and "efficiency" prevails. The law we are told, as if by magic, has for decades been serving this laudable goal by ensuring that B gets paid (either by awarding him compensatory damages or an injunction as a bargaining chip).

As with any economic analysis, one can respond in one of two ways. The first is to reject the morality-neutral analytical tool "efficiency", on the grounds that it is simply not appropriate to countenance pollution in the name of "efficient" use of resources in a context of finite resources and a fragile world. The second is to adopt the economists' approach (and its jargon) and follow it through. Any thorough economic analysis requires its efficiency sums to be based on a proper 'internalisation of costs' and in particular the 'social cost'. With its 'social cost' properly on-board, it may well be that pollution is not so "efficient" after all. But the crux is that we cannot adequately measure 'social cost' anyway.

The fact that Parliament has seen fit to criminalise polluting activities lends support to all these observations about inadequate common law models. But the existence of a statutory offence, even (or perhaps especially) with an unlimited power to fine, does not of itself identify the proper conceptual basis for the liability. Criminology and penology are riddled with conflicting theories of punishment: deterrence; retribution; reparation; rehabilitation; prevention; and so on.

It all depends on how environmental offences are viewed: see for instance Atkinson, *The Regulatory Lacuna: Waste Disposal and the Clean-up of Contaminated Sites* Journal of Environmental Law Vol.3

No.2 265, on the deterrence/compensation dichotomy presented by the criminal and civil law. Some of the 'trigger terms' in the statutory environmental offences, with which we deal in the next part, are suggestive of a strict liability. And some of the caselaw is supportive of a strong judicial policy commitment. But wherever you look you find a dilemma as to the sort of 'criminality' which attaches to environmental offences. Put bluntly, the dilemma is how seriously we should take pollution crimes.

For instance, the judicial uneasiness with strict criminal liability has produced the view that only in exceptional circumstances is it appropriate. The classic authority is *Sherras v De Rutzen* [1895] 1 QB 918 at 922 where Wright J formulated three exceptions to the presumption that criminal liability requires 'mens rea'. The first concerned "a class of acts which ... are not criminal in any real sense, but are acts which in the public interest are prohibited under a penalty". The second (strikingly) was "public nuisances", and the third "cases in which, although the proceeding is criminal in form, it is really only a summary mode of enforcing a civil right".

The second of these is inherently environmental, but begs the question of why liability is strict. To the environmentalist, the first would presumably be quite unacceptable allowing pollution to retain an image that it is 'not a real crime', with consequentially light penalties imposed, and the giant polluter's corporate image to remain relatively untarnished. To the polluter, it would presumably be seen as a recognition of the public benefit of his wealth-generation or even waste-disposing activities, and a refusal to straight-jacket him in these laudable pursuits. As we shall see, it is precisely the notion which has been used in the pollution context.

A good example of the dilemma is presented by *Alphacell v Woodward* [1972] AC 824, which we discuss more fully below. That was a 'strict' river pollution case where the House of Lords held that it was unnecessary for the prosecution to prove either knowledge or negligence. The environmentalist would welcome the strong policy acknowledgment of Lord Salmon (at 848):

> "It is of the utmost public importance that our rivers should not be polluted. The risk of pollution, particularly from the vast and increasing number of riparian industries, is very great ..."
>
> "If this appeal succeeded and it were held to be the law that no conviction could be obtained under the Act of 1951 unless the

> prosecution could discharge the often impossible onus of proving that the pollution was caused intentionally or negligently, a great deal of pollution would go unpunished and undeterred to the relief of many riparian factory owners. As a result, many rivers which are now filthy would become filthier still and many rivers which are now clean would lose their cleanliness. The legislature no doubt recognised that as a matter of public policy this would be most unfortunate ..."

However, the other side of the dilemma is presented by what Lord Salmon said between the two passages just cited,

> "The offences created by the Act of 1951 seem to me to be prototypes of offences which 'are not criminal in any real sense, but are acts which in the public interest are prohibited under a penalty': *Sherras v De Rutzen* [1895] 1 QB 918 per Wright J. at p.922, referred to with approval by my noble and learned friends, Lord Reid and Lord Diplock, in *Sweet v Parsley* [1970] AC 132, 149, 162. I can see no valid reason for reading the word "intentionally", "knowingly" or "negligently" into section 2(1)(a) and a number of cogent reasons for not doing so. In the case of a minor pollution such as the present, when the justices find that there is no wrongful intention or negligence on the part of the defendant, a comparatively nominal fine will no doubt be imposed. This may be regarded as a not unfair hazard of carrying on a business which may cause pollution on the banks of a river. The present appellants were fined £20 and ordered to pay, in all, £24 costs. I should be surprised if the costs of pursuing this appeal to this House were incurred for the purpose of saving these appellants £44."

Similarly, the Court in *Southern Water Authority v Pegrum* (discussed later) applied and echoed the 'strict liability' and strong policy aspects of *Alphacell*, but also adopted the first *Sherras v De Rutzen* exception as explaining the criminality of pollution. What the Courts have done, then, is to acknowledge a strong policy in favour of imposing criminal liability (strict liability), but 'sweetening the pill' by down-playing the culpability of the polluter.

This is more than a dilemma. It produces a paradox. The readily-imposed strict liability may be of little significance if the *Sherras v De Rutzen* idea means that penalties imposed on polluters are modest. The real villain in the environmental protection story is the cynical or calculating polluter. It would be paradoxical indeed if the fact that prosecutors are not required by Parliament to prove 'mens rea' make it harder to secure a meaningful penalty in cases where they would have been able to show an intentional or deliberate act of environmental damage.

In the end the question is whether the law wants certain environmentally damaging activities to stop. Even harsh fines are likely to be seen by large industrial concerns as simply part of the cost of the process. And deterrence is weaker where proof is hard or policing authorities lack adequate resources. Is the environmental criminal sanction merely to operate as a kind of tax: the 'cost' of polluting (as a parking ticket is to some the 'cost' of parking) ? Or is the aim more serious ? How do you ensure that the chemical plant, which deliberately dumps its waste in the river, stops ? The answer, we suggest, is that you seize the profits it has made from the process.

Of course, the very existence of the injunction in the context of nuisance is suggestive of the law's recognition that some activities should stop rather than simply pay for the damage they cause. The problem is the inadequacy of the common law, and its built-in conservatism, both of which we have discussed above.

There is a powerful statutory analogy presented by the profit-seizing provisions of the Housing Act 1988 sections 27 and 28. The policy considerations relating to eviction of residential occupiers have long required the obtaining of a Court order (Protection of Eviction Act 1977). But Parliament has recognised that the only way to stop the calculating landlord from ignoring the law, deciding that his profit will exceed any compensatory damages payable, is to allow the evicted occupier to sue for any profits made through the eviction, with startling results: see *Tagro v Cafane* [1991] 1 WLR 378.

Unlike unlawful eviction of course, environmental harm does not present an individual 'victim' to whom profits can be awarded. Moreover, it is doubtful whether such 'jackpot' awards are the most sensible mechanism in this context. The ideal might be seized-profits going into a central fund to be used for environmental protection and clean-up.

Further support can be seen to come from the Hodgson Committee, whose 1984 report "*The Profits of Crime and Their Recovery*" was the forerunner to the DTOA and the CJA Part VI. What the Committee had in mind when proposing the profit-seizing regime was that it apply to "profitable non-victim crimes". Some would say this is a term which fits perfectly the conduct of those who make profits from processes which pollute the environment.

Finally, and ironically, we return to where we started, the inadequacies of the common law. The intellectual coherence of the concept of profit-seizing is supported by the underlying theme of a group of cases which are scattered throughout the law of obligations, and where the insight is precisely that compensation notions are an inadequate response to those who disregard the law.

These are cases which are now sought to be re-housed under the "unjust enrichment" umbrella of the new faith 'restitution' (see for example Birks, *An Introduction to the Law of Restitution* 1985, chapter 10). We offer simply a brief synopsis of some examples where orthodoxy has been extended, relaxed or manipulated to order payment of what the Defendant has profited, notwithstanding no real suggestion that it is the accurate measure of the Plaintiff's loss or damage:

- Waiver of tort. *Lamine v Dorrell* (1701) 2 Ld Ray 1216: Defendant selling Plaintiff's property required to pay price obtained.

- Damages. *Whitwham v Westminster Brymbo* (1896) 1 Ch 894: Defendant dumping colliery spoil onto Plaintiff's land required to pay value to him of use of the land. *Strand Electric v Brisford* [1952] 2 QB 246: Defendant using Plaintiff's theatre lighting equipment, required to pay value of hire. *Penarth Dock Engineering v Pounds* [1963] 1 Lloyds Rep. 359: Defendant mooring boat in Plaintiff's dock required to pay value of using dock. *Swordheath Properties v Tabet* [1979] 1 WLR 285: Defendant occupying Plaintiff's property required to pay value of staying.

- Damages in lieu of injunction (tort). *Bracewell v Appleby* [1975] Ch 408: Defendant building house and disregarding lack of access over Plaintiff's property required to share profit from building house. *Carr-Saunders v McNeil* [1986] 1 WLR 922: Defendant building property in disregard for Plaintiff's right to light required to share profits of so doing.

- Damages in lieu of injunction (contract). *Wrotham Park Estates v Parkside Homes* [1974] 1 WLR 798: Defendant having built houses in wilful disregard of restrictive covenant in Plaintiff's favour required to pay profits.

- Exemplary / punitive damages. *Cassell v Broome* [1972] AC 1027: Defendant deliberately defaming Plaintiff for profit, required to pay that profit to Plaintiff. Note that the possibility of exemplary damages in the context of private (but not public) nuisance has recently been countenanced if a polluter (or supplier of polluted matter) has deliberately gone ahead with the harmful activity calculated to make a profit exceeding compensatory damages: *Gibbons v South West Water Services* The Times 26th November 1992.

- Equitable account / fiduciary relationship etc. *Edelsten v Edelsten* (1863) 1 De Gex J & Son 185: Defendant using Plaintiff's Trade Mark required to pay profits; *My Kinda Town v Soll* [1983] RPC 407: Defendant doing business under Plaintiff's trade-name required to pay profits; *Peter Pan v Corsets Silhouette* [1964] 1 WLR 96: Defendant using Plaintiff's manufacturing techniques required to pay profits; *Reading v AG* [1951] AC 507: Defendant army officer required to pay the Crown bribes received for guiding smugglers; *Boardman v Phipps* [1967] 2 AC 46: trustee Defendant required to pay to trust profits from share purchase using information acquired qua trustee; *English v Dedham Vale* [1978] 1 WLR 93: Defendant purchaser required to pay to Plaintiff vendor benefit from planning permission obtained through impersonating Plaintiff.

The point is that these cases are not readily explainable on the basis of 'compensation' orthodoxy. There was no real suggestion in the *Penarth Dock* line of cases that the Plaintiff could have hired his property to a third party; it was impossible in *Boardman v Phipps* for the beneficiary to acquire the shares; the Crown in *Reading v AG* could hardly say that it was deprived of the bribes; and *Cassell v Broome* turned precisely on the fact that compensatory damages would have left the Defendant with an undeserved profit. The theme, then, is the recognition on the part of the Courts that the only way to deter the wrongdoing was to confiscate the Defendant's profits.

To conclude, the CJA is likely to appear in the environmental context, at least in cases concerning 'conscious' pollution. And we think it perfectly conceivable that policing authorities will be bold enough to pursue, and Crown Courts bold enough to make, profit-seizing orders against companies who have decided that their profit levels justify disregarding environmental law.

PART III

LENDER LIABILITY

CHAPTER 7

ISSUES FOR LENDERS

Having surveyed it, what is the significance of the domestic environmental law scene for lenders ? Many of the important questions are obvious already. We discuss here some of the issues, and aims, which arise for lenders.

(1) General observations

The impact and effectiveness of the statutory environmental protection regimes will turn on questions of practicality and policy, not law. A central issue is the enviro-jingle, 'command and control'. The obvious, but critical factors include the following:

- the attitude and effectiveness of the policing authorities;
- the approach of the courts;
- the delay in implementation of statutory machinery;
- the availability of insurance for environmental risks;
- the availability of environmental assessment experts.

The effectiveness of the policing authorities will in turn depend on two things: resources and resolve. As to the first, providing the statutory machinery is quite simply not enough unless the authority has the funds, training and staff to use it.

As to the second, environmental enforcement machinery including the 'clean-up' provisions of the PHA in 1936 and then COPA in 1974 has traditionally rarely been used. Prosecution has been seen as a last resort, and policing authorities have preferred what can be called a 'cooperative' rather than a 'confrontational' approach. Moreover, the reluctance to prosecute corporate polluters has been accompanied by an even greater reluctance to pursue individuals (such as directors) or third parties having some connection with the activity, to the comfort of lenders and mortgagees. It may be said that the *Sherras v Rutzen*-type notion, that polluters are 'not really criminals', has been one recognised not only by Judges but by environmental policemen.

Similarly, past experience of the operation of environmental registers has suggested a lack of effectiveness and dynamism on the part of policing authorities. An empirical study of the water registers under COPA found disappointing levels of promotion, access, usefulness and enforcement, concluding that the registers were "little more than symbolism" (see Burton, *Access to Environmental Information: the UK experience of Water Registers* Journal of Environmental Law Vol. 1 No.2 p.192).

There is a widely-held perception though that it is all changing, that there is a new determination, even ruthlessness, on the part of the policing authorities. The NRA in particular is widely considered to be both well-resourced and bold. Whether this will be an apt description of HMIP remains to be seen. It may be that a honeymoon period is over, signified perhaps by the Mersey Oil spill, which led to a £1 million fine (and massive clean-up) for Shell in 1990.

The question of resolve goes not only to issues of enforcement, but licensing and clean-up. Requirements of assurances and information to accompany licence applications, refusal of licences, conditions imposed upon licences granted, and methods to be used in conducting clean-up duties are all matters of the policing authority's discretion. These are powerful bodies indeed, challengeable only on the deferential administrative law bases for judicial review (cast in the *GCHQ* case [1985] AC 374 as "illegality", "irrationality" and "procedural impropriety").

Fears about delayed implementation are already being fuelled by the shelving of the 'contaminated land' Register, which was due to come into force in April 1992 (for compilation, with publication in April 1993). As we have said, it was always rather ominous that the 1974 COPA regime for water registers took until August 1985 to come into force.

We have mentioned the question of insurance and environmental assessment expertise. We do not propose to discuss these at length: they could (and no doubt will) lead to books in their own right, and a consideration of each would benefit from its own "trans-atlantic glance". But we pause to mention that environmental insurance is fraught with difficulties as to the reluctance to underwrite potentially enormous risks, and the hurdles (or evasion techniques) of 'non-disclosure' and 'deliberate act'. As for 'environmental auditors', they may be in a period of learning/exploring the significance of the environmental protection regimes, like lenders (and practically everybody else), which ironically adds to the importance of insurance.

Some hints as to the attitudes in the higher Courts will arise in our discussion of 'trigger terms' below. But it is worth underlining the importance of the attitude of criminal courts of first instance, and especially the country's magistrates. The realities of enforcement depend on the boldness of prosecutors coupled with that of the Courts. And again, the past can be said to have been characterised by lenient penalties.

Of course, if magistrates are prepared to commit pollution prosecutions to the Crown Courts then questions of environmental liability will (in the first place, at least) be in the hands of juries, and an unlimited power to fine, together with the prospect of profit-seizing, in the hands of the sentencing Crown Court judge. The results are potentially dramatic. But how "green" the Courts are, or how ready to indulge in the 'search for a deeper pocket' is, like much else, a matter of speculation.

A final observation is that it would be wholly wrong to characterise developments in environmental law as being capable only of exposing or attacking lenders. Several component parts of the statutory machinery can be seen to assist lenders: for example, the availability of pollution registers, the requirements in connection with licensing applications, the conditions attached to licences, and the provisions as to surrender of licences. All of these are capable of being deployed by lenders to assist them in what we have identified as their dual objective: knowing the lender, and avoiding liability.

(2) Clean-up costs and priority

One specific and important issue which arises concerns the status of a liability to pay clean-up costs. How does that liability relate to other debts, both secured and unsecured ?

We start with some observations about the statutory scheme. Neither the EPA nor the WRA has done what Parliament has done elsewhere, that is to make clean-up costs registrable as a charge on the land. Three cases illustrate the kind of scheme which Parliament could have incorporated into the EPA and WRA (and did not):

- *Maguire v Leigh-on-Sea UDC* (1906) 70 JP 479, concerning

the Private Street Works Act 1892. Under that Act the cost of works done by the local authority were registrable and operated as a charge, capable of allowing the authority to precipitate a sale, providing that they had served the correct "owner".

- *Westminster CC v Haymarket* [1981] 1 WLR 677, where the Court considered the General Rate Act 1967, under which the authority had registered a legal charge over property, to secure an outstanding rating surcharge.

- *Southern Water Authority v Nature Conservancy Council* [1992] 1 WLR 775, involving the Wildlife and Countryside Act 1981. There it was not clean-up costs but the service of a notification prohibiting certain operations on the land which was registrable as a land charge. Lord Mustill stated that this mechanism served to counteract any suggestion of hardship on the part of an "innocent purchaser", since he was "presumed to have notice" of the charge.

Of these, *Westminster CC v Haymarket* is the most startling for lenders. There the Court of Appeal held that the rating authority was entitled to its surcharge ahead of the mortgagee bank, even though the bank's interest had been registered first, the concept of the authority's "charge on the land" being interpreted widely.

The fact that no such regime is included in the EPA and WRA suggests that clean-up costs are to be treated as mere 'debts' and that the policing authorities (local authority, waste regulation authority, HMIP, NRA etc) have the status of unsecured creditors.

The problem is that this, of course, was precisely what the receiver and secured creditors thought in *Panamericana v Northern Badger*. There, as we have seen, the Canadian Court rejected an 'insolvency' analysis and held that the ERCB's 'clean-up' Order in Council had a status of imposing on the receiver a duty to pay the environmental authority first, to the dismay of the secured creditor.

The question is whether it would be open to an English Court to hold that the status of a Court Order secured by a policing authority is such that it prevails over the interests of other (even secured) creditors. Put another way, the question is who in English Law would win the clash between 'insolvency law' and 'environmental law'. As we have seen, in *Panamericana v Northern Badger* it was the former at first instance and the latter in the Alberta Court of Appeal.

One important aspect of *Panamericana v Northern Badger* which ought to be explored is the distinction between clean-up debts and clean-up duties. It could turn out to be a vital one. The Alberta Court of Appeal was able to reject MacPherson J's characterisation of the ERCB as "a creditor seeking to have its claim preferred" because the ERCB was seeking to enforce an order that the Receiver carry out clean-up operations, not an order for recovery of clean-up costs already incurred by the ERCB itself. Laycraft C.J.A. said this (at 291):

> "It is true that the board has the power by statute to create in its own favour a statutory debt if it chooses to do so. It may ... do the work ... itself and become a creditor for the sums expended. But the board has not done so in this case. Rather, it is simply in the course of enforcing observance of a part of the general law of Alberta ... In my view, the board is not, at this point, a "creditor" of Northern Badger with a claim provable in its bankruptcy. The problem presented by this case is not to be solved, therefore, by determining whether the board ranks as creditor of Northern Badger before or after the secured creditors. Rather, it must be determined whether the Receiver, which was the operator of the oil wells in question, had a duty to abandon them in accordance with the law."

The 'clean-up debt' situation was therefore left open in *Panamericana v Northern Badger* but with a hint at least that the result might be different in such a context. Were such a distinction to appear in English law, the lesson is obvious: the well-advised policing authority may well prefer to delay its own clean-up operations and rely instead upon the "public duty" of clean-up. Accordingly, policing authorities would have a stronger hand in an insolvency context were they to rely upon clean-up orders (eg. EPA ss.26(1); 82(2)) or possibly offences of non-compliance with clean-up notices (eg. EPA ss.38(9); 59(1); 80(1); WRA s.92(1)(b)) rather than orders for payment of clean-up-costs (EPA ss.27(1)(b); 59(6)(8); 61(8); 81(4); WRA s.161(3)).

(3) Knowing the borrower

What arise for the lender from an understanding of domestic environmental liability can be characterised as the dual aims of knowing the borrower and avoiding liability. Unfortunately there is some prospect that steps prudent in relation to the first of these may be fatal in relation to the second. We discuss these dual-aims here, first separately and then focusing on their interrelationship.

The essential requirement of successful lending is understanding the risk. Bankers are well-practised in the art of identifying an acceptable balance of resources and prospects. The fact that there is borrowing at all means that there are inevitably on the part of the borrower financial resources which are in some sense limited: the borrower does not borrow unless he needs the money. Conversely, there must be some basis for security and/or prospect of success of the borrower's endeavours. The borrower will not be permitted to borrow unless there is a prospect of recovery of the debt. Somewhere in the middle of it all is the perfect balance: the borrower can repay the lender, but not too easily; at least not before he has gained what he considers a healthy amount of interest. The vital thing for the lender is that it knows what the risk is.

We state the obvious because of its common sense implications in the environmental sphere. The successful lender needs to know prior to the lending what environmental liabilities or potential liabilities the borrower has, the scale of those liabilities and the prospects that they will be enforced effectively. For example, what are the chances of having to pay clean-up costs ? How much would they be ? What are the chances of a licence being revoked and the borrower going out of business altogether?

The lender also needs to know the nature and value of the borrower's assets, particularly any intended security, and so the effect or potential effect on those assets of environmental issues. What are the chances that the borrower's land will be registered as contaminated land ? How would this affect its value and marketability?

Then there is the position during the lending: when to call in the loan. The lender's monitoring function, reviews of its exposure and security coverage, require assessment from a position of knowledge. What dealings have there been with the policing authority ? What notices have been served ? What entries on the public registers made ?

There is a further point. Prudent lenders and deposit-takers must be concerned with far more than commercial return. Indeed they have the watchful eye of their own policing authorities to worry about, formally and primarily the Bank of England, informally but importantly the media, and somewhere in between the Banking Ombudsman. The perils of involvement with 'dirty money', and the need for heightened scrutiny, are well-understood in the banking community. The question is what degree of shift, if any, would be required in the criminalisation and public perception of pollution for its exploitation and profits to move alongside that of drug traffickers and pornographers. In this respect the issue is similar to that raised with regard to profit-seizing (the special implications of which are discussed below).

(4) Avoiding liability

The second of the dual-aims relates to what to lenders is the spectre, and to environmentalists perhaps the dream, of a lender (or receiver etc), incurring liability. It is this notion of course which spawned the phrase 'lender liability'. In other jurisdictions the notion is a reality, as *US v Fleet Factors* and *Panamericana v Northern Badger* demonstrate. What is clear from those illustrations is that the greatest risk appears to fall upon those seeking to enforce securities.

There is also the question of insolvency. We will mention below the concepts and consequences of preferences and wrongful trading under the Insolvency Act 1986. The simple observation is that environmental liabilities introduce a new element in the balancing of the "prospective or contingent liabilities" side of the insolvency equation, an equation which is a matter of concern not only for lenders and insolvency practitioners, but directors and auditors as well.

It will be clear already that the extent to which this direct 'lender liability' will develop on the domestic scene, depends largely on definitional matters: when does a bank or receiver "carry on" a business, or "cause" or "permit" it ? Can pollution be due to an "act or default" by the lender who sustains or supports it ? Is such a lender a "person responsible" for the pollution ? (When) is a mortgagee an "occupier" or "owner" or "owner for the time being" ? Can a lender be a "similar officer" or "purport to act" in that capacity ? We will call terms such as these 'trigger terms'. We say more about their importance later in the chapter, and then consider them in depth in the next two chapters.

(5) The "dilemma": knowing the borrower and avoiding liability

In case it is not already obvious, we should identify a central dilemma produced by the relationship between the ideas of knowing the borrower and avoiding liability. It is a dilemma which can arise at two different stages: the time of lending and the time of debt-collecting.

The dilemma is how closely to become involved in the borrower's activities. The lender has the "dual aims" of wanting to know the borrower without incurring liability itself. The dilemma arises because in "scrutinizing" or "monitoring" the borrower, it may incur precisely such direct liability.

The "dual aims" are well illustrated with reference to an important 'environmental' speech given by Lord Alexander of Weedon QC to the Chartered Institute of Bankers in Bristol on 26th November 1991. Lord Alexander stressed the importance of scrutiny:

> "It is a matter of good business sense that our lending policies and practices should reflect the potential damage a customer's business might do to the environment. This reflects the responsibility we owe as a business to our shareholders, to our staff, to our customers and the communities in which they operate, to contribute to a healthier environment. It is also becoming ... an important aspect of the assessment of risk in any business proposal."

He went on to emphasize the role of banks in giving to "small businesses ... assistance in the development of more environmentally responsible working practices" and to acknowledge that:

> "lenders ... have clear responsibilities. Banks must take all proper steps to evaluate the environmental risk and comply with standards which were current at the time when the loan was made."

Finally, though, came the recognition of the second of the "dual aims", avoiding a level of scrutiny or involvement such as to attract potential liability:

> "But it is not our role to act either as "environmental police", or to run a customer's business. Indeed, there would be an important detriment to business if the liability on the banks went too wide ... We need a secured creditor exemption which holds the balance between requiring banks to do business on a responsible basis without imposing a liability which would be an active deterrent to the provision of finance."

the time of lending

The first stage, then, at which the dilemma can be said to arise is at the time of lending (or continuing to lend). Here it is similar to 'the CERCLA dilemma' encountered in the United States and discussed in chapter 2. In essence the problem is this: the more actively the lender takes steps to know its borrower and the more carefully the lender monitors the borrower's activities, the more likely the lender is to become liable himself for the borrower's pollution. Thus, a bank which takes prudent steps to find out about its lender's business, may find itself saddled with criminality, and massive clean-up costs.

A further question is whether a bank can in these circumstances come under a duty to its borrower, or prevented from being able to recover monies loaned. These are cases which show that a banker owes no duty to protect its customer from himself (eg. by pointing out the potential risks of his activities). There is Ralph Gibson J. in *Williams & Glyns Bank v Barnes* [1981] Com. LR 205 (at 207):

> "no duty in law arises upon the Bank either to consider the prudence of the lending from the customer's point of view, or to advise with reference to it ... even if the Bank knows or ought to know that the borrowing and application of the loan, as intended by the customer, are imprudent ...";

And Saville J. in *Redmond v Allied Irish Banks* [1987] 2 FTLR 264 (at 267):

> "[there is no duty] to advise or warn a customer that there are risks attendant upon something which the customer wishes to do ...";

Then there is the dictum from Lord Scarman in *Tai Hing Cotton Mill v Liu Chong Hing Bank* ([1986] 1 AC 80 at 107):

> "Their Lordships do not believe that there is anything to the advantage of the law's development in searching for a liability in tort where the parties are in a contractual relationship ... Their Lordships do not, therefore, embark on an investigation as to whether in the relationship of banker and customer it is possible to identify tort as well as contract as a source of the obligations owed by the one to the other ..."

But equally familiar are the notions of 'special circumstances' which are said to be capable of allowing a 'duty to warn' to arise: 'unusual circumstances' (*Mackenzie v Royal Bank of Canada* [1934] AC 468); the customer specifically seeking advice (*Woods v Martins Bank* [1959] 1 QB 55); the bank volunteering advice (*Hedley Byrne v Heller* [1964] AC 465); a special fiduciary relationship (*Lloyds Bank v Bundy* [1975] QB 326; *Redmond v Allied Irish Banks*, above); and the "implied representation and reliance, having regard to the terms of advertisements frequently used by Banks" (*Williams & Glyns v Barnes*, above). Moreover, in the context of "personal customers", many of these can be used alongside the assumption of responsibility contained in the new Banking Code (effective from March 1992), in which banks acknowledge the duty to consider information as to the customer's financial affairs and past dealings with a view to avoiding over-commitment.

Putting these 'windows for argument' alongside the potential effects of liability for environmental harm, it is easy to imagine the arguments likely to be deployed against a bank: that the Bank through its investigation of the nature and extent of the potential environmental risks was in a position to warn its borrower of those risks and ought to have done so.

The question as to whether an 'investigative' lender may incur a liability is clearly not simply the lender's dilemma, but the law's. From the point of view of the legislator formulating, or judge interpreting (or in the case of the common law formulating), the law, where should the emphasis lie? If it is in encouraging responsible borrowing or discouraging lending to polluters, this may not be achieved by deterring lenders from investigating and monitoring the activities of their borrowers, for fear of being penalised by direct liability themselves.

As a lender's dilemma, this is similar to other types of dilemma in other banking contexts which are already all too familiar. For example, in the context of taking security the law (at present) seeks to protect a bank who takes steps to ensure that a security document is executed in the presence of a solicitor who is other than that of the bank (eg. cases like *Bank of Baroda v Shah* [1988] 3 All ER 24). But if the bank takes too many steps, and interferes too much in communicating with the solicitor or 'instructing' him, the solicitor may be deemed to have been the bank's agent so that the bank is tainted by things said or known by the solicitor (eg. cases like *Kingsnorth v Bell* [1986] 1 WLR 119). Similarly, the cases dealing with a duty to explain security documents have acknowledged the Bank's potential "dilemma of having to choose between, on the one hand, risking the security being unenforceable, and, on the other hand, undertaking a duty of care" (*Barclays Bank v O'Brien* [1992] 3 WLR 593 at 621 per Scott LJ).

These are difficult paths for the bank to tread. So is lending to polluters. Our view is to favour fully researched lending. If the environmental assessment shows an unacceptable risk then the bank must decline to lend. If the risk only emerges subsequently the bank should not be at fault and/or should look to a remedy against its experts.

the time of debt-collecting

The second stage when the dilemma can arise concerns debt-collecting, and particularly the enforcement of security. This is really just one part of the responsible borrower's monitoring function: the all-important question of when to call in the loan, but it gives rise to questions about whether and how to collect the debt. When should a lender make demand, foreclose, take possession, sell, or appoint a receiver ?

Ordinarily, when the prospects of success of a business and repayment of the debt are becoming too slim the lender will call a halt, make demand and look to its security. In the context of environmental harm, where a polluter has reached a position where his potential environmental liabilities render his position hopeless, one might think that the law ought to encourage the person who controls the money supply not only to cut that off, but to intervene immediately.

The problem is that this is precisely the situation where a lender may be least inclined to become involved, since the most obvious warning signs as to direct 'lender liability' are concerned precisely with those enforcing securities. The situation is likely to stagnate, and not just metaphorically, especially if the policing authority is without the resources to conduct a major clean-up in circumstances where it is unlikely to recover its costs from either borrower or lender.

The reason for the dilemma is well-illustrated by the attitude of the US Court in the *US v Maryland Bank* case, and the Canadian Court in *Panamericana v Northern Badger*. The reasoning in each of these was that if a bank or receiver chooses to step into the polluter's shoes by enforcing a security, it must 'take the rough with the smooth'. It cannot 'pick and choose', expecting simply to sell off assets for its own benefit and ignore the environmental responsibilities. And, in the case of banks anyway, if anticipated problems at the enforcement stage create a powerful incentive for earlier monitoring and intervention long before, prior to the time of the lending and preferably before the pollution takes place, so much the better.

(6) Special implications of profit-seizing

Our profit-seizing analysis from Chapter 6 has some special implications of its own for lenders. The possible characterisation of pollution proceeds as 'dirty money' and analogous to drug trafficking proceeds is, of course, a matter of great potential anxiety for lenders for several reasons. In the first place, 'knowing the borrower' must extend to an awareness of whether his business is likely to be ruined through the seizure of his profits. Second, avoiding 'involvement' must extend to the impact of a seizure order, not least the bad publicity.

Third, even a completely innocent lender may find itself significantly affected by the seizure provisions. It may hold assets which are suddenly the subject of a confiscation order, frozen by a restraint order (CJA s.77) or encumbered by way of a charging order (s.78). There then arises the question of third party protection under the confiscation order and 'criminal Mareva' scheme. In many respects the extent of this is unclear. But from the indications so far, some of which are outlined here, the suggestion is that third party protection is somewhat limited:

- The CJA states that a third party is to be allowed to "retain or recover the value of any property held by him" (s.82(4)). In *re Peters*, [1988] QB 871 at 879 Lord Donaldson MR considered this wording (as mirrored in the DTOA) and concluded that its:

  > "purpose is somewhat clearer than its wording. That purpose appears to be to safeguard the legitimate rights of third parties in property which is held by them, but which, because of an interest of the defendant (either legal or equitable), is capable of being the subject matter of a restraint order".

- However, a restraint order can be made over any property in which the Defendant has "an interest" (CJA s.102(7); and see *re the Drug Trafficking Offences Act 1986*, 26th March 1987, Webster J. unreported, (LEXIS), on the equivalent DTOA provision and property co-owned by spouses).

- An affected third party can apply to discharge or vary any restraint order (CJA s.77(7); RSC Order 115 r.5).

- However, there may be a reluctance to allow a discharge / variation even where the third party can establish sole interest. Indeed, the Hodgson Committee's position (Report p.128) was that an application could be made by third parties:

  > "to free their property from a pre-trial freezing order ... but only if the judge is persuaded that their application can be determined without prejudice to the defendant's pending criminal trial"

- A landlord can forfeit a lease held by the Defendant notwithstanding a restraint order, this being an "unfettered right" (*In re R* [1990] 2 QB 307).

- A bank may have a similar "automatic" right to combination or set off notwithstanding a restraint order, though an application to vary is prudent. This issue arose in *re K* [1990] 2 QB 298, where Otton J. referred (at 305) to the:

  > "rights of the bank ... who had acted in good faith and in ignorance of the tainted source of the deposited money ... to combine or to set off the indebtedness against the credit balance ... [otherwise] the vested rights of the bank would be in peril".

- There may be a variation of a restraint order to allow payment by the defendant of accrued debts. In *re Peters* (above) the Court allowed a variation to pay school fees.

- Otherwise, unsecured debts are apparently overridden by a restraint order and ex hypothesi a confiscation order, including that in favour of a bona fide third party judgment creditor (*In re W* The Times 12th September 1990, per Buckley J., applying s.82(6): "no account shall be taken of any obligations of the defendant ... which conflict with the obligation to satisfy the confiscation order").

- Also overridden are voluntary arrangements as to the defendant's estate under the Insolvency Act 1986 (*In re M*

(Restraint Order) [1992] 1 QB 377).

- However, the Court of Appeal has held that a confiscation order should be based only on the equity in a mortgaged property (*R v Chapman* The Times 18th November 1991).

- Finally, despite the strength of the Mareva analogy (recognised in *re Peters*; *re the Drug Trafficking Offences Act 1986* above; and *re I*, 13th July 1988, MacPherson J., unreported (LEXIS)), a restraint order does not carry an undertaking in damages in favour of the Defendant (see *re Peters*; RSC Order 115 r.4(1)). More importantly, nor does it involve an implied undertaking by the prosecutor to pay the reasonable expenses of third-party compliance (*re R*).

(7) The importance of 'trigger terms'

As we have said, what is of crucial importance is the question of the 'trigger terms' under the environmental protection regimes. These terms divide neatly into two types: those which relate to the polluting activity, and those which relate to the land on which that activity takes place. In the first group are terms like "permitting" and "connivance" etc., and in the second group the concepts of "owner" and "occupier".

Accordingly, whether a lender has direct liability for environmental harm will depend on whether the lender satisfies these 'trigger terms'. When is a lender's relationship with an activity such that he "permits" or "connives" at it ? When is a lender's relationship with land such that he is "owner" or "occupier" of it?

Both areas, 'relationship with activity' and 'relationship with land', can be approached in two different ways. The first is to look at sources of law which involve lenders in relationship with activities or land, and particularly those where that relationship results in liability, whether or not they raise the same matters of definition as are contained in the environmental protection regime. This involves looking at cases like *re a Company ex parte Copp*, *American Express v Hurley*, *Midland Bank v Conway* and *Meigh v Wickenden*, all of which are discussed below. Cases like these, then, can readily be seen as cases relating to 'lender liability', though often not in an environmental context.

The second way is to look at cases which concern the particular statutory triggers, cases on what is meant by terms like "permitting" or "occupier". Most of these will be from non-lending contexts, and it will be a question of assessing the various approaches and the strength as analogies in the context in which they occur.

Putting all this together, we will seek to analyze the way in which the various statutory triggers are likely to be interpreted in their environmental context, and what it all means for lenders.

In discussing some of the cases there will be a secondary agenda, trying to discern the underlying judicial mood in relation to two things: making lenders liable for wrongdoing in general; and the policy commitment of the Courts in environmental protection cases. For example, it is helpful to know if the Courts are resistant to making lenders liable for wrongful trading as a result of involvement in their borrower's activities, or resistant to making lenders liable to pay rates as a result of their relationship with land. It is also helpful to know how the Courts treat environmental cases generally, especially in the face of arguments that the chosen defendant is not an 'active' or 'knowing' polluter.

Before doing any of this, the kind of 'lender' roles which we have in mind in deciding whether/when a lender may fall foul of a 'trigger term' should be identified. The possible roles of the lender to be borne in mind include the following:

- The investigator
- The profit-sharer
- The manager
- The adviser
- The shadow director
- The security holder
- The security enforcer
- The receiver
- The receiver's appointer or indemnifier

Finally, before we turn to consider the statutory terminology, there are four matters to raise by way of warning about the limitations of the exercise we are about to conduct.

First, there is the potential relevance of EC terms, such as "deemed producer" under the Waste Directive. Such terms may overlap with those which we consider below. But one should beware before placing too much emphasis on an analysis of English construction of such terminology. The true perspective would presumably be that of the ECJ, driven by teleological rules of interpretation and overt policy concerns.

Second, there are the triggers potentially relevant to the common law. As for nuisance and *Rylands v Fletcher*, the notions are broadly of "control" (the ability to stop the nuisance, control of the substance) similar to those which we discuss below. As for breach of statutory duty, the relevant terms are identical to those we discuss below. However, negligence depends not upon an identification of who the Defendant is but his relationship with the Plaintiff, and whether that relationship satisfies the malleable "duty of care".

Third, in some ways more important than the way in which the Courts would interpret the relevant triggers, is the way in which the environmental policing authorities will do so. Much of the triggers serve to identify those upon whom these authorities think fit to serve compliance notices. And potential liability attaches to such persons immediately, who will ignore the compliance notice at their peril and be prepared at the very least to seek to have the notice set aside or defend an ensuing prosecution.

Fourth, under the statutory regimes some provisions are apparently definition-free. For example, there are offences of obstructing officers from exercising rights of entry in order to inspect a facility. One need satisfy no definitional trigger other than to be a person who has obstructed an officer.

CHAPTER 8

RELATIONSHIP WITH THE ACTIVITY

(1) Lenders and activity

We look here at some examples of the way in which the law has treated the relationship between lenders and the activities of borrowers, particularly the question of when the lender's involvement with the activities may be sufficient for it to incur a liability. We do so before turning to consider the various definitional triggers contained in the domestic framework of environmental liability.

We will discuss two main areas: shadow directors and negligent receivers. Neither is environmental. However, the critical themes in both areas are the extent of the lender's "participation" in or "control" over activities. These concepts are of course ones which are of vital importance in lender liability, as is illustrated by both *US v Fleet Factors* in the USA and *Panamericana v Northern Badger* in Canada. They fit in with the "control" factor which governs the "deemed producer" under the EC Waste Directive. Most importantly, as we will show later, they fit in with the 'trigger terms' under environmental law.

The cases which we mention here are we think helpful analogies in considering the prospect of lender liability for environmental harm. Indeed, they may take on a new significance in that context.

shadow directors

The first context where 'lender liability' based on "participation" or "control" has been discussed, comes from insolvency and concerns the role of the "shadow director" in the Insolvency Act 1986.

A "shadow director" is defined in section 251 of the Act, as "a person in accordance with whose directions or instructions the directors of the company are accustomed to act (but so that a person is not deemed a shadow director by reason only that the directors act on advice given by him in a professional capacity)". His significance is, in outline, that he is both a "connected person" who triggers the presumption of a desire to prefer (s.239) and a "director" who may be liable for wrongful trading (s.214).

Both preference and wrongful trading are concepts of risk based upon participation in the company's activities, the first a risk of increased exposure and the second one of direct liability. They therefore fit in well with several of the environmental statutory triggers which we consider below. Moreover, the fact that under the scheme of the Act there is some prospect that a participating lender's debt could be ordered to be postponed behind all the other debts of the company and/or the lender ordered to make a contribution towards the company's assets makes the analogy with *Panamericana v Northern Badger* (where the secured creditors were ordered to rank behind the company's clean-up liability) readily apparent.

Accordingly, any case where a bank has been argued to be a "shadow director" is likely to take on a new significance. Indeed, any such case could be characterised as already a 'lender liability' case. Enter *Re a company No. 005009 of 1987 ex parte Copp* [1989] BCLC 13; 4 BCC 424.

The company's liquidator had brought a claim against a bank, alleging that the bank's debenture was invalid as a preference and that the bank was guilty of wrongful trading, pleading that the bank had been at the material times a "shadow director". The bank was applying to strike out.

The one thing which emerges clearly from *re a Company ex parte Copp* is that Knox J considered that a bank was capable of constituting a shadow director for the purposes of section 251. This is important for our purposes. It represents a recognition that a banker may exert a level of control sufficient to satisfy the "directing or instructing" trigger term, such that it may incur direct liability (for wrongful trading) and increased exposure (losing its security).

The crucial question is obviously "when ?". What sort of conduct on the part of the bank would serve to make it a "shadow director" ?

Re a Company ex parte Copp reveals little more. In the first place, there is no clear description in the case as to what the bank's "participation" was, though it appears that the Bank was asserting an influence by making recommendations and giving instructions as to the management of the company, as a condition of the bank not appointing an administrative receiver.

Second, Knox J declined to say anything at all about why the bank might be or when a bank could be a shadow director. It was sufficient for the purposes of the application to hold that the liquidator's claim was not "obviously unsustainable", ([1989] BCLC at 21):

> "I have come to the conclusion that what I can, perhaps, conveniently call the 'obviously unsustainable test' is not satisfied in relation to the claim that the bank acted as a shadow director. It follows from that conclusion of mine that the possibility of there being further material before the court makes it wholly undesirable that I should state the conclusion which I have in fact reached on the basis of the material before the court in the light of the full, careful and helpful arguments addressed to me. That in turn, in my view, means that I should not give my reasons for stating the conclusion on the 'obviously unsustainable' test which I have expressed. To do so would, in my view, merely embarrass the judge who will have to determine the question at the trial."

Unfortunately, the claim was not continued against the bank so that the question of participation was not determined.

negligent receivers

The second context concerns the three-party-situation of banker, receiver and company, and the receiver's role of realising assets. Potentially, two things come out of this context. The first is the question of the receiver's liability for his "participation" and "control". The second is the position of a debenture-holding bank: when is its involvement such that liability attaches to it for the acts of the receiver?

It is worth starting by stressing that the role of a receiver is inherently characterised by a high degree of "participation" and "control". The Insolvency Act 1986 Schedule 1 contains wide management powers for administrative receivers, which include "the power to carry on the business of the company". Similar roles are played by a receiver appointed under the Law of Property Act 1925 (expressly the agent of the mortgagor) and under a debenture. The latter's powers typically include the power to get in assets, receive income, manage the company's business and dispose of assets.

These powers depend, of course, on the terms of the debenture and appointment, which are vital in two further respects. First, they will usually make clear that the receiver is to be the agent of the company and not the bank. Second, the appointment may contain an indemnity given to the receiver by the bank against any liability incurred in connection with the receivership.

The relationship between a bank, a receiver and the company in respect of the activities of the company was considered in *Standard Chartered Bank v Walker* [1982] 1 WLR 1410 and *American Express v Hurley* [1985] 3 All ER 564.

These cases tell us rather more about banker "participation", than that of receivers. They concern allegations by guarantors of negligence by receivers in the realisation of assets, so that the 'liability' involved is akin to the *Cuckmere Brick v Mutual Finance* ([1971] Ch 949) duty of care owed by an asset-realiser to a surety. Indeed, there is nothing particularly special about *Standard Chartered Bank v Walker* and *American Express v Hurley* from the point-of-view of the receiver's duty. What is more enlightening is the consideration in those cases of the bank's role. In both cases the Court held that the bank was capable of incurring liability through the acts of the receiver it had appointed, and notwithstanding the usual contractual 'agency' provisions.

Standard Chartered Bank v Walker was a bank's claim for summary judgment under a directors' guarantee. The guarantors alleged that there had been a sale at an undervalue by a receiver appointed by the bank under its debenture, and that this infected the bank by reason of agency. The bank's argument was that it could not be liable for any acts of the receiver since the debenture had the usual term stating that the receiver was to be the agent of the debtor company.

The Court of Appeal held that the Defence raised triable issues, including whether the receiver had interfered sufficiently in the conduct of the receivership so as to constitute the receiver its agent. Fox LJ stated (at 1418):

> "Apart from intervention in the conduct of receivership, the bank can rely on the provisions of the debenture making the receiver the agent of the company. But, it is said, if the bank gave directions to the receiver as to the conduct of the sale, the receiver became the agent of the bank; and, it is said, in such an event, if the receiver was negligent, the bank was liable."

And Lord Denning MR (at 1415-16):

> "So far as the receiver is concerned, the law is well stated by Rigby LJ in *Gaskell v Gosling* [1896] 1 QB 669 ... The receiver is the agent of the company, not of the debenture holder, the

> bank ... The debenture holder, the bank, is not responsible for what the receiver does except in so far as it gives him directions or interferes with his conduct of the realisation. If it does so, then it too is under a duty to use reasonable care towards the company and the guarantor."

In *American Express v Hurley* the complaint was the same: a guarantor alleged a negligent sale of assets by a bank-appointed receiver, that the receiver was the bank's agent, and that he was not therefore liable to the bank under the guarantee. There the receiver had continued to act both before and after the liquidation of the company, an event which was characterised as critical by Mann J (at 568):

> "A receiver appointed under the common form of charge here employed acts as the agent of the mortgagor ... If the mortgagor is put into liquidation then the agency terminates ... If the receiver continues to act he does not automatically become the agent of the mortgagee ... but he may become so if the mortgagee treats him as such"

Mann J. reached the following three conclusions: (1) that a bank is not responsible for what the receiver does while the company's agent (ie. pre-liquidation) unless the bank directed or interfered with the receiver's activities (*Standard Chartered Bank v Walker*); (2) that the bank is responsible for what the receiver had done while the bank's agent and acting as such (ie. here, post-liquidation); and (3) that the receiver was liable under an implied term, to indemnify the bank in respect of any liability arising from the receiver's conduct, there being no express provision in the 'contract of agency'.

He held that there had been a negligent asset-sale, subsequent to liquidation, and that the bank in correspondence had treated the receiver as acting on its behalf. Accordingly, the bank was liable to the guarantor, but the receiver liable to the bank (via the implied term).

The irony of the last point is obvious. Having reached a point of concern for lenders, that they can be infected directly be a receiver's conduct not just liable under an indemnity, they may themselves be protected by an indemnity.

The principle which may be said to arise from *Standard Chartered Bank v Walker* and *American Express v Hurley* is a corrosive one. It can be expressed as follows: notwithstanding 'agency' provisions which seek to protect it, a debenture-holding bank may find itself caught with whatever liability its receiver has incurred in his conduct of the receivership, if the bank gives him directions, interferes with his function or, after liquidation, assents in his continuing to act.

If nothing else, this emphasizes the importance of banker-receiver negotiations as to their inter se obligations, particularly indemnities.

(2) The trigger terms

We turn then to consider the most important terms (largely the statutory ones) which relate to a relationship with the polluting activity, and as to which a lender or receiver will want to ask the question 'could that mean me' ? And we do so at some length, notwithstanding the 'anti-analogy principle' recently expressed by the House of Lords (see Chapter 9, below), not least because behind the definitions the caselaw shows a great deal about the mood and policy-orientation of the Courts, and the tensions and choices arising in the environmental sphere.

"CARRYING ON"

This is the statutory trigger for liability in respect of air pollution under Part I of the EPA. The person requiring authorization under section 6, upon whom an enforcement notice can be served under section 13 or a prohibition notice under section 14, and who can be made liable for clean-up costs under section 27, is a person "carrying on" a prescribed process.

There is no definition of "carrying on" in the EPA, but it is a phrase which occurs frequently in various other statutory schemes (from the Mayor's Court Procedure Act 1857 s.12 to the Income and Corporation Taxes Act 1970 s.109) and in the context of restrictive covenants. There is therefore plenty of case-law on "carrying on", though much of it is concerned solely with questions of geography (whether the person concerned was "carrying on" an activity in a particular place or area, for purposes of tax, jurisdiction, restrictive covenants, etc.) and is of little help.

who carries on ?

The vital question for our purposes is who can be said to be "carrying on" an activity. The classic definitions in this respect state that what is required is that such persons exercise control and direction over the process (*Lewis v Graham* (1888) 22 QBD 1), and that mere contemplation, proposal or intention, and even active preparation are not sufficient (*Commissioner of Taxation v McPhail* (1968) 42 ALJR 150).

An example of the absence of the necessary control and direction may be the 'third party' case of *Lewis v Graham*. There, in the context of the Mayor's Court Procedure Act 1857, it was held that to "carry on" a business primarily meant one's own business, so that a salaried clerk did not carry on business at the offices of his employer.

The need for a high level of participation to satisfy the "carrying on" trigger is supported by the following argument. Other statutory schemes have chosen, and ensuing case-law been concerned with, the trigger not of a person "carrying on" but one said to "engage in" (eg. *Rolfe v Rolfe* 15 Sim 88) or be "concerned in" (eg. *Jones v Heavens* (1876) 4 ChD 636) or "concerned or interested in" (eg. *Newling v Dobell* 38 LJ Ch 111) the activity. The fact that these alternatives were not chosen by Parliament in Part I of the EPA is indicative of a close "participation" and "control" in that context.

Moreover, the concept of "carrying on" a polluting activity rather than, say, "causing" pollution requires a degree of continuity: involvement with an isolated act will apparently not suffice. This fits in with another classic definition of "carrying on", as involving "a repetition or series of acts" in *Smith v Anderson* (1880) 15 ChD 247.

receivers and insolvency

To the receiver, the most compelling example of a "carrying on" case is perhaps *re Sarflax* [1979] Ch 592. That case actually involved directors of a company who had collected assets and distributed proceeds following a resolution by the company that it was ceasing to trade. The question was whether in acting in this way the directors could be said to have been "carrying on" a business for the purposes of section 332 of the Companies Act 1948 (preference). Oliver J said (at 599):

> "I feel quite unable to say that the expression 'carrying on any business' in the section is necessarily synonymous with actively carrying on trade or that the collection of assets acquired in the

course of the business and the distribution of the proceeds of those assets in the discharge of business liabilities cannot constitute the carrying on of 'any business' for the purposes of the section ..."

To the receiver, the question raised by these words is obvious. Supposing that during the collection of assets and distribution of proceeds the company's plant causes air pollution, could the receiver then be said to have "carried on the process". *Re Sarflax* suggests that the receiver could be so liable and we consider it right in principle that he should be.

Finally, there are cases relating to the concept of "carrying on" business in the context of insolvency. They present something of a mixed message. For example, *Shorthorn Dairy v Hall* 31 SJ 479, suggests that once insolvent a company ceases to "carry on" business, though that case may well be confined to its particular context. It concerned a restrictive covenant not to carry on any business similar to that of a company for so long as the company "carried on" such business. The company was in liquidation and its business was being continued with a view to its sale as a going concern. This was held to be insufficient to constitute "carrying on" business for the purposes of triggering the contractual obligation. Contrasting with *Shorthorn Dairy v Hall* is *Theophile v Solicitor-General* [1950] AC 186, a case under section 4 of the Bankruptcy Act 1914 where it was held that a person "carries on business" within that provision until all his debts are paid.

"CAUSING"

The notion of causation is, of course, a dominant one in the common law context. Moreover, the principal offender under the water pollution regime in Part III of the WRA is someone who "causes or knowingly permits" pollution of controlled waters. Such a person can be guilty of the section 85 offence, and liable to pay section 161 clean-up costs.

The wording "causes or [knowingly] permits" has a long history of use in environmental statutes, going back to the Salmon Fisheries Act 1861. It is a phrase which implies two independent offences (*McLeod v Buchanan* [1940] 2 All ER 179), the relationship between which was well illustrated by *Price v Cromack* (below). It was discussed in *Alphacell v Woodward* [1972] AC 824 where Lord Wilberforce said (at 834) that it:

> "evidently contemplates two things - causing, which must involve some active operation or chain of operations involving as the result the pollution of the stream; knowingly permitting, which involves a failure to prevent the pollution, which failure, however, must be accompanied by knowledge... In my opinion, "causing" here must be given a common sense meaning ..."

And Lord Cross said (at 846):

> "the contrast drawn in the section between 'causing' and 'knowingly permitting' shows that a man cannot be guilty of causing polluting matter to enter a stream unless at the least he does some positive act in the chain of acts and events leading to that result ..."

a "mental element" ?

The keys to "causing", then, are an "active operation" or a "positive act". Do these need to be accompanied by fault or knowledge ? The House of Lords emphatically rejected any need for such elements in the context of a pollution "causing" offence, in *Alphacell v Woodward* (above). This is undoubtedly the leading case on "causes" for the purposes of section 85 of the WRA. It has the force of being a House of Lords pollution case, concerned with a near-identical statutory provision: ie. "causes or knowingly permits to enter a stream any poisonous, noxious or polluting matter" under section 2 of the Rivers (Prevention of Pollution) Act 1951. It is worthy of detailed consideration for these reasons, and because the approach which it illustrates may be of general significance.

Alphacell Ltd was a paper-manufacturing company which had a settling tank on the bank of the river Irwell. The tank was prevented from overflowing into the river by two pumps. When the river authority's inspector came, pollution was pouring out of the tank into the river. It transpired that the pumps had become blocked with leaves in the 45 minutes between the foreman's fourth inspection of the pumps that day and the inspector's visit. The company was convicted of the "causing" offence under section 2, and appealed on the basis that the pollution had occurred without either knowledge or negligence on its part.

The House of Lords was unimpressed. "Causes" was to be given its common sense meaning. Parliament had deliberately not qualified it by the word "knowingly" and 'mens rea' notions were irrelevant, with Lord Pearson thinking that intention, knowledge or negligence as to the pollution would simply make causation "easier to decide".

Any need for 'culpability' or a 'guilty mind' was satisfied by the deliberate and intentional conducting of the potentially-polluting process. It was not necessary to intend, or be aware of, the actual pollution. It was enough that the process was a deliberate activity, and that its operation had led to the pollution. Lord Wilberforce (at 834):

> "In my opinion, this is a clear case of causing the polluted water to enter the stream. The whole complex operation which might lead to this result was an operation deliberately conducted by the appellants and I fail to see how a defect in one stage of it, even if we assume that this happened without their negligence, can enable them to say they did not cause the pollution. In my opinion, complication of this case by the infusion of the concept of mens rea, and its exceptions, is unnecessary and undesirable ..."

Viscount Dilhorne, similarly (at 839-40):

> "It was the operation of the works which led to the flow of liquid to the tanks. It was that operation which, with the system they had installed, led to the liquid getting into the river ...
>
> Without their acts there would have not have been this pollution. It was their operation of their works that led to the liquid getting into the tanks and their failure to ensure that the pumps were working properly that led to the liquid getting into the river ...
>
> Here the acts done by the appellants were intentional. They were acts calculated to lead to the river being polluted if the acts done by the appellants, the installation and operation of the pumps, were ineffective to prevent it. Where a person intentionally does certain things which produce a certain result, then it can truly be said that he has caused that result ..."

And Lord Salmon (at 847):

> "The appellants had been responsible for the design of the plant; everything within their works was under their control;

> they had chosen all the equipment ..."

We suggest that the use of the word "causing" in WRA section 85, being in juxtaposition with "knowingly permits" in that section and, by the comparison with "knowingly causes" by Part II of the EPA, imposes strict liability and that the courts are unlikely to require "knowledge" as an additional ingredient (cf. *R v Tolson* (1889) 23 QBD 168). It is to be noted that in *Alphacell v Woodward*, *Sherras v De Rutzen* (discussed in Chapter 6, above) with its emphasis on 'mens rea' as an essential ingredient of every criminal offence, was distinguished on the basis of the environmental exceptions it presents: public nuisance for Lord Cross, and acts "not criminal in any real sense" but penalised "in the public interest" for Viscount Dilhorne and Lord Salmon.

Alphacell v Woodward is instructive not least because it can be viewed as an environmentally-aware House of Lords recognising strict liability, for strong policy reasons, notably the public importance of being able readily to secure convictions. Viscount Dilhorne said of the argument that a superadded requirement of intention should be read into "causes" (at 839):

> "I cannot think that was the intention of Parliament for it would mean that a burden of proof would rest on the prosecution that could seldom be discharged."

And Lord Salmon said (at 848):

> "It is of the utmost public importance that our rivers should not be polluted. The risk of pollution, particularly from the vast and increasing number of riparian industries, is very great ...
>
> If this appeal succeeded and it were held to be the law that no conviction could be obtained under the Act of 1951 unless the prosecution could discharge the often impossible onus of proving that the pollution was caused intentionally or negligently, a great deal of pollution would go unpunished and undeterred to the relief or many riparian factory owners. As a result, many rivers which are now filthy would become filthier still and many rivers which are now clean would lose their cleanliness. The legislature no doubt recognised that as a matter of public policy this would be most unfortunate ..."

However, as we have shown when discussing the possibility of profit-seizing (see Chapter 6) the strictness of *Alphacell v Woodward* was mitigated by the level of the penalty. In the midst of Lord Salmon's policy reasoning was his reference to the "minor pollution" of the present case and the absence of negligence or knowledge justifying the "comparatively nominal fine" imposed (£20 plus £24 costs).

The policy message is nevertheless clear. Under *Alphacell v Woodward* liability is strict, the House of Lords being keen that there should not be a great "burden" on prosecutors and that pollution must not "go undeterred". Two main questions remain. The first is the nature of the "active" or "positive" act of the defendant. The second concerns the significance of 'independent causes'.

how "active" ?

What sort of conduct will be sufficiently "active" or "positive" to satisfy the *Alphacell v Woodward* test of "causing" pollution ?

It is easy in cases like *Alphacell*, where the defendant is clearly the operator of the polluting facility. However, take the example of the lender who knows the activity in which his borrower is engaged, and supports the business by providing the necessary cash.

There is presumably a spectrum of activities which range in degrees of "positive" or "active" conduct. Least "active" or "positive" are situations where the defendant has 'stood by with knowledge'. Some offences have attracted hints that this conduct could be "causing". For example, in *R v Chainey* [1914] 1 KB 137 Sir Rufus Isaacs CJ said that:

> "If it was proved that a father, knowing that his daughter was consorting with persons of known immoral character, stood by and allowed such intimacies to continue when it was in his power to prevent them, that might furnish evidence of causing or encouraging her unlawful carnal knowledge".

Were this the appropriate analysis then the question would be to what extent banker is to customer as father is to daughter. This is not though an approach applied to "causing" offences generally and the Courts have in the main been hostile to 'standing by' notions of "causes" (eg. *Kelly's Directories v Gavin & Lloyds* [1902] 1 Ch 631).

At the opposite end of the spectrum from *R v Chainey* is the approach adopted in relation to offences of 'causing another person to do something'. This tends to require a high degree of participation. Thus, for example, the offence of causing another to use an uninsured vehicle under the Road Traffic Acts was characterised in *Shave v Rosner* [1954] 2 QB 113 as requiring "control, dominance or compulsion".

In the pollution context, "causing" seems to lie somewhere between *R v Chainey* and *Shave v Rosner*. Certainly, more is necessary than merely 'standing by'. The vital observation is that such conduct will not, and need not, constitute "causing" in the pollution context precisely because it will amount to the partner term, "knowingly permitting".

This point is demonstrated by *Price v Cromack* [1975] 1 WLR 988, which concerned the same statutory offence as *Alphacell*. There, the owner of land over which effluent had passed was held to be not guilty of "causing" it to enter a river because the requisite *Alphacell* "positive act" was not present on his part, but merely acquiescence, which was held to be insufficient. Nevertheless, the Divisional Court did indicate that the alternative "knowingly permitting" would have been available (see below).

The recent decision in *Wychavon DC v NRA* The Times 17th September 1992 is to like effect. There the Court rejected a failure to discover the source of pollution or to take effective action, even though amounting possibly to negligence, as conduct sufficiently "positive" to constitute "causing". Again, it was implied that the conduct would have amounted to "permitting" the pollution. (See too *NRA v WDA* The Times 29th December 1992.)

There is then no need for a *R v Chainey* approach to causation. The only tension which arises is in one of two situations. The first is where the defendant has been charged by the prosecuting authorities with the wrong offence (*Price v Cromack; Wychavon DC v NRA*). The second is where the defendant has 'stood by' with a state of mind which was something less than "knowingly", since there the partner trigger will be unavailable. Of these two tensions, the Courts have refused to release the former, while the latter is perhaps satisfactorily dealt with by a flexible approach to "knowingly" (below).

'independent causes'

Notwithstanding his "active operation" or "positive act" in the process which led to pollution, the defendant may seek to blame an 'independent cause'. How significant must such a factor be in order for a defendant to escape liability ?

The starting-point is *Impress v Rees* [1971] 2 All ER 357, another case under section 2 of the Rivers (Prevention of Pollution) Act 1951. In that case evidence that pollution had resulted from a valve being "opened by some unauthorised person for purposes unconnected with the appellant's business" meant that there was no offence by the company of "causing" the pollution. The Court was able to deploy notions of 'novus actus interveniens' ("an intervening cause ... of so powerful a nature that the conduct of the appellants was not a cause at all") and avoid both policy and 'mens rea' issues.

It is right to say that *Alphacell v Woodward* treated *Impress v Rees* with some circumspection and even hostility. In *Alphacell* an argument that the blocking leaves represented an 'independent cause' was rejected. The House of Lords held that whether such causes save the operator of the installation from liability depends on notions of "a proper attribution of responsibility" (Lord Wilberforce); whether there were events "which could not reasonably be foreseen" (Lord Salmon); or events "which could fairly be regarded as being beyond their ability to foresee or control" (Lord Cross). It is rather ironic that these negligence-type principles found this back-door way into the very case which holds that negligence is irrelevant to an offence of "causing" pollution.

The issue arose again more recently in *Southern Water Authority v Pegrum* [1990] JP 581. A stream in Kent had been polluted as a result of an ingress of rain water into what was elegantly called a 'lagoon' of pig effluent. The Pegrums were prosecuted under section 31(1) of COPA for "causing" polluting matter to enter the stream. The Magistrates acquitted them, on the basis that four days' rain was an act of God.

The Divisional Court allowed the Water Authority's appeal and directed the magistrates to convict. Henry J reasserted the 'strict liability' approach of *Alphacell*, relying both on the ancient beginnings of strict liability and the analogy of *Rylands v Fletcher* strict liability at common law. He characterised the inch and a quarter of rain in 4 days as being "not so very extraordinary". Finally, he rejected an argument that the collection and drainage of effluent were to be treated as separate, and that the "active operations" under *Alphacell* related solely to the former (and the pollution to the latter). His general theme was a restrictive view of 'independent cause', (at 588):

> "It was the respondents' drain, and its blockage caused the escape of their polluting matter. For such escape they are strictly liable under the Act unless they can point to that blockage being caused by an intervening cause so powerful as to render their own pollutant collection and storage operation merely part of the surrounding circumstances. The failure of their own drains to cope cannot be so described. As it was their own drainage system which failed, and they cannot in law attribute such failure to act of God or act of a trespasser, they are strictly liable for (in the judicial language of 300 years ago) 'the trespass of their dirt' ..."

The emphasis on 'independent causes' as having to be this "powerful" may tie in with what is said in other contexts as to multiple causes, for example in the context of an offence of causing death by reckless driving, that the Defendant's conduct need not be the sole, but simply "a substantial", cause: *R v Hennigan* [1971] 3 All ER 133.

What is clear is that this all fits in with a pro-liability mood in the context of offences of "causing" pollution. It ties in with a judicial refusal to allow arguments that what occurred was different from that which was expected or contemplated, and so avoids any inroad into the *Alphacell* rejection of the need for mens rea: see eg. *Wrothwell v Yorkshire Water Authority* [1984] Crim LR 43.

"KNOWINGLY PERMITTING"

This is the partner of both the water pollution trigger "causing" (Part III WRA) above, and the waste on land trigger "knowingly causing" (Part II EPA) below. We will discuss its two component parts separately.

permitting

The "permitting" offence can be viewed in contrast with its "causing" partner (above): see eg. *Shave v Rosner* [1954] 2 QB 113. One starts then with Lord Wilberforce's *Alphacell* interpretation, that whereas "causing" requires "some active operation", "knowingly permitting ... involves a failure to prevent the pollution ... accompanied by knowledge".

Similarly, as to the offence by someone who "causes or permits" false invoices under the Fertilizers and Feeding Stuffs Act 1893, Lord Alverstone CJ discussed the contrast in *Korten v West Sussex County Council* 88 LT 466 as follows:

> "'causes' would prima facie involve the man taking part in the act. But the legislature has put in the wider word 'permits', which was inserted in order to include the case of a false description - a description, false in fact, which has been sent out by the permission of the person whose goods are being sent out with it, or who is the manager of the works from which the goods go out".

In the same case, Channell J held that permitting the invoice to be false would include taking no steps to ascertain whether or not it was true.

Perhaps the best illustration of both "permitting" and its contrast with "causing" is presented by *Price v Cromack* (above). That was the case where the owner of land agreed to allow a neighbouring landowner's effluent to flow across his land and into a river. He was acquitted of "causing" river pollution (above) because his acts amounted merely to "acquiescence". However, whilst Lord Widgery CJ stated simply "it is not for us to decide whether the defendant would have been found guilty of knowingly permitting had the offence been so framed", Ashworth J went rather further ([1975] 1 WLR 988 at 994-5):

> "It seems to me, although it is unnecessary to express any concluded view, that it would have been difficult for the present defendant to provide an answer if indeed he had been charged with knowingly permitting the effluent to escape into the river ... though it is obiter, I cannot resist saying that I do not see what answer the present defendant could conceivably have had in the circumstances of this case."

Similarly, in the recent *Wychavon DC v NRA* case (above) there was some suggestion that the defendant's conduct, failure to discover the source of the pollution or take effective action, would have amounted to "permitting" the pollution.

The above cases yield notions of "permitting" which are both active and passive. The active notions are those of the grant of permission or the activities of a manager (Lord Alverstone CJ in *Korten*). The passive ones are the failure to prevent (Lord Wilberforce in *Alphacell*), the failure to investigate (Channell J in *Korten*), and acquiescence (*Price v Cromack*).

These two senses of "permitting" are also reflected in the authorities which consider the phrase not in contrast with "causing" or some other trigger, but in its own right. These cases emphasize control in the sense first, that the defendant's go-ahead is needed for the activity, and second, that the defendant had the power to stop the activity.

Accordingly, there is the formulation from *Berton v Alliance Economic Investment* [1922] 1 KB 742, where to "permit" was held (by Atkin LJ at 759) to be either "to give leave for an act which without that leave could not legally be done, or to abstain from taking reasonable steps to prevent the act where it is within a man's power to prevent it". This is the approach adopted in cases like *Commercial General Administration v Thomsett* (1979) 250 EG 547 which concerned a tenant's covenant "not to do or to permit to be done ... anything which may be ... a nuisance".

Some cases have emphasized only the first part of the *Berton* approach, the need to give the go-ahead. In *Tophams v Sefton* [1967] 1 AC 50, Lord Upjohn stressed (at 75) that "permits" is "a word connoting on the part of the one whose permission is asked the right effectively to refuse and on the part of the applicant the necessity to ask for and obtain permission, so as lawfully to undertake his proposed course of action".

Others have concentrated on the second part of the *Berton* test, the power to prevent. Significantly, it was the "power to prevent" which was stressed by Lindley LJ in a pollution context in *Yorkshire West Riding v Holmfirth* [1894] 2 QB 842. There are plenty of examples from a range of other contexts too. In *Barton v Reed* [1932] 1 Ch 362 Luxmoore J said (at 377) that "in certain circumstances a man may permit the continuance of an act if he can prevent it by taking legal proceedings and refrains from doing so." In *Holloway v Hill* [1902] 2 Ch 612 a person bound by a covenant not to "permit or suffer" a prohibited user, was liable for letting the premises for the prohibited purpose since he could or might have prevented it. And in a case under the Dangerous Drugs Act 1965 concerning the trigger "permitting" the use of premises for drug activities, the House of Lords emphasized the need for "an unwillingness ... to use means available to him to prevent [the activities]" (Lord Diplock in *Sweet v Parsley* [1970] AC 132 at 162). All this ties in, of course, with Lord Wilberforce's emphasis in

Alphacell on the failure to prevent, since it can be said that this notion must imply the power to do so.

The best view may be that the first part of the *Berton* test is in any case merely a species of the second part. In other words, if a person's go-ahead (or "permission") is necessary for the activity to take place then he will always have the power to prevent it. Of course, he may be able to prevent things other than those needing his go-ahead.

The concern for lenders will be that if they exercise a sufficient degree of control the Court may say that they had the power to prevent a polluting activity, and so "permitted" it.

knowingly

In the cases involving drugs it has been held that the preface "knowingly" before an offence of "permitting" is superfluous in that knowledge of some kind is an essential element of permission anyway: see *R v Thomas*, *R v Thomson* (1976) 63 Cr App R 65. Whether or not it is necessary, in the WRA and the EPA Parliament has expressly chosen the prefix "knowingly".

Two issues arise, each of which relates to the strictness of the offence. First, what is "knowledge" for these purposes ? How flexible is it? Could it include 'shutting one's eyes' or 'not bothering to find out'? Second, to what must the "knowledge" relate? How much detail must the defendant "know"? Specifically, must he know simply of the act which constitutes the offence, or must he also know of its illegality?

who knows?

There are cases on "knowingly" offences which show that the person who 'shuts his eyes' or 'fails to supervise' the activity in question is liable. Good examples are cases in the licensing context, where "knowingly" has been interpreted as sufficiently flexible to incorporate notions of negligence.

In *Vane v Yiannopoullos* [1965] AC 486 it was held that for "knowingly permitting" liquor-sale offences deliberate disregard of events would suffice and actual knowledge was not necessary. Similarly, in *R v Winson* [1969] 1 QB 371 it was held that the holder of a licence could not evade his responsibilities by delegating management functions to another person, and that he had "knowledge" under the Licensing Acts if that other person knowingly sold liquor in breach of the licence (see too *Howker v Robinson* [1973] QB 178).

These cases can be seen to turn on notions of irresponsible delegation or inadequate supervision. It would make sense then if, conversely, a defendant could avoid liability by showing that he had taken all reasonable steps to avoid the occurrence of the offence. And so in *Buxton v Chief Constable of Northumbria* (1984) 148 JPL 9 it was not fatal that a licensee was aware that inevitably some under-age drinkers would be served in his establishment, it was enough that he had introduced reasonable steps to avoid this happening.

Accordingly, whether a person permits something "knowingly" translates into issues of how careful or careless he has been. It would seem that the idea of negligence which was not necessary for the "causing" offence (*Alphacell*) is sufficient for the "knowingly permitting" one.

Indeed, in *Croyalgrange* (below) Lord Bridge referred to the person who "had deliberately shut his eyes to the obvious or refrained from inquiry because he suspected the truth but did not want to have his suspicion confirmed".

what must he know: act or illegality?

The second issue concerns the detail to which the "knowledge" must relate. Must the defendant "know" everything, including the nature and extent of the pollution? Specifically, is it enough that he knows about the polluting act, or must he know of its illegality ?

Here there can be seen to be two conflicting judicial approaches. The first is represented by the Divisional Court in *Ashcroft v Cambro Waste Products* [1981] 1 WLR 1349, and has the advantage of being an environmental case. The second is found in *Westminster City Council v Croyalgrange* [1986] 1 WLR 674, which is more recent, a decision of the House of Lords, but non-environmental. *Ashcroft* was not cited in *Croyalgrange*, which may support the contention that each is confined to its own context.

Before turning to those cases, it is worth mentioning some 'criminal possession' cases which illustrate a range of the extent of requisite knowledge. These are all cases where the defendant knew some but not all of the facts making up the offence. In *R v Hussain* [1969] 2 QB 567 and *R v Ellis & Street* (1987) 84 Cr App R 235 smugglers were held to have been guilty of being "knowingly concerned in" the fraudulent importation of goods despite being unaware, or mistaken, about the identity of the goods being smuggled. *R v Taaffe* [1984] AC 539 was a curious situation where a smuggler who believed that the illegal substance X which he carried was a different, legal substance Y, while mistakenly believing that substance Y was illegal too, did not satisfy the "knowingly" trigger. In *R v Hallam* [1957] 1 QB 569 it was held that the offence of "knowingly" possessing an explosive substance was triggered only by both knowledge of having the substance and knowledge that it was explosive.

Ashcroft

In *Ashcroft v Cambro Waste Products* the Defendant was a company operating a waste disposal site with a licence from Derbyshire County Council under the COPA regime. The terms of the licence imposed conditions, including that oil waste be covered with overburden and blue asbestos with incombustible material. The local authority found that these terms were not being complied with, and the company was prosecuted under section 3 of COPA, for "knowingly permitting" the deposit of waste other than in accordance with the conditions of the licence. The company was acquitted on the ground that whilst its foreman was aware that the conditions were being breached, the company was not, nor was it infected by the foreman's knowledge since he was not a "directing mind" of the company. The prosecutor appealed.

The Divisional Court allowed the appeal, dealing solely with the issue of the extent of necessary knowledge to satisfy the offence, and holding that it was necessary for the prosecution to prove only that the company had "knowledge" of the act constituting the pollution, and that it need not be proved to have known that such act was outside the terms of any licence. Boreham J stated (at 1355-6):

> "It seems to me that the meaning of section 3(1) is clear. Both the structure of the section itself and the words themselves impel me to the conclusion that they mean what the prosecutor in this case contends that they mean, namely, that it is prohibited to deposit or cause to be deposited or knowingly permit the deposit of controlled waste on any land unless in fact such deposit is in accordance with the conditions of a valid

licence".

It may be possible to argue that *Ashcroft* turns simply on the burden of proof. The case establishes that the prosecution need prove knowledge only of the polluting act not its illegality. The critical issue is whether it would have been open to the company to prove the absence of knowledge of the illegality, or perhaps a bona fide belief that there was a licence and compliance with its terms.

In this respect the decision is obscured, or explained, by the statutory defence under COPA for a Defendant who can prove "that he took all such steps as were reasonably open to him to ensure that the conditions were complied with", on which the Court relied. What, then, would the position be where a statute had no such provision ? The "knowingly causing" offence under section 33 of the EPA (waste on land) is accompanied by a general "due diligence" defence. Does this allow for the *Ashcroft* strictness ? On the other hand, the "knowingly causing" offence under section 85 of the WRA (water pollution) carries no such defence. Does that mean that the *Ashcroft* approach does not apply and that the prosecution must prove knowledge of both the act and its illegality ?

On a 'strict' reading of *Ashcroft* it turns neither on the burden of proof nor on the existence of the 'reasonable steps' defence. On this interpretation "knowingly" permitting a pollution offence is triggered by knowledge of a polluting act which is in fact illegal (subject to any statutory defence, of course), so that knowledge that the activity is illegal is unnecessary and belief that it was legal irrelevant.

Croyalgrange

In *Westminster City Council v Croyalgrange* the Court was concerned with the offence under schedule 3 of the Local Government (Miscellaneous Provisions) Act 1982 of "knowingly permitting" the use of premises as a sex establishment other than in accordance with a licence. Importantly, the Act also provided that there was no offence if an application for a licence was pending. The Defendant was the owner of property used by its sub-tenant as a sex establishment. In fact the sub-tenant had no licence, nor had it taken steps to apply for one. The Defendant knew that the premises were being used as a sex establishment, but adduced evidence that through its director it had honestly believed that a licence application was pending. It was acquitted.

In short, the critical issue concerned whether knowledge of use was sufficient, or of illegality necessary. The parallel with *Ashcroft* is obvious. The House of Lords upheld the acquittal, holding that for the purposes of the Act it was necessary for the prosecution to prove both knowledge of the use of the premises as a sex establishment and knowledge that such use was other than in accordance with a licence. The leading judgment was given by Lord Bridge.

Lord Bridge's first line of reasoning was a construction argument. Under the Act there was a separate offence of knowingly contravening a term of a licence, for which the Defendant had to be shown to have acted "without reasonable excuse". Lord Bridge considered that this showed that where a licence had been obtained the prosecution would have to prove knowledge of more than that the premises were being used as a sex establishment, and thought it "curiously anomalous" if it did not have to do so where no licence application had been made.

The main thrust of Lord Bridge's judgment was remarkably simple (at 682) and amounted to a bare conclusion that "knowingly" must mean a knowledge of illegality:

> "If the argument for the council were accepted, it would lead to the conclusion that paragraph 20(1)(a) had in effect created an offence of strict liability. The offence would consist in the unlawful use of premises as a sex establishment and even an honest belief in facts which, if true, would make the use lawful would afford no defence. It is trite law that the legislature's intention to create an offence of strict liability must be signified by clear language. To find such an intention in paragraph 20(1)(a) with its iteration of the word "knowingly" is obviously impossible. The only meaning of which the language is reasonably capable makes knowledge that the use of premises as a sex establishment is in contravention of the prohibition imposed by paragraph 6 a necessary ingredient of the offence".

The necessary ingredients of the offence, then, included both knowledge of the act and its illegality. This reasoning, if applicable in the environmental sphere, would make *Ashcroft* wrong, even it would seem if *Ashcroft* were said to turn on the burden or proof and certainly if the 'strict' view of *Ashcroft* is the correct one.

Croyalgrange must then be seen to represent a less strict approach than that in *Ashcroft*. Indeed, whilst recognising the policy issues, Lord Bridge made clear that he would not countenance a stricter approach without express guidance from Parliament. In considering the submission that the Act "should be construed ... to avoid frustrating the policy of the Schedule and to enable authorities who have adopted the Schedule to maintain effective control of sex establishments", Lord Bridge concluded (at 683) that "if the problem of controlling sex establishments is so acute as to require the creation of an offence of strict liability, it is of course for Parliament ... to take that step".

However, policy issues were also taken into account because Lord Bridge recognised that the defendant may be "in the best position to know whether application for a licence ... was made by him or on his behalf". He sought to comfort the local authority, and perhaps himself, with the indication that if the test for "knowingly" was not flexible then the means for satisfying it was, stating that in certain situations "the defendant's knowledge of the true position in regard to the licensing of the use of the premises can properly be inferred".

The most relaxed approach to the state of mind necessary for the person to "know" is found a little later in Lord Bridge's judgment (at 684):

> "it is perhaps worth remarking, in the hope that it may further allay the anxiety of the council about the enforcement of licensing control of sex establishments, that it is always open to the tribunal of fact, when knowledge on the part of a defendant is required to be proved, to base a finding of knowledge on evidence that the defendant had deliberately shut his eyes to the obvious or refrained from inquiry because he suspected the truth but did not want to have his suspicion confirmed."

Further, Lord Brightman in a short concurring judgment said (at 684), that:

> "although the onus of establishing all the ingredients of the offence must lie on the prosecution ... [where] there are no circumstances which sufficiently suggest absence of knowledge, the court may properly infer without direct evidence that the defendant did indeed possess the requisite knowledge. For this reason the fear expressed by the council that Parliament's intention to establish an effective licensing system will be frustrated by the severity of the onus of proof burdening the prosecution, is I think groundless."

the choice

As to the extent of the necessary "knowledge", there is then a straight choice between *Ashcroft* and *Croyalgrange*. But these cases illustrate far more than that. They go to the heart of the jurisprudence of environmental protection. The prefix "knowingly", like many of the other trigger terms, is flexible and its interpretation will reflect the nature of a judicial policy-commitment.

Ashcroft uses that flexibility to take a 'strict liability' approach which is consistent with *Alphacell* and *Southern Water v Pegrum*, and the importance of deterring pollution and not over-burdening prosecutors.

The justification for such an approach is policy-based and simple. It is for a potentially-polluting company to make sure that it is aware of its legal obligations and make sure they are complied with. There is simply no room for mistaken beliefs or assumptions. And potential polluters must take responsibility for what their employees actually do. "Reasonable steps" are not enough.

Croyalgrange takes the opposing view, that the deliberate choice of the prefix "knowingly" suggests a less strict approach, requiring an awareness of both the act and its illegality. But even in *Croyalgrange* the Court's policy-awareness was sufficient to introduce a relaxed test as to who is a person with "knowledge".

One of the problems with the 'strict' reading of *Ashcroft* is that knowledge of the act comes strikingly close to *Alphacell*, where the need for "knowledge" was expressly ruled out but where the Court emphasized nevertheless the intentional or deliberate nature of the process (above). The question here is how different the *Alphacell* process is from the *Ashcroft* act. The closeness may indicate the real principle that the defendant knew enough to be in a position to take steps to avoid an environmental offence taking place.

There is then at the heart of environmental law an important policy choice. Should the Courts support strict liability, even in the face of triggers like "knowingly", as in the strict view of *Ashcroft*? This presents a dilemma, not least because it would penalise a defendant who knows of the act, but has taken 'all reasonable steps' to ensure there is no illegality.

The Court in *Ashcroft* itself appears to have acknowledged this 'strict liability' dilemma, citing Lord Diplock in *Tesco Supermarkets v Nattrass* [1972] AC 153, where he referred (at 194) to:

> "the rational and moral justification for creating in the field of consumer protection, as also in the field of public health and safety, offences of 'strict liability' for which an employer or principal, in the course of whose business the offences are committed, is criminally liable, notwithstanding that they are due to acts or omissions of his servants or agents which were done without his knowledge or consent or even were contrary to his orders. But this rational and moral justification does not extend to penalising an employer or principal who has done everything that he can reasonably be expected to do by supervision or inspection, by improvement of his business methods or by exhorting those whom he may be expected to control or influence to prevent the commission of the offence ... What the employer or principal can reasonably be expected to do to prevent the commission of an offence will depend upon the gravity of the injury which it is sought to prevent and the nature of the business in the course of which such offences are committed."

Finally, both *Ashcroft* and *Croyalgrange* can be seen to turn on construction of the specific provisions of the Acts in question, and to support the notion that each case is confined to its own narrow context. Indeed, in *Ashcroft* Boreham J stated that he found "little assistance, save by way of general approach, from authorities or decisions which relate to other statutory provisions". This ties in with the 'anti-analogy principle' discussed in the next chapter. If *Croyalgrange* is just a sex shop case, then either *Ashcroft* is the environmental approach, or *Ashcroft* is the waste disposal approach (or just the COPA approach).

"KNOWINGLY CAUSING"

Like "causing" this is part of an alternative test, this time under the waste on land regime of Part II of the EPA, embracing both the section 33 crime and in turn the section 73 (civil) statutory duty to compensate. Both of these are triggered by any person who shall "knowingly cause or knowingly permit" waste, without the requisite waste management licence. Again, there are two separate offences (*McLeod v Buchanan* above).

Having already discussed "causing" and "knowingly" at length, the former in its own right and the latter in the context of "knowingly permitting", there is little to add. Indeed, the hypothetical person who 'stands by' need not feature at all: the partner trigger "knowingly permitting" will be the appropriate offence here, and no more disadvantageous to prosecutors since both alternatives have the same "knowingly" prefix.

Presumably then, "causing" will need a "positive act" or "active operation", and is to be decided in a common sense way (*Alphacell* above). Moreover, an 'independent cause' will have to be foreseeable/ controllable (*Alphacell*) or "so powerful" to make the defendant's activities pale into insignificance as "merely part of the surrounding circumstances" (*Southern Water v Pegrum*).

The question is then whether "knowingly" adds the 'mens rea' requirement rejected as necessary in *Alphacell*. We have seen that "knowingly" has a certain flexibility, in two senses. First, the question of who has knowledge turns on negligence-type notions of adequate supervision and investigation, leading to Lord Bridge's person who "had deliberately shut his eyes to the obvious or refrained from inquiry because he suspected the truth but did not want to have his suspicion confirmed" (*Croyalgrange*).

Second, the question as to the extent of knowledge presents a choice between *Ashcroft* (knowledge of the act) and *Croyalgrange* (knowledge of the illegality). The question here, then, will be whether the defendant need "know" not only the nature of the act he is "causing", or also of its illegality.

The extent to which this flexibility is used by the Courts will reflect a policy-commitment. And it is the comparison between the WRA's "causing" and the EPA's "knowingly causing" which is striking. As we have seen, the 'strict' view of *Ashcroft* minimizes the impact of the "knowingly" prefix. Indeed, whether there is any impact at all depends on whether "act" in *Ashcroft* and "process" in *Alphacell* are different.

One feature of the "knowingly causing" offence under EPA section 33 compared with the "causing" offence under WRA section 85 is that for the former Parliament specifically provided a "due diligence" defence. Since the courts tend to treat more strictly offences for which specific defences have been provided, this could also serve to minimise the difference between the two trigger terms.

"PERSON RESPONSIBLE"

A "person responsible" for a nuisance can be served with an abatement notice under section 80 of the EPA (although where there is a structural defect the correct person is the "owner", below).

Here there is a statutory definition. Section 79(7) defines the "person responsible" as "the person to whose act, default or sufferance the nuisance is attributable". These are all considered below.

We pause to make one short but important point. Notwithstanding the section 79(7) definition's use of the words "the person" and "attributable", it is clear that there can be several "persons responsible". Section 81(1) states that: "where more than one person is responsible for a statutory nuisance section 80 above shall apply to each of those persons whether or not what any of them is responsible for would by itself amount to a nuisance".

"CONSENT OR CONNIVANCE [or] ATTRIBUTABLE TO ANY NEGLECT ON THE PART OF"

This is part of the scheme for third party liability applying to each of the 4 statutory regimes, and found in section 157(1) of the EPA and section 217(1) of the WRA. The person whose "consent", "connivance" or "neglect" in relation to the pollution is a "director, manager, secretary or other similar officer of the body corporate or a person who was purporting to act in any such capacity". As to the meaning of these terms, see below.

The meaning of "consent" and "connivance" has been considered in various contexts, many of which are of little help. In relation to "consent" these include formal examples like a requirement of consent by trustees (s.65 Settled Land Act 1925) and semi-formal matters like change of user of leasehold property, where "consent" is more than mere acquiescence and requires a positive affirmative act: *Bell v Alfred Frank & Bartlett* [1980] 1 WLR 340. A key theme is knowledge: "you cannot consent to a thing unless you have knowledge of it" (Jessel MR in *re Caughey ex parte Ford* (1876) 1 Ch D 521 at 528).

As for "connivance", much of the caselaw is in the context of divorce, where "connivance" in a conjugal offence requires willing consent or culpable acquiescence: *Phillips v Phillips* 1 Rob Ecc 157.

The most helpful cases are those relating specifically to "consent and connivance" by a director. Here a notable interpretation is that contained in *Huckerby v Elliott* [1970] 1 All ER 189 at 194 where Ashworth J endorsed the following approach:

> "where a director consents to the commission of an offence by his company, he is well aware of what is going on and agrees to it ... where he connives at the offence committed by the company he is equally well aware of what is going on but his agreement is tacit, not actively encouraging what happens but letting it continue and saying nothing about it".

Turning to "neglect", it is tempting to say that this is the most passive of the three 'triggers'. In fact, it is a little hard to describe but may represent something of a 'catch-all' term.

"Neglect" is the first of several statutory triggers whose definitions can be accused either of question-begging or circularity but which on any view present flexible tools suitable for the achievement of judicial policy. Indeed, it has been defined simply as the "failure to perform a duty which the person knows or ought to know" (*Re Hughes* [1943] 2 All ER 269 per Simmonds J at 271).

Accordingly, whether there has been "neglect" by a defendant will turn on identifying his duty, and the criminality can be said to arise from, in traditional language, "not doing that which he ought to have done". The reality must be that the "act or default ... of any other person" represents the equivalent of the common law 'duty of care' readily applied to justify the imposition, or not, of liability.

In this regard cases like *Huckerby v Elliott*, and *Re City Equitable Fire* [1925] Ch 407 are important, both of which considered the duties of directors. In the latter case Romer J said that ascertaining a director's duties depends on considering the nature of the company's business and the way in which its work is distributed between the directors and other officers. Similarly, in *Armour v Skeen* [1977] IRLR 310 the Court emphasized that what is important is not whether the person was the target for a statutory "duty", but whether in reality he had that responsibility.

What "neglect" is may then all depend on who the "director, manager etc" is, and what his role is. We discuss these next.

"DIRECTOR, MANAGER, SECRETARY OR OTHER SIMILAR OFFICER OF THE BODY CORPORATE OR A PERSON WHO WAS PURPORTING TO ACT IN ANY SUCH CAPACITY"

This, then, is the person whose "consent or connivance" or "neglect" triggers the first two third party liability options, as is provided for in section 157(1) EPA and section 217(1) WRA.

The purpose of the provision is obvious. It enables a prosecution to be directed at a company's representative in his personal capacity, either instead of or along with the company. Thus, in *Croyalgrange* (the sex shop case, above) Westminster City Council had prosecuted both the company and its director (unsuccessfully in both cases, as things turned out), under a provision in similar terms to the WRA and EPA provisions. We have observed that the liability of an "officer" will depend very much on how his duties are characterised (*re Hughes*; *re City Equitable Fire* above).

The term "director" is fairly straightforward, being a formal status recognised in companies legislative and registration regimes.

As we have seen, the concept of "neglect" is viewed simply as a 'breach of duty'. What conduct will amount to a director's breach of duty ? The issues raised are to what extent directors are entitled to delegate responsibility for compliance with the law, similar to those raised in the context of "knowingly permitting" (see cases like *R v Winson* and *Buxton v CC Northumbria*, above).

A useful starting-place is *Croyalgrange* itself. There, the Court held that the director, despite being in the "best position" to do so, had no general duty to ensure that the appropriate licence was held. Similar to this is *Huckerby v Elliott* where magistrates had convicted several directors on the basis that as a matter of policy they were each in a position to ensure that the appropriate gaming licence was held. The Divisional Court upheld an appeal by one of the directors, whose evidence had been that she knew a licence was necessary but had trusted her co-director that one had been obtained. The Court held that director's liability required more than some degree of control, that there was no general duty "to see that the law is observed", nor to supervise a co-director.

Also seemingly straightforward is the purpose of the phrase "purporting to act in such capacity". This can be seen to be aimed at situations where a director's appointment is irregular or defective: see eg. *Dean v Hiesler* [1942] 2 All ER 340.

More difficult are the notions of "manager" and "other officer". One can start with the position of shareholders. Under both the EPA and the WRA there are provisions expressly providing that a "member" of a company is to be liable where the company's affairs were "managed by its members" for his "acts or defaults ... in connection with his functions of management as if he were a director" (EPA s.158; WRA s.217(3)). It is therefore unlikely that a shareholder could satisfy "officer" as well, and for the sake of completeness cases like *Macnee v Persian Investment Corporation* (1890) 44 Ch D 306 can be said to be resistant to such a possibility. There a shareholder who sought an injunction against the company to restrain an allegedly illegal activity, lost on the ground that he had no potential vulnerability to criminal prosecution from the activity and so had an insufficient 'interest'.

"officer"

A useful authority on the liability of an officer is *Mancetter Developments v Garmanson* [1986] QB 1212. That was a case concerning the tort of waste, where along with the company its managing director was liable, because of his knowing participation in the tort. Dillon LJ referred to the principle (at 1217) that:

> "if a director of a company gives instructions for the commission of a tort by the company, the director may be personally liable in damages to the injured party for the tort although the tort was the act of the company... directors [will be] .. liable if they have themselves directed or procured the commission of the tortious act ..."

Mancetter may be treated as presenting a general principle in this respect, that any person who has "directed or procured" an offence is a "manager ... or other similar officer" for the purposes of liability.

company law statutes

The most helpful place to look is undoubtedly the way liability through "involvement" in a company's affairs has been treated in the company law sphere itself. First, some examples of useful statutory triggers and definitions are set out:

- the Companies (Winding Up) Act 1890 section 10 referred to "any past or present director, manager, liquidator or other 'officer' of the company"

- "officer" in section 721 of the Companies Act 1985 is defined in section 744 as including "a director, manager or secretary"

- "person connected with the company" in section 239 of the Insolvency Act 1986, is defined in section 249 as " a director or shadow director of the company or an associate of such a director or shadow director or ... an associate of the company"

- "associate" is defined in section 435, and includes the situation where "the same person has control of both [companies]"

- "shadow director" under s.251 of the Insolvency Act 1986 (wrongful trading/ preference) is "a person in accordance with whose directions or instructions the directors of the company are accustomed to act (but so that a person is not deemed to be a shadow director by reason only that the directors act on advice given by him in a professional capacity ..."

company law cases

Then there are the cases which are concerned with these concepts. We mention two, which may do little more than show that the statutory triggers are flexible and their meaning depends on the context and purpose of the particularly provision in which they are found.

First, there is *re B. Johnson & Co* [1955] Ch 634, which took a narrow view of "officer", holding that a receiver and manager was not to be an "officer" for the purposes of sections 333 and 455 of the Companies Act 1948 (misfeasance).

Second, there is *re a Company No.00996 of 1979* [1980] Ch 138, which took a wider view. The Court held that "officer" in section 441 of the 1948 Act (the predecessor to the Companies Act 1985 s.721) was not to be narrowly construed and included a subordinate departmental manager in the company. The critical factor was the scheme and policy of the legislation, which allowed an order for production of documents from a person who had "while an officer of the company, committed an offence in connection with the management of the company's affairs". Lord Denning MR said (at 143):

> "The general object of the Act is to enable the important officers of the state to get at the books of the company when there has been a fraud or wrongdoing. It seems to me that whenever anyone in a superior position in a company encourages, directs or acquiesces in defrauding creditors, customers shareholders or the like, then there is an offence being committed by an officer of the company in connection with the company's affairs ..."

Shaw LJ added (at 144):

> "The expression 'manager' should not be too narrowly construed. It is not to be equated with a managing or other director or a general manager. As I see it, any person who in the affairs of the company exercises a supervisory control which reflects the general policy of the company for the time being or which is related to the general administration of the company is in the sphere of management. He need not be on the board of directors. He need not be subject to specific instructions from the board. If he fulfils a function which touches the central administration of the company, that it sufficient in my view to constitute him an 'officer' or 'manager' of the company for the purposes of section 441 of the Act ..."

The policy reasoning came from Templeman LJ (at 145):

> "Section 441 is dealing with crime. It is dealing with power to prevent crime being hidden behind a facade and the corporate activity of a company; and, for the reasons which Shaw LJ has already pointed out, unless the normal meaning of the words of section 441 are to be applied in their wider connotation the section can have very little effect ..."

bankers and others

The general rule can be said to be that solicitors, bankers, auditors and so on are not "officers". For bankers this general rule is expressed in cases like *re Imperial Land Co* LR 10 Eq 298 where a banker was held not to be an "officer" of a company for the purposes of section 165 of the Companies Act 1862. If that case is strengthened by the fact that Malins V-C would have been delighted to find otherwise (he was "grieved" by what he regarded as "disgraceful" conduct by the bank), it may be weakened in that the Court regarded its hands tied by the fact that section 100 of the same Act juxtaposed "receiver, banker ... or officer".

A useful general approach is that in *re Liberator Permanent Benefit Building Society* (1894) 71 LT 406 where Cave J stated (at 407):

> "It seems to me that merely because he was appointed solicitor to the society, without more, the solicitor does not become an officer of the society any more than it has been held that a banker does if he is appointed banker to the society, or a broker if he is appointed broker to the society, or the auditor if he is appointed auditor to the society. All these persons render services to the society, but they cannot be said to be in the employment of the society so as to make them 'officials'."

However, in "special circumstances" this can change. The solicitor in *re Liberator Permanent Benefit Building Society* was held to have become an "officer", having acted as the company's "financial manager". Similarly, an auditor has been held to be an "officer", both soon after *re Liberator* (see *re Kingston Cotton Mill* [1896] 1 Ch 6, applying *re London & General Bank* [1895] 2 Ch 166) and more recently (*R v Shacter* [1960] 2 QB 252).

These "special circumstances" tie in with the concept of "shadow director". The warning sign for banks is of course *re a Company ex parte Copp*, which we discussed at the beginning of this chapter, on the question of whether a bank can by its participation in the management of the company become a "shadow director". The picture is developed by the recent case of *re Tasbian Ltd* (No.3) [1992] BCC 358. There, the Court of Appeal had to consider the identical shadow director provision in s.22(5) of the Company Director Disqualification Act 1986. The alleged 'shadow director' was a chartered accountant and 'company doctor'. He became a consultant to the company, and amongst other things he negotiated with creditors, monitored trading, became a signatory on the bank account and advised a transfer of the company's labour force to a shell company. The Court of Appeal was clear that activities such as monitoring the Company's trading and controlling its bank account led to an inference that the consultant was controlling the affairs of the company. The issue to be determined was whether:

> "for whatever purpose ... [the consultant] was controlling the company's affairs in a manner going beyond the province of

> a company's professional advisor and in such a manner as to make him ... a shadow director."

Although it is unlikely that a bank will become as directly involved in the affairs of a company as this, it is common for bankers to direct a customer as to the creditor bill it can pay and to control the bank account. When these matters are accompanied by more general business advice, the risk that a bank will become a shadow director is real.

summary

The key element here seems to be a direct influence and control, captured by the *Mancetter* notion of one who has "directed or procured" the offence, and the "function which touches the central administration of the company" (*re a Company No.00996 of 1979*). The peace of mind of bankers depends on how reliable the old protection for bankers etc (*re Liberator Permanent*) remains, or whether the "special circumstances" can readily be met. But *re a Company ex parte Copp* will rightly be seen as giving rise to both anxiety and uncertainty on the part of banks.

As for receivers, the usual 'agency' provisions would seem to be sufficient to put them in the position of "officer or manager", and *re B. Johnson & Co* is best regarded as confined to its particular context.

Finally, *re a Company No.00996 of 1979* illustrates the potential for the Courts to view the question of "officer" simply from the point of view of the policy of the statute. Again, the important factor will be the judicial mood, and the way in which the Courts are prepared to regard lenders in the context of environmental protection.

"ACT OR DEFAULT"

This trigger has two functions. The first is as a further type of third-party liability, whilst the second is as part of the definition of a "person responsible" for a statutory nuisance.

third-party liability

We have discussed already the third-party liability represented by "consent, connivance or neglect" of a "director etc". The further type is where an offence is "attributable" to the "act or default" of "some other person" (EPA s.158(1) and WRA s.217(3)).

"Act" is fairly straightforward and suggests notions of *Alphacell* "causing". As for "default", this, like "neglect" can be criticised as adding little as a trigger of culpability. Thus in *re Young & Harston's Contract* (1886) 31 Ch D 168, Bowen LJ said (at 174):

> "default, is a purely relative term, just like negligence. It means nothing more, nothing less, than not doing what is reasonable under the circumstances; not doing something which you ought to do, having regard to the relations which you occupy towards the other persons interested in the transaction ..."

And in *re Bayley-Worthington & Cohen* [1909] 1 Ch 648, Parker J said (at 656):

> "default must, I think, involve either not doing what you ought or doing what you ought not, having regard to your relations with the other parties concerned in the transaction; in other words, it involves the breach of some duty you owe to another or others ..."

What is obvious is that this type of third-party liability is extremely general: "any other person" potentially includes anyone; and "act or default" allows liability to be attached where the Courts consider it appropriate. "Attributable" may suggest a strict view of "causation", but as we see in a moment does not have a very strict meaning elsewhere in the EPA.

Tromans in his book *The Environmental Protection Act 1990* says of this trigger that it "could be used, for example, to prosecute employees whose acts cause offences on the part of their employer or a waste producer who deliberately misdescribed waste so as to cause a waste contractor to commit an offence".

More significantly, it might be used to attach liability to a bank who controlled and directed a polluter's finances or a receiver taking control.

"person responsible"

"Act or default" is also part of the definition of the "person responsible" for a nuisance (section 79(7) EPA), upon whom a nuisance abatement notice can be served under EPA section 81 and from whom clean-up costs can then be recovered.

Here there are cases which are specifically concerned with the phrase "act or default" under statutory nuisance regimes. An example is the consideration of the phrase in section 259 of the PHA in *Neath Rural District Council v Williams* [1951] 1 KB 115, where the Court's approach was similar to that in *Price v Cromack* and where what was said to be required was something akin to the *Alphacell* "positive act".

The situation in *Neath RDC v Williams* was this. A mountain stream ran alongside the defendants' land and had become silted up by natural processes. One of the statutory nuisances under the Act related to a "watercourse ... which is so choked or silted up as to obstruct or impede the proper flow of water and thereby cause a nuisance", but with a proviso that there was no liability "on any person other than the person by whose act or default the nuisance arises or continues". The defendants' acquittal was upheld on the grounds that they had committed no "act or default". Lord Goddard said (at 126-7):

> "I cannot construe the word 'default' here in the way in which we have been asked to construe it by the rural district council. I do not think that in this case "default" could mean merely doing nothing, unless an obligation to do something were imposed by the Act. There was no act of the defendants which caused the obstruction either to arise or to continue. I can well understand that there might be a case where it might be said that a person who failed to do something which he ought to have done, such for instance, as failing to prevent obstructive matter from going into a river from his own premises, had caused an obstruction by his default. In the present case ... there is nothing to show that the defendants did anything which caused this obstruction to arise or to continue; nor do I think that there is anything which can properly be called a default on their part ..."

Importantly, the "person responsible" cannot be all that strict in section 80, for notwithstanding the (repeated) reference to "the [person responsible]", section 81(1) states expressly that "where more than one person is responsible", section 80 applies to them all.

"SUFFERANCE"

This is the remaining component used to identify a "person responsible" for a nuisance who can be served with an abatement notice under sections 79 & 80 of the EPA, the full definition being the "person to whose act, default or sufferance the nuisance is attributable". "Act and default" have already been discussed.

"Suffering" is apparently rather like the second part of the *Berton* test for "permitting", emphasizing the power to prevent the activity.

A useful starting-point is the pollution case of *R v Staines* 60 LT 261, where it was said that: "a man cannot be said to 'suffer' that which he has no right to prevent". There the Court was concerned with the Thames Navigation Act 1866 under which it was an offence to "cause or suffer" sewage to flow into the Thames. It was held that a local board was not guilty of such an offence where its sewers were used to carry sewage by a person who had acquired a prescriptive right to do so, there being no power to prevent the use.

Indeed, in the statutory phrase "do or suffer" the latter term has been interpreted as having a passive sense in contradistinction to the former: *Roffey v Bent* LR 3 Eq 759. This is rather like the contrast for "causing or permitting" presented by Lord Wilberforce in *Alphacell* or illustrated by *Price v Cromack*.

The power to prevent was emphasized in *Barton v Reed*, a case concerned with a restrictive covenant, though it is interesting that there "sufferance" was regarded as a looser trigger term than "permitting". Luxmoore J said ([1932] 1 Ch 362 at 375) that:

> "The word 'suffer' is a wide term. It seems to be wider than the word 'permit' ... At any rate it must cover allowing something to be done which the covenantor has the complete power to prevent".

The concept of "sufferance" may fit in well with the notion of continuation of a nuisance on land owned by the Defendant, notwithstanding that it was begun by a third party, prior to that ownership commencing (like *Clayton v Sale Urban District Council* [1926] 1 KB 415 and 'continuation' of common law nuisance cases like *Sedleigh-Denfield v O'Callaghan* [1940] AC 880 and *Leanse v Lord Egerton* [1943] 1 KB 323).

A useful further illustration is presented by the "default" case *Neath RDC v Williams* (above), in much the same way as the "causing" case *Price v Cromack* illustrated "permitting" trigger. *Neath RDC v Williams* was the welsh mountain stream which had become silted up, the defendants having refused to remove the obstruction. The council's problem was that whereas the statutory nuisance offence provision of the Public Health Act (s.259) required an "act or default", the abatement notice provision (s.93) referred to "act, default or sufferance". The Court held that this was a critical distinction and that the defendants' conduct did not amount to a "default", so that there was no offence, but hinted strongly that it would have constituted a "sufferance".

"IMPORTS, PRODUCES, CARRIES, KEEPS, TREATS OR DISPOSES [of waste] OR, AS A BROKER, HAS CONTROL"

The statutory duty of care in respect of waste on land, under section 34 of the EPA, attaches to a person who "imports, produces, carries, keeps, treats or disposes of controlled waste or, as a broker, has control of such waste". The first six notions seem straightforward, identifying the person having direct and active involvement with the particular process. "Broker" must then be considered.

This is apparently a specific role, deliberately chosen by Parliament in preference to the more general and passive terms found elsewhere: for instance those of "permitting" and "sufferance". The EPA says two things about the broker. First, he is only caught by the provision if he has "control" of the waste. Secondly, his duty is tailored to his capacity: a duty "to take all measures applicable in that capacity as are reasonable in all the circumstances".

The concept of "broker" is concerned with control via a contract. In *Milford v Hughes* (1846) 16 M & W 174 at 177, brokers were defined as "those who contrive, make, and conclude bargains and contracts between merchants and tradesmen for which they have a fee or reward". Presumably it would have to be a contract to "import, produce etc" waste. This could be important, since a lender whose terms allow supervision of the borrower's activities could be said to have control via a contract.

In this respect the "code of practice for the purpose of providing to persons practical guidance on how to discharge the duty imposed on them" under section 34(7) of the EPA may comfort lenders. The

Department of the Environment issued a Consultation Paper and Draft Code of Practice, *Waste Management: The Duty of Care*. Paragraph 3 of this document suggests the kind of person who may be regarded as the "broker", stating:

> "where a large expert waste producer delivers to a new disposer waste which he has been producing for many years, whose properties he knows and whose disposal he has arranged with other disposers, he can reasonably be expected to have some idea of the disposal method likely to be permitted by a Waste Management Licence ..."

(3) Discussion

What does it all mean, then, for lenders ? When is the relationship between a bank, or a receiver, and a polluting activity likely to satisfy the various statutory trigger terms ? We will discuss this question with reference to what we see as three vital themes which can be extracted from the various cases which we have just discussed: control, policy and duty. These themes indicate the way in which the trigger terms are likely to be approached by the Court.

the control factor

The first theme which comes from the cases is the significance of control. Thus, the extent to which a lender is likely to become liable under the various trigger terms will depend on the extent to which that lender controls the activity. But that need not mean absolute or even primary control. There is apparently a range of necessary control, corresponding to the range of statutory terms. And it may well be that for some of them the capacity to control is sufficient, in other words that the American *US v Fleet Factors* principle is applicable to English Law.

Indeed, it should be noted that precisely the same theme can be seen to be raised by questions of common law liability, whether in nuisance, *Rylands v Fletcher* or indeed negligence.

As we have seen, the concept of "control" features expressly in section 34 of the EPA, where the "broker" is one who "has control". Moreover, there are statutory triggers where the concept of ultimate or primary control is implicit: one who "imports, produces, carries, keeps, treats or disposes" of waste (EPA s.34), a "manager" (EPA s.157(1) & WRA s.217(1)), a "member" of a company whose affairs are "managed by its members" (EPA s.158 & WRA 217(3)).

It would appear though that the control factor features in all of the other 'activity' triggers too. Broadly speaking, those triggers can be seen to fall into two categories, which correspond to a higher and a lower level of requisite control.

The higher level is represented by the following:

- "carrying on" (air pollution): interpreted in *Lewis v Graham* as needing control and direction over the activity;

- "causing" & "knowingly causing" (water pollution & waste on land): which need a "positive act" or "active operation" according to *Alphacell*, and are not satisfied by mere "acquiescence" according to *Price v Cromack*;

- "act or default" (statutory nuisance & third-party liability): like *Price v Cromack*, approached as needing more than passive acquiescence in *Neath RDC v Williams*;

- "consent, connivance or neglect" by a "director" etc (third-party liability): treated in *Mancetter Developments* as needing the defendant to have "directed or procured" the offence, and in *re a Company No.00996 of 1979* as requiring "a function which touches the central administration of the company";

The lower level of requisite control can be seen to be represented by the following concepts:

- "knowingly permitting" (water pollution & waste on land): interpreted as requiring the power to prevent the activity, in *Berton, Price v Cromack, Alphacell*; and

- "sufferance" (statutory nuisance), treated as needing the power to prevent, but being wider than "permitting", in *Barton v Reed*.

The fact that there may be two levels of control does not mean that lenders can simply conclude that they must be safe in respect of situations which we have suggested need the higher level. Two illustrations are helpful.

The first concerns "act or default". That term appears in the statutory nuisance and third-party liability provisions and may appear at first sight to be quite strict. After all, in the statutory nuisance regime the "act or default" must be that of "the person responsible" for the nuisance. Moreover, that person must apparently exercise greater control than simply passive acquiescence (*Neath RDC v Williams*). And both there and in the third-party liability provisions, Parliament has used the word "attributable". All of this may seem to suggest that "act or default" refers to ultimate or primary control, but this is not so. In the first place, there is the very fact that the third-party liability regime uses the term to apply to the catch-all "any other person". "Other", that is, than the rest of the trigger terms: "other" than a person who has "caused" pollution, "carried on" the process, been a "producer, importer" of waste, and so on. What is more, the statutory nuisance regime expressly makes clear that there can be more than one "person responsible", more than one person to whom the offence is "attributable".

The second illustration is the case with which we started this chapter, *re a Company ex parte Copp*. That case relates to the "director ... officer" context, where we have characterised *Mancetter* and *re a Company No.00996 of 1979* as requiring a 'higher' level of control. What is clear from *re a Company ex parte Copp* is that the Courts are prepared to countenance a bank satisfying that type of criterion.

A receiver who continues to operate the activities of a polluter company would we think satisfy the 'higher' level of control. Moreover, if the *re Sarflax* approach is of general application, then a receiver who collects and distributes assets and their proceeds will be seen to exercise the requisite degree of control.

More startlingly perhaps, it is perfectly conceivable the a bank could fall foul of the 'higher level' trigger terms if during the lending it exercises a control like that contemplated in *re a Company ex parte Copp*, or during a receivership interferes in a way as contemplated in *Standard Chartered Bank v Walker*.

It must follow that if lenders are at risk under the 'higher level' terms, then the risks must be greatly increased in respect of those we have labelled as requiring a 'lower level' of control. Here, then, a bank may not have to exercise the *re a Company ex parte Copp* and *Standard Chartered Bank v Walker* types of control.

So, it would be possible to argue that a bank facilitated, supported, or acquiesced in a polluting activity. It may certainly be arguable that the bank could have prevented the pollution, either directly through powers of supervision reserved in loan agreements, or indirectly in the decision whether to lend or continue to lend.

the policy dimension

The opportunity, indeed the need, for an overt policy analysis can be seen to be presented by the flexibility of many of the statutory terms we have considered. Sure enough, in discussing many of the cases, particularly those concerned in the context of environmental protection, we have paused to consider the nature of the policy reasoning deployed.

Thus, we have seen the recurring question of how strict liability should be, and is readily attached to a given defendant. The best examples in the environmental context are:

- *Alphacell*, where the strict test for "causing" was the result of a desire to ensure that there was not too great a "burden" on prosecutors (Viscount Dilhorne) and a recognition that "it is of the utmost public importance that our rivers should not be polluted" (Lord Salmon);

- *Southern Water v Pegrum*, where the resistance to 'independent cause' and the distinction between parts of the process were fuelled by what was acknowledged as a "policy" justification for strict liability.

- *Ashcroft*, with Lord Diplock's "moral justification" for strict liability from *Tesco Supermarkets v Nattrass* leading to the restriction in the requisite degree of knowledge to satisfy the 'trigger' "knowingly".

A good example in the non-environmental sphere was the wide interpretation of "officer" in *re a Company No.00996 of 1979*, achieved in recognition of what Templeman LJ articulated as a strong policy-commitment based on the perceived importance of the statutory purpose.

Moreover, the contrast between *Ashcroft* and the sex shop case *Croyalgrange* illustrates the flexibility of a term like "knowingly". Ironically, in *Croyalgrange* the policy considerations were articulated too, and the importance of what Lord Brightman called "an effective licensing system" resulted in dicta encouraging a rather relaxed attitude to the nature of evidence.

Despite these policy considerations, it would be quite wrong to give the impression that the English courts have shown themselves to be engaged in an exercise whose paramount consideration is attaching liability or finding a 'deep pocket'. This is clear from cases like *Price v Cromack* and *Neath RDC v Williams*, where Courts driven solely by policy considerations would surely have been tempted to fit a "permitting" offence into the category "causing" (*Price v Cromack*) or a "sufferance" offence into the category "default" (*Neath RDC v Williams*). Indeed, we have mentioned in the context of licences that the Courts' attitude to both conditions and enforcement is if anything rather restrictive (referring to cases like *AG's Reference No.2 of 1988* and *Leigh Land v Walsall*, though see now *ex p. London Waste* The Times 14th January 1993 where *Leigh Land* was held to involve an "unnecessary erosion" of the environmental protection regime).

The critical matter is therefore how the Courts will view lenders in policy terms. This leads on to the concept of duty, which we consider next.

the duty perspective

We have shown how several of the trigger terms are so flexible that they really do no more than identify liability as being when a defendant has 'not done that which he should have done'. The prime examples of this are the concepts of "default" (*re Young & Harston's Contract*; *re Bayley-Worthington*) and "neglect" (*re Hughes*).

Moreover, other triggers involve notions of unreasonableness or negligence: for example the delegation and supervision factor in the test for "knowingly" (*Vane*; *Winson*; *Buxton*, epitomised by Lord Bridge's example of failure to investigate in *Croyalgrange*, where a defendant "had deliberately shut his eyes to the obvious or refrained from inquiry because he suspected the truth but did not want his suspicion confirmed".

These examples suggest that it is possible to re-cast the trigger terms for liability for environmental harm in terms of "duty" language similar to that found in the common law. Accordingly, some triggers may represent a 'reasonable care' duty corresponding to negligence, but others will be a stricter *Rylands v Fletcher*-type of duty. Importantly though, the duty is not owed to a particular plaintiff and may be best viewed as one owed to the environment.

When looked at in this light, the emphasis of several of the cases changes. *Alphacell* and *Southern Water v Pegrum* become cases where the Court recognised a duty on the part of any person who has an "active" or "positive" role in a potentially-polluting process, to ensure that no pollution in fact takes place. It is not necessary that the person know that the pollution has taken place. It is enough that his involvement (his control, above) is such that he can be said to be under a 'duty' to prevent it. Moreover, the policy of protecting rivers from pollution (above) demands that the duty be strict. It is not enough that the person has taken "reasonable steps" to prevent the pollution, only that it has occurred. The fact that this is similar to *Rylands v Fletcher* was of course recognised in *Pegrum* where that common law principle was expressly used.

It is worth recalling too how the duty perspective pervaded the 'independent cause' aspect of *Alphacell*, dealt with by Lord Wilberforce on the basis of "a proper attribution of responsibility".

Similarly, *Ashcroft* becomes a case which recognises the duty on the part of a person who knows of a polluting act, to investigate it fully and ensure that the act is not being conducted illegally: that it is covered by and in compliance with the terms of the relevant licence. And again, the duty can be characterised as a strict one. Ironically, the policy consideration which best supports this "duty" analysis is found in *Croyalgrange* where Lord Bridge recognised that the defendant may be "in the best position" to conduct such investigations.

Indeed, this is precisely the notion which can be said to have swayed the American courts. In *US v Maryland Bank* it was said that lenders "have the means to protect themselves, by making prudent loans. Financial institutions are in a position to investigate and discover potential problems in their secured properties".

Viewed in this way, the crucial question is therefore this: in what circumstances is a lender to be viewed as owing a duty to protect the environment from harm ?

Can it be said that a lender is in an appropriate position, perhaps "the best position", to carry out the necessary investigations to ensure that a borrower is not committing pollution offences, or that the borrower holds and is complying with the relevant licence ? Should such a lender then be encouraged to do so ?

This analysis fits in with some of the defences presented by the environmental protection statutes. Accordingly, there is the provision in the waste on land regime under which it is a defence to prove the exercise of "due diligence". To what extent does the position of lenders make it appropriate to put them under a duty to exercise "due diligence"?

In our view it is questions like these, rather than questions of definition or interpretation, which will determine the scope and direction for lender liability in English Law.

CHAPTER 9

RELATIONSHIP WITH THE LAND

(1) Lenders and land

In Chapter 8 we considered the trigger terms which relate to the relationship between the defendant and the polluting activity, terms like "knowingly permitting" and "default". We referred to the cases which we consider likely to prove significant as to lender liability, because they concern the relationship between lenders/receivers and corporate activity. In this chapter we turn to consider the triggers (again largely from their statutory perspective) which relate to the relationship between the defendant and the land where the pollution is, or has, taken place: the terms of "owner" and "occupier". We will start, though, by discussing some cases in which the relationship between lenders and land has been considered. These, then, are the sort of cases (or, the approach in them) which we consider may take on a new significance in the context of lender liability for environmental harm.

mortgagees

We start with the most obvious relationship between a lender and land, that of mortgagee. As we shall see, there is a critical distinction between a mortgagee not in possession and a mortgagee in possession.

First, we consider the mortgagee not in possession. It is trite law that such a person has an interest in land, taking effect as a term of years, and which is registrable on the title of the property. The mortgagor retains immediate possession and the right to receive rents and profits, and can execute subsequent mortgages.

It is also trite law that the mortgagee not in possession has a prima facie entitlement to possession "before the ink is dry on the mortgage" and at any time thereafter, statute and contract aside (*Four-Maids v Dudley Marshall* [1957] Ch 317; *Birmingham Citizens Building Society v Caunt* [1962] Ch 883; *Western Bank v Schindler* [1977] Ch 1).

The question is whether that entitlement to possession represents a relationship with the land sufficient to found 'lender liability'. The most obvious example would be a liability which attaches to an "owner", where that term is defined as a person "entitled to possession".

This was precisely the situation in *Westminster City Council v Haymarket Publishing* [1981] 1 WLR 677, where the Court was resistant to the notion of a mortgagee not in possession being liable, despite such a statutory definition. The issue was whether a bank, which was a mortgagee not in possession, was liable to pay the rating surcharge on an unused commercial building. The trigger term under the relevant legislative scheme, the General Rate Act 1967, was "owner". And the problem for the bank was that under section 17A of the Act, that term was defined as "the person entitled to possession".

Notwithstanding this provision, the bank was held not to be liable to pay the surcharge. Lord Denning MR reasoned that there should only be one person "entitled to possession" for the purposes of the Act, holding (at 680) that:

> "unless and until the mortgagee enters into possession, in accordance with the mortgage law, and takes the rents and profits, the mortgagor is the person entitled to possession. He is the person who is entitled to put up advertisements, to let and do all that is necessary to let, unless and until the mortgagee interferes. It seems to me that the owner under s.17A is not two, three or more people. It is the one who really has control of the letting. In this case it means the mortgagor ..."

It is noteworthy that the council prevailed against the bank in *Westminster v Haymarket*, though in a different way. Under the statutory scheme, the mortgagor's liability to the council for the surcharge was registrable as "a charge on the land" (like the scheme in *Southern Water Authority v Nature Conservancy Council*, below). The council had registered that liability on the land charges register, and the Court held that the charge took priority over the bank's interest as mortgagee. This 'priority' victory is not unlike the type of 'lender liability' illustrated by the Canadian case of *Panamericana v Northern Badger*.

The importance of the mortgagee in possession / mortgagee not in possession distinction is clear already. *Westminster v Haymarket* makes clear that it has a significant impact in the context of who is an "owner", it being clear from the passage we have quoted from Lord Denning's judgment, that a mortgagee who had entered into possession would have been liable for the rating surcharge.

Cases like *Maguire v Leigh-on-Sea UDC* (1906) 95 LT 319 illustrate similar kinds of responsibilities consequent upon the taking of possession by a mortgagee. That case concerned the Private Street Works Act 1892. Under the Act, the appropriate person liable for costs of works performed by the local authority, and upon whom the relevant notice should be served, was the "owner". The question was whether that term included a mortgagee in possession. Unusually, that lender was arguing that it did satisfy the trigger. It was seeking an injunction to prevent a sale of the property by the authority, which was looking to recover its costs secured by a legal charge. The lender's argument was that the authority had wrongly served the mortgagor and so was not entitled to sell. The Court held that a mortgagee in possession was the "owner" for the purposes of the Act and granted the injunction.

As with "owner", a mortgagee's taking of possession will have an important impact on the question of who is "occupier" of the property, at least where possession is taken by re-entry. This is illustrated by the unusual case of *Poland v Earl Cadogan* [1980] 3 All ER 544.

Commander and Mrs Poland had left their leasehold property for an extended period, and were apparently sailing their yacht around the world. Arrears having built up, their lender-mortgagee had gone into possession of the property. On the Polands' return differences were resolved and the property surrendered back to them. The issue was whether they had "occupied the house as their residence" for a sufficient period to entitle them to acquire the freehold under the Leasehold Reform Act 1967, which all turned on the correct view of the position during the world sailing trip.

The Polands lost. The Court held that at the time when the lender had been in possession, the Polands had ceased to be "occupiers", since "the mortgagees had lawfully taken possession and would have lawfully prevented the tenants from residing in the house if they had sought to do so".

Of course, one view would be that if the Polands had ceased to be "occupier" then the implication is that the mortgagee in possession was the "occupier" during the period in question. Whether this was the right view may depend on the question of whether a property can be without an occupier, which we discuss later.

If the taking of possession is of such significance, then it becomes crucial to identify precisely when a mortgagee enters into possession. In the context of peaceable re-entry or court proceedings for possession this would seem to be straightforward. But what about the situation where the property has been let ? Possession is taken over the rents and profits: does that mean that any receipt of rents and profits will suffice?

The classic authority here is *Noyes v Pollock* (1886) 32 ChD 53. There the issue was whether the London Life Association, which was receiving cheques in respect of rents on the property, was to be treated as mortgagee in possession and so had a duty to account to its mortgagor. The test formulated by the Court emphasized whether the mortgagee had "deprived the mortgagor of the control and management of the property". Accordingly, Bowen LJ stated (at 64) that:

> "in the case where an estate is let to tenants, of course the mortgagee does not enter upon actual occupation of the demised premises. He may fall under the principle [of a duty to account] as a person who enters and takes possession of the rents and profits; but only, as it seems to me, if he does something which goes beyond the mere receipt of sums of money to which the rents and profits may amount, and reaches a point at which he displaces, for the purpose of realising the security, the mortgagor from the control and dominion of the reversion of the estate which is demised. Unless the dominion and control is taken in that sense, the mere receipt of the produce of the management may be taken by the mortgagee, and yet he may stop short of taking the management itself. He may take the rents; that is not enough unless he takes the rent in such a way to take upon himself, and out of the hands of the mortgagor, the business and the duty of collecting and being diligent in that respect ..."

receipt of rents

Noyes v Pollock establishes that mere receipt of rents by a mortgagee does not make him a mortgagee in possession. What is needed is taking the "management" of the land, that is "dominion and control" over it.

But receipt of rents may have a life of its own. Even if it does not make the lender a mortgagee in possession, it is a relationship with land which can be seen to be sufficiently close to trigger liability, especially where the relevant term is expressly defined as including a "person ... receiving the rackrent of the premises" and all the more if this includes receipt of rents "whether on his own account or as agent or trustee for any other person".

This leads us to the context in two rent receipt cases, one where a receiver who handled rents was held not to be liable for the purposes of a statutory duty to provide a fire escape, the other where a bank which handled rents escaped liability for disrepair.

The receiver case was *Solomons v Gertzenstein* [1954] 2 QB 243. There the Court of Appeal held that a Law of Property Act receiver appointed by a mortgagee did not constitute an "owner" of land for the purposes of liability for breach of statutory duty to provide and maintain a fire-escape under the London Building Acts.

The case presented a clash of statutory definitions. The duty was found in the 1939 Act (s.133) and attached to the "owner", defined in that Act (s.33) as:

> "the person for the time being receiving the rack-rent of the premises whether on his own account or as agent or trustee for any other person, or would so receive it if the premises were let at a rack-rent".

However, the 1939 Act was expressly to be read in conjunction with the 1930 Act, which stated (s.5) that 'owner':

> "includes every person in possession or receipt either of the whole or any part of the rents or profits of any land or tenement or in the occupation of any land or tenement otherwise than as a tenant from year to year or for any less term or as a tenant at will."

The Court held that the receiver satisfied the 1939 Act "owner", but not that in the 1930 Act. The crucial thing was the presence in the 1939 Act, but absence in the 1930 Act, of the words "as agent". Had just the 1939 Act applied, the receiver would have been liable "notwithstanding his purely representative capacity", indeed precisely because of it: "collects the rents as agent for the mortgagor".

However, there was the 1930 Act, as to which it was held that the receiver did not satisfy the trigger precisely because there was no mention of receipt "as agent". Somervell LJ said (at 252):

> "One is faced with a general and a special definition. The latter expressly includes an agent and the former does not. One could not possibly in a partly penal statute imply an agent into the former definition. If a statute is plain, ours not to reason

why ..."

It is interesting that the Court did not find the result very satisfactory. Indeed, Somervell LJ renewed his call (from *R v Housing & Local Government, ex parte Corporation of London* [1954] 1 QB 140) that the 'receipt as agent' statutory wording defining "owner" should be reconsidered. As we shall see, Parliament either ignored or disagreed with him.

The bank case was *Midland Bank v Conway* [1965] 1 WLR 1165. This is in many ways the best example of an existing authority on the scope of lender liability, and can even be seen as concerning environmental harm: there the bank was served with an abatement notice.

A property in Caernarvon was owned by a Mrs Griffith who lived in Peru. She had both let it to a Mr Jones and mortgaged it to the bank. The bank was in regular receipt of rent cheques from Mr Jones to Mrs Griffith, which it credited to Mrs Griffith's bank account. The property had fallen into disrepair and the local council wanted to serve an abatement notice under the Public Health Act 1936. It made sense to choose the bank for this purpose, not least because s.343 of the Act defined "owner" as "the person for the time being receiving the rackrent of the premises ... whether on his own account or as agent or trustee for any other person". The bank failed to comply with the notice, and was made subject to a nuisance order made by the Caernarvonshire justices. Lender liability indeed.

On appeal by way of case stated, the bank succeeded in having the nuisance order quashed, it being held that the Bank was not "owner" of the land despite the wording of the Act. It was not enough that the bank handled rent cheques, nor that it knew that the cheques constituted rent. It was held as a matter of construction that "in this context, a person receiving rent as agent must mean someone who does more than act as a mere conduit pipe, but who receives in circumstances where the natural view is that it is not the other person who is receiving".

Lord Parker CJ began by discrediting the policy arguments put forward by counsel for the local authority, to justify the attaching of liability to any person who handled rent monies (at 1169):

> "It is, as he said, a matter of great importance to local authorities, particularly in the case of absent owners, to find

> somebody who can be served and whom the local authority can in the end look to for expenses. It is, as he points out, an artificial definition; it has nothing to do with whether the person served is capable of abating the nuisance or has the authority to abate the nuisance. It is solely to enable the local authority to find someone upon whom to serve a notice ..."

Both Lord Parker and Sachs J used an 'office boy' analogy from cases like *Watts v Battersea Corporation* [1929] 2 KB 63, and the 'conduit pipe' metaphor from cases like *Bottomley v Harrison* [1952] 1 All ER 368, while Browne J doubted whether the bank "would be particularly pleased at being described as a conduit pipe or compared with an office boy". Surprisingly it appears that *Solomons v Gertzenstein* was not cited. And to complete the conundrum, *Bottomley v Harrison* had not been cited in *Solomons v Gertzenstein.*

Crucially perhaps, all three judges stressed that the case simply concerned "the normal relationship of banker and customer", and equally all three suggested (obiter) that there could be liability on the part of the bank if there had been "special circumstances ... which would bring these bankers into such a special relationship with the freeholder as to constitute them her agents for the purposes of this section".

There was no guidance as to the extent or nature of the "special circumstances" or "special relationship" which could be sufficient to attach liability to the bank. When would a bank handling rents be sufficiently 'involved' with its customer as to render it liable ? We suggest that it could be the kind of involvement contemplated in the "shadow director" case *re a Company ex parte Copp*, discussed in the last chapter. Ironically, as we saw, there was no guidance there either.

receivers and "occupation"

We have already considered a case which concerned the relationship of a receiver with land and the question of liability for breach of statutory duty: *Solomons v Gertzenstein.* There the receiver did not satisfy one statutory definition of the trigger term "owner", but would have satisfied another. We turn now to three cases which concern the relationship between receivers and land in the context of the term "occupier". These show a marked contrast of approach. In the first and third the receiver was held liable for the purposes of statutory duties. By contrast, in the second the receiver escaped liability for rates.

The first case is *Meigh v Wickenden* [1942] 2 KB 160, where strong policy considerations drove the Court to the conclusion that the receiver was an "occupier" for the purposes of the Factories Act 1937.

The Act imposed a duty on the "occupier" of a factory to provide a guard for machinery. The defendant had been appointed receiver and manager of a company by a debenture-holder. During the receivership the business continued to be conducted at the factory, and was controlled by the directors and works manager of the company. An employee was injured by unguarded machinery and the receiver was successfully prosecuted.

The receiver argued that the company was the "occupier", relying on the following facts: that the company had remained in existence, that it was controlled by its directors and manager, that he was not in physical occupation of the premises, and that in any case he was expressly agent of the company under the usual debenture terms.

The 'strict liability' policy reasoning, with the need to find someone on whom to "fasten responsibility", was expressed by Viscount Caldecote CJ (at 164-5):

> "The occupier's responsibility under the Act does not depend on proof of personal blame or even on knowledge of the contravention. The policy of the Act seems to be to fasten responsibility, in the first instance, on the occupier. The occupier, however, may bring the person who is alleged to be 'the actual offender' before the court, and if this person is found to have committed the offence, the occupier may be found not guilty: see s.137. The Factories Act 1937 is drastic in its provisions. It is clearly framed in such a way as to make it certain that someone can be found who can be convicted of an offence in the event of a contravention ..."

Accordingly, the receiver was "occupier" for the purposes of the Act, because of his potential power of management and control, rather than any need for the actual exercise of control. Shades of *Fleet Factors*. Viscount Caldecote a little later said (at 166):

> "He was appointed, not to receive directions from the directors, but to give directions. He might at any time remove them and appoint someone to take over their duties. He might himself perform those duties, if he had the necessary technical qualifications. It may, indeed, be said with accuracy, I think,

> that he took the place of the directors and was responsible in their stead for the management of the affairs and business of the company even while he permitted them to manage the business under him. No doubt, the company continued to exist, and, unless and until steps were taken to wind up the company's affairs and to liquidate the company, it would continue to be answerable for engagements into which the company had entered before the appointment of the appellant as receiver and manager ..."

The second case is *Ratford v North Avon District Council* [1987] QB 357 where the Court was also concerned with the question whether a receiver and manager appointed pursuant to a debenture was "occupier". Here the context was liability for rates under the General Rate Act 1967. It was held here that the company and not the receiver was rateable occupier, with the receiver here (unlike in *Meigh v Wickenden*) being saved by the usual 'agent of the company' terms in the debenture and appointment.

The approach of the Court was that given the 'agent of the company' provisions of the debenture and appointment, it was for the council to show that "the receivers had dispossessed the company", which they had failed to do. The facts had showed that (per Slade LJ at 378-9):

> "the receivers had had representatives on the property from time to time during their receivership, that they had managed the company's business and authorised the payment of various outgoings, that the company had at their direction disposed of the company's assets, including, eventually, the leasehold interest in the premises, and that during the receivership they had control of those of the company's assets covered by the debenture ... these facts are quite consistent with the company remaining in legal possession and rateable occupation of the premises ... [and do] not indicate or establish any action on the part of the receivers in relation to the premises beyond management of the company's business and control of its assets, as in any typical receivership where the receiver decides to continue the business as a going concern ..."

It is worthy of note that *Ratford* (like *Solomons v Gertzenstein* and *Meigh v Wickenden*) had an important further dimension: the position of the debenture-holder, in *Ratford* a bank. It was the terms of the debenture which dictated the result so that the contest was not between the company and the receiver, but between the company and the bank.

Thus, Slade, LJ (at 371):

> "a receiver appointed out of court by a debenture holder, in exercise of powers contained in the debenture granted by a company, in properly carrying out his functions, will ordinarily be under no personal liability. The reason is that, ordinarily, depending on the terms of his appointment, he will be acting simply as agent either for the debenture holder or for the company ..."

The third case is a decision of the Scottish Outer House, *Lord Advocate v Aero Technologies Ltd* [1991] SLT 134. It is consistent with *Meigh v Wickenden* and contrasts with *Ratford*.

The story was as follows. A debenture-holding lender had appointed receivers over a factory which produced explosives. Under the Explosives Act 1875 there was a statutory duty on the "occupier" of such a factory to act with "due precaution" to secure the factory and prevent accidents. The receivers informed the Health and Safety Executive that they intended to leave the premises and take no further step as regards its security.

Faced with an application by the HSE for an interlocutory injunction, the Receivers argued that the "occupier" of the factory was the company, relying on the usual debenture term which stated that they were agents of the company.

The HSE obtained their injunction. Lord Sutherland found there to be a prima facie case that the receivers were "occupier" for the purposes of the Act, the 'balance of convenience' taking care of the rest.

In a judgment which had all the hallmarks of a Scottish *Panamericana v Northern Badger*, Lord Sutherland stressed the public policy considerations and the responsibilities incumbent on those acting in a management capacity (at 136):

> "In my opinion in deciding who is the occupier of this factory the reality of the situation must be looked at. The provisions of s.2 of the Explosives Act 1875 are there in the interests of public safety and should not in my opinion be elided on some highly technical ground ... Having regard to the fact that the receivers are acting as managers for the company they are for practical purposes in occupation of the premises in order that

they can carry out their task. The requirement to comply with statutory duty is a management function and accordingly I see no reason in principle why the receivers should not be occupiers for the purposes of the Explosives Act."

the problem with comparisons

The fact that there is the contrast between *Solomons* and *Midland Bank v Conway*, and between *Meigh v Wickenden /Lord Advocate v Aero Technologies* and *Ratford*, indicates a preference on the part of the courts to treat each context separately.

Indeed the central heading in Slade LJ's judgment in *Ratford* was "The authorities relating to the liability of a receiver for rates". *Meigh v Wickenden*, not a rating case, was referred to briefly as supporting the contentions that "there is no rule of law that a receiver appointed by debenture holders may not be in rateable occupation ... and that the usual agency provision does not necessarily prevent him from being in occupation for rating purposes", all of which Slade LJ accepted. Conversely, *Ratford* was considered unhelpful in *Lord Advocate v Aero Technologies*, and distinguished as a 'rating case'.

An anti-comparison feeling has been expressed recently by the House of Lords in *Southern Water Authority v Nature Conservancy Council* (see below). The safest way to treat the cases is simply as providing different examples of different kinds of approach to the relationship with land in the context of liability. *Meigh v Wickenden* and *Lord Advocate v Aero Technologies* for example, are best seen as examples of a possible approach to "occupier", fuelled by strong policy considerations and notions of strict liability, but which may or may not reflect the likely judicial attitude in the context of the EPA.

(2) The trigger terms

"OWNER"

The importance of being "owner" arises in the waste and statutory nuisance schemes. An "owner" will be liable as follows:

- to be fined for breach of an abatement notice in respect of a statutory nuisance, unless he has a "reasonable excuse". Such a notice can be served on him under s.80 of the EPA in any of three situations: where the nuisance is a "structural defect"; where the 'person responsible' for the nuisance cannot be found; or where the nuisance has not yet occurred;

- for clean-up costs incurred by a local authority in abating a statutory nuisance, following service of an abatement notice. These costs are recoverable under s.81, where the nuisance was caused by the act or default of an owner of the land, from the person who is "for the time being" the owner;

- for clean-up costs incurred by a waste regulation authority in taking steps to avoid pollution by waste in the context of a build-up of "noxious gases" or "noxious liquids" under s.61 of the EPA. Again, recovery is from the owner "for the time being", unless he can show costs were incurred unreasonably, hardship, or that the authority had accepted a surrender of a licence for the site.

There are two crucial issues, and we discuss each in turn.

questions of chronology

It is necessary to determine when a person must be, or have been, the "owner" to satisfy the statutory triggers. There are various possibilities: when the acts occurred which caused or allowed the waste or nuisance to develop; when any abatement notice was served; when the authority took the relevant steps; or finally at the time when clean-up costs come to be demanded. This is a vital issue for a lender who may become "owner", a mortgagee who has taken possession perhaps, between two of these various stages. To what extent will such a person avoid liability because he can say he was not owner at an important earlier stage ?

There are cases relating to the timing of liability in the context of earlier cost-recovery regimes. Two of these concern the 'clean-up' provisions of the Public Health Acts, where the relevant trigger term was "owner in default". This was held to mean the owner at the time when the local authority completed the works the cost of which it was seeking to recover: *R v Swindon* (1878-9) 4 QBD 305; see also *Millard v Balby-with-Hexthorpe* [1905] 1 KB 60. By contrast, there is *Croydon Corporation v Oldaker* [1937] 1 KB 337, concerning a similar provision in the Croydon Corporation Act 1884. There, liability was held to attach only to an owner at the time of service of the notice requiring the work to be done, not the date of its completion.

In fact, a plain reading of the EPA suggests that liability is capable of attaching to the "owner" at one of the later of the possible dates, and that lenders (and purchasers) should therefore beware.

Section 80 liability would appear simply to be that of the "owner" at the time when the abatement notice was served, even though Parliament did not incorporate the phrase "for the time being".

Sections 81 and 61 are more difficult. The use of the phrase "for the time being" in connection with "entitled to recover the cost" suggests that the relevant time may be the time when recovery is sought. Parliament could easily have said "at the time that the expenses were incurred". Thus, it would not matter that the person had become "owner" after the clean-up operations had taken place. It seems to turn on whether "incurred" means "which have been incurred" or "which are incurred". In section 61 the word "exercises" would support the latter interpretation. And the former could be said to allow an absurd situation where a local authority delays, or resurrects, a claim for clean-up costs to catch an unsuspecting purchaser (or perhaps lender). Finally, the same issue arises in respect of "occupier" and the second type of clean-up recovery under section 59. There is an interesting construction argument in favour of needing to be "owner" at the time of clean-up costs and not recovery (see below). That could be deployed here, as a 'favoured EPA scheme', though one consideration is that section 59 does not use "for the time being".

Accordingly, the person who has become "owner" after a nuisance began, may find himself served with an abatement notice. And a person acquiring "ownership" of land may be liable for clean-up costs relating to either nuisance or waste where the polluting acts, service of an abatement notice (in the case of nuisance), entry onto the land by the authority, and possibly (though probably not) the incurring of the costs.

This chronology angle illustrates the policy-orientation of the statutory provisions, in two senses. First, that the liabilities are strict, an observation which is supported by the limited defences selected by Parliament: under section 80 "reasonable excuse", under section 61 hardship (unlikely to be satisfied by lenders) or a formally-accepted surrender, and under section 81 not even these. Second, the clear message that the onus is on the person thinking of acquiring "ownership" of the land to investigate environmental matters. That translates to a responsibility to investigate, to which we will return at the end of this chapter.

who is "owner" for the purposes of the EPA?

Who then is vulnerable to these risks or under these duties ? When does a person, in particular a lender, constitute an "owner" under the EPA?

There is no definition of "owner" in the EPA. That is rather odd, at least from the point of view of statutory nuisance, since the predecessors to the EPA Part III (PHA and COPA) both had statutory definitions of this trigger term. The WRA also has a statutory definition of "owner". This is ironic, because "owner" is not an express trigger term for water pollution (Part III): its relevance in the WRA is to water abstraction (Part II).

Indeed, legislation frequently defines "owner", and three sets of examples are noteworthy for lenders:

- First, some definitions have included reference to the receipt of rents, whether or not including the phrase "as agent", which we have seen was vital in *Solomons v Gertzenstein*, being present in one of the London Building Acts but absent in the other. Examples of statutes including the definition of receipt of rents and including the phrase "as agent", were the Nuisances Removal Act 1855 (s.2) and Public Health Act 1936 (s.343) before *Solomons* and (notwithstanding the exhortations of Somervell LJ in *Solomons*) both COPA (s.105) and the WRA (s.221).

- Second, some statutes have expressly included receivers, either in general or those appointed by a court. An example of the former is the Mines & Quarries Act 1954 s.181:

> "Where the business of a person who, by virtue of the foregoing provisions of this section is, for the purposes of this Act, to be taken to be owner of a mine or quarry is carried on by a liquidator, receiver or manager, or by some other person authorised to carry it on by an order of the court of competent jurisdiction, the liquidator, receiver, manager or other person shall be

taken for the purposes of this Act to be an additional owner of the mine or quarry."

And an example of the latter is the Nuisances Removal Act 1855 s.2:

> "'owner' includes any person receiving the rents of the property in respect of which that word is used from the occupier of such property, on his own account or as trustee or agent for any other person, or as receiver or sequestrator appointed by the Court of Chancery or any order thereof, or who would receive the same if such property were let to a tenant"

It is significant that "receiver or sequestrator" was dropped in the Public Health Act of 1875 (and thereafter), a fact which was held in *Corporation of Bacup v Smith* (1890) 44 ChD 395 to be a compelling argument against holding a court-appointed receiver to be an "owner" under that Act.

- Thirdly, some definitions of "owner" have related directly to mortgagees. We have seen how in the General Rating Act 1967 s.17B the term was defined as "the person entitled to possession", but which the Court of Appeal in *Westminster City Council v Haymarket* held excluded a mortgagee not in possession.

  What the Court achieved in *Haymarket* has been achieved directly by Parliament in several statutory definitions of "owner" as expressly excluding "a mortgagee not in possession", of which examples include the Agricultural Statistics Act 1979 s.6(1), the Highways Act 1980 s.325 and the Housing Act 1985 s.56. As we shall see, the WRA definition contains a partial exclusion of mortgagees not in possession. Of course, if mortgagees not in possession are expressly excluded, the implication is that mortgagees in possession are included.

  The Town & Country Planning Act 1947 s.119 went one step further, excluding mortgagees in possession too.

Of these, it is most tempting to rely on the definitions in COPA and the WRA. COPA, which was the predecessor of the EPA statutory nuisance regime (and which in turn followed its predecessor the Public

Health Act 1936 s.343), can be perceived as deploying a 'wide' definition of "owner" (s.105). It is certainly familiar:

> "the person for the time being receiving the rackrent of the premises ... whether on his own account or as agent or trustee for another person, or who would so receive the rackrent if the premises were let at a rackrent".

As for the WRA definition (albeit concerned with abstraction of water), WRA s.221 states:

> " 'owner', in relation to any premises, means the person who -
>
> (a) is for the time being receiving the rack-rent of the premises, whether on his own account or as agent or trustee for another person; or
>
> (b) would receive the rack-rent if the premises were let at a rack-rent,
>
> but for the purposes of Schedule 2 of this Act, Chapter II of Part II of this Act and the related water resources provisions does not include a mortgagee not in possession, and cognate expressions shall be construed accordingly"

These, then, can be seen as the "environmental" meanings of "owner". One might conclude then that in the "environmental" field, including the EPA, "owner" includes the notions of receipt of rents as considered in *Solomons* and *Midland Bank v Conway*. Thus, were *Solomons* the preferred approach, lenders would need to think carefully before handling rents. If it is *Midland Bank v Conway* which points the way forward, then the crucial question will be what was meant there by the "special relationship" which will serve to attach liability to a bank who has become too involved with its customer.

The use of the COPA/PHA definition of "owner" can be supported by Viscount Dilhorne's approach in *Newbury Council v Environment Secretary* [1980] 1 All ER 1731: that in the context of a continuing scheme one would expect an intended change in statutory definition to have been made clear by Parliament. We are told that this argument has proved sufficient to persuade Hampstead Magistrates' Court to impose statutory nuisance liability on an LPA receiver (*Weston v London*

Borough of Camden 20th February 1992, unreported).

Moreover, the WRA definition at any rate would indicate that a mortgagee in possession is an "owner", which is supported by cases like *Maguire* and *Haymarket*. It is arguable that since the mortgagee exclusion from the WRA definition is partial, perhaps a mortgagee not in possession is to be included, at least for some purposes. *Haymarket* of course, can be seen as hostile to such liability, but then *Haymarket* is distinguishable as a rating case.

The problem, of course, is that the existence of these other statutory definitions is something of a double-edged sword. They are, after all, ways in which Parliament could have approached "owner" in the EPA, but did not. In the first place, the very fact that there is such a range of definitions makes it difficult to be confident that any one of them is helpful in relation to the EPA. Even if COPA and the WRA are the best examples of "environmental", it is an inescapable observation that Parliament, having used those definitions in those Acts, appears (one interpretation of "owner" assumes deliberately) not to have selected them in the EPA.

That, in turn, presents a paradox. The refusal to adopt the wide definition from COPA may suggest either that Parliament contemplated a narrower alternative or an even wider one. As to the latter, if the 'strict liability' policy which we identified in the last chapter is allowed to dominate then one can imagine a relaxed definition, approached in a similar way that we saw *Meigh v Wickenden* approach the term "occupier", driven by the desire "that someone can be found who can be convicted of an offence in the event of a contravention".

The same double-edged characteristic is evident in the WRA definition of "owner". On the one hand it may be comforting for those who lend to polluters that Parliament has provided (albeit 'elsewhere') a specific indication that "mortgagees not in possession" are not included. But if this is seen as a special protection, it is one which was not chosen in the EPA. Moreover, the very fact that the WRA definition is so specific about parts of the Act in which "owner" does not include mortgagee in possession suggests that generally (and perhaps elsewhere in environmental protection legislation) "owner" does include "mortgagee not in possession".

Finally, it could be that there is a 'control' perspective here, as elsewhere. The key hints could be seen to be those of Lord Parker LJ in *Midland Bank v Conway* when he dismissed the prospect of lender liability by pointing out that the proposed interpretation of the bank as "owner" was artificial because it had "nothing to do with whether the person served is capable of abating the nuisance or has the authority to abate the nuisance". If this is the way forward then the question is when a lender does demonstrate such capability or authority.

"OCCUPIER"

Like the "owner" of land, its "occupier" has a special interest in the waste and statutory nuisance regimes of the EPA, and should be aware of the following:

- First, he may be served with an ordinary waste removal notice under section 59, non-compliance with which will render him criminally liable (and liable for clean-up costs) unless he has a "reasonable excuse" or can persuade a Court to quash the notice since he did not deposit, knowingly cause or knowingly permit the waste. This provision corresponds to the fact that under section 35(2) the relevant person for the purposes of holding a waste disposal licence is a person "who is in occupation of the land".

- Second, even if not served with such a notice, he may be pursued under section 59 for clean-up costs where the waste regulation authority decided that emergency steps were necessary. It is a defence for the occupier to show that he did not deposit, knowingly cause or knowingly permit the waste.

- Third, there is an abatement notice under section 80. In this respect the "occupier" is alongside the "owner" as a person on whom such a notice can be served where the "person responsible" for the nuisance cannot be found or the nuisance has not yet occurred. Again, a "reasonable excuse" will save the "occupier" from liability.

We should add that the "occupier" of land is the relevant trigger for the purposes of common law nuisance, though only where there is a continuing nuisance of which he ought to know and has the power to prevent: *Sedleigh-Denfield v O'Callaghan* [1940] AC 880.

Like "owner", "occupier" is not defined in the EPA. Moreover, whilst both the PHA and COPA used it as a trigger term, neither defined what "occupier" meant. There are, however, various cases which consider what is meant by "occupier", for example:

- *Poland v Earl Cadogan* (above), where a lender-mortgagee going into possession displaced the "occupation" of the borrower;

- *Harris v Birkenhead* [1976] 1 WLR 1380, where a local authority which served a compulsory purchase order in respect of premises which were subsequently vacated was held to have become "occupier" for the purposes of the Occupier's Liability Act;

- *Wheat v Lacon* [1966] 1 AC 552, where the House of Lords treated "occupier" under the Occupier's Liability Act as turning on the question of "control";

- *Meigh v Wickenden* (above), where a receiver was treated as "occupier" for the purposes of breach of statutory duty under the Factories Acts; and

- *Ratford v North Avon DC* (above), where a receiver in a "typical receivership" was held not to be "occupier" for the purposes of rates.

However, any discussion must be tempered by a recent warning from the House of Lords.

the anti-analogy principle

We start then with Lord Mustill's statement in the recent case of *Southern Water Authority v Nature Conservancy Council* [1992] 1 WLR 775, a case which concerned the term "occupier" in an environmental protection context. He said in relation to the question whether the defendants had been "occupiers" (at 781):

> "No useful progress can be made towards an assessment of this argument by looking up in dictionaries the words "occupy" and "occupier", or by inquiring what meaning the courts have given them in reported cases, for they draw their meaning entirely from the purpose for which and the context in which they are used ..."

This echoes the words of Lord Denning in *Wheat v Lacon* (at 577):

> "At the outset, I would say that no guidance is to be obtained from the use of the word "occupier" in other branches of the law: for its meaning varies according to the subject-matter ..."

However, in that case Viscount Dilhorne apparently thought analogies did provide some help, (at 573):

> "although it is possible to draw distinctions between occupation for the purposes of taxation and rating and occupation for the purposes of the Occupiers' Liability Act 1957, in all these cases the same question has to be determined, namely, who was the occupier at the relevant time ..."

Lord Mustill's statement also compliments the mood in *Ratford*, where as we have seen Slade LJ confined his discussion to "the authorities relating to the liability of a receiver for rates", narrower even than "occupier in the context of rates".

We acknowledge this approach because some of the analysis of the cases (here and indeed, elsewhere) may be said to serve what Lord Mustill called "no useful progress". In truth, all that Lord Mustill has said is that it is an 'open game', that no particular approach will be of general application, and that the most important factor is the specific statutory context with which one is concerned: here the EPA.

What is vital is that ideas plucked from the caselaw be treated with great caution. But what can nevertheless, we think, be "useful" is to identify the kinds of approach which Courts have taken, and could take in the context of the EPA, and some important themes which have arisen.

a "control" approach

We start with *Wheat v Lacon*, though cited (and implicitly repeated) in *Southern Water Authority v Nature Conservancy Council*. The point of course, to emphasise it again, is that while any Court concerned with the EPA will be completely free to adopt a different approach, such a Court is equally completely free to adopt the *Wheat v Lacon*-type approach. Moreover, there are reasons which make such an approach fit neatly into environmental protection.

Mr Wheat had died in a fall at "The Golfers' Arms" in Great Yarmouth and his widow was suing the brewing company who owned the pub, for damages under the Act. The House of Lords held that the company was "occupier", through its servant-manager, and so owed the statutory duty of care. The claim however failed because there was no evidence of any breach of that duty.

The Court adopted a relaxed test for "occupier", based on "control" and which was sufficiently flexible to accommodate notions of variant "duties". This is consistent with the themes identified from the cases on relationship with activity: "control" and "duty".

So, in *Wheat v Lacon* the Court recognised an intimate link between "occupier", "control" and "duty", the critical question being characterised as whether "the brewery company had a sufficient degree of control over the premises to put them under a duty to a visitor" (Lord Denning at 580).

The essence of the Court's approach is captured in a passage from Lord Denning MR (at 578):

> "wherever a person has a sufficient degree of control over premises that he ought to realise that any failure on his part to use care may result in injury to a person coming lawfully there, then he is an 'occupier' ... In order to be an 'occupier' it is not necessary for a person to have entire control over the premises. He need not have exclusive occupation. Suffice it that he has some degree of control. He may share the control with others. Two or more may be "occupiers". And whenever this happens, each is under a duty to use care towards persons coming lawfully onto the premises, dependent on his degree of control. If each fails in his duty, each is liable to a visitor who is injured in consequence of his failure, but each may have a claim to contribution from the other."

It should be acknowledged that *Wheat v Lacon* would be readily distinguishable from the current context even without Lord Mustill's warning in *Southern Water Authority v Nature Conservancy Council*. The notion of "control" necessarily had a high profile in the context of the 1957 Act with which *Wheat v Lacon* was concerned. There, the s.1(1) duty attaches to "an occupier", but s.1(2) says that the regime regulates "the nature of the duty imposed by law in consequence of a person's occupation or control" (see Lord Pearson at 589).

Wheat v Lacon is consistent with other "occupier" cases, for example under drugs legislation. In *R v Mogford* [1970] 1 WLR 988 it was held that an "occupier" for the purposes of the Dangerous Drugs Act 1965 must have legal possession and control over the premises. And in *R v Tao* [1977] QB 141 an "occupier" under the Misuse of Drugs Act 1971 included anyone in occupation whose degree of control over the premises was such that he was capable of excluding anyone likely to commit an offence.

Perhaps its greatest attraction is that *Wheat v Lacon* would reflect the approach to common law nuisance, and that seen in *Meigh v Wickenden* and *Lord Advocate v Aero Technologies*, in both of which liability for statutory duty was seen to be capable of attaching to a receiver as "occupier" because of his potential power of control. And to complete the linkage, the strong policy reasoning of the 'strict liability' approach in *Meigh v Wickenden* fits closely with *Alphacell v Woodward* and the 'control' perspective discussed in Chapter 8, above. All of which would of course contrast with cases like *Ratford* and *Midland Bank v Conway*.

the "comprehensive and stable relationship"

Ironically perhaps, Lord Mustill's warning (above) means that we may need to be wary of the approach to "occupier" taken by him in *Southern Water Authority v Nature Conservancy Council* itself. Nevertheless, that case is seemingly irresistible, having the compelling force of being a recent House of Lords' authority on the question of "occupier", in the context of concerned with environmental protection. Moreover it can be seen to turn on statutory machinery not dissimilar to that under the EPA. Perhaps the "purpose" and "context" are sufficiently close even for Lord Mustill's strict test of what is "helpful".

Hill Heath Ditch lay between the land of 2 farmers and near land owned by the Southern Water Authority. In 1982 the Nature Conservancy Council notified the farmers and the Authority that part of their land, including the Ditch, had been designated a Site of Special Scientific Interest (SSSI) under the Wildlife and Countryside Act 1981. The notification included a list of operations which were prohibited on the site likely to cause damage to flora and fauna. In 1987, following requests from the farmers, the Authority dredged the Ditch, causing considerable damage.

Section 28 of the Act provided that "the owner or occupier of any land which has been notified ... shall not carry out or cause or permit to be carried out, on that land any operation specified in the notification". The Authority was convicted and fined heavily, but appealed on the ground that it had never been an "occupier" of the Ditch. The council argued that in carrying out the dredging operations, which had taken several weeks, the Authority had been "occupier" of the Ditch.

The Divisional Court, Court of Appeal and House of Lords all held that the convictions should be quashed, rejecting the suggestion that the Authority's carrying out of dredging operations had been sufficient to render it "occupier".

We return later to the parts of the Act which Lord Mustill held to be particularly significant in approaching the term "occupier".

The heart of the judgment, though, was as follows (at 782):

> "The section contemplates that the elaborate machinery of notices, waiting periods, agreements and so forth will be set in motion by a notification under section 28(1) to an owner or occupier. The juxtaposition with "owner" shows, to my mind, that the occupier is someone who, although lacking the title of an owner, nevertheless stands in such a comprehensive and stable relationship with the land as to be, in company with the actual owner, someone to whom the mechanisms can sensibly be made to apply. A stranger who enters the land for a few weeks solely to do some work on it does not fall into this category".

This approach is not unlike that of the Alberta Court of Appeal in *Panamericana v Northern Badger*, that the Receiver was the entity with whom it was appropriate for the ERCB to deal (see Chapter 2, above).

It is worth observing that *Southern Water Authority v Nature Conservancy Council* tells us one important thing about the current judicial mood, that 'merits' and 'policy' influences alone are not enough for a wide reading of statutory triggers. The House of Lords resisted policy temptations of two kinds. In the first place, the 'merits' of the prosecution case were obvious: the Authority was clearly 'culpable' in that, by the coincidence of owning nearby land, it knew of the designation and prohibition. Lord Mustill described the authority's conduct as an "act of ecological vandalism", acknowledging that (at

778):

> "There is no doubt that these were operations falling within the scope of the notification. The result was to cause grave damage to those natural features of the ditch which the notification had been designed to protect ..."

The second policy feature was the suggestion that Courts should avoid interpreting the Act in such a way that made it (at 783):

> "insufficient to penalise the "fly-tipper", a notorious threat to the countryside, whose methods involve a hasty and furtive dumping of rubbish ..."

Given these factors, a policy-driven Court would have been tempted to squeeze into the definition of "occupier" a person whose presence on the land had been solely to conduct the damaging acts. The House of Lords did not. Lord Mustill concluded that the statutory scheme was "flawed" in more than one respect and declined to "force on the statute the interpretation advanced by the council", which interpretation in any case he thought would not have been sufficient to include the "fly-tipper".

no occupier / several occupiers?

We wish to mention next two significant issues which arise from the caselaw. The first is whether there will normally always be an "occupier", or whether the Courts readily will countenance situations where there is a 'lacuna': no one to whom liability can be attached. If there is to be no lacuna then it would have to be enough that the defendant has a 'closer' relationship with the land than others. Lenders will have in mind situations like that of the mortgagee not in possession, where the mortgagor has abandoned the land, ceased his operations there, or perhaps is insolvent. Can such land be without an occupier ? In the rating context, it is clearly readily contemplated that land may have no "occupier". A classic definition for rating purposes is that of Lush J in *R v St Pancras Assessment Committee* (1877) 2 QBD 581 (at 588):

> "Occupation includes possession as its primary element, but it also includes something more. Legal possession does not, of itself, constitute an occupation. The owner of a vacant house is in possession, and may maintain trespass against anyone

who invades it, but as long as he leaves it vacant he is not rateable for it as an occupier. If, however, he furnishes it, and keeps it ready for habitation whenever he pleases to go into it, he is an occupier, though he may not reside in it one day in a year..."

This issue arose too in the context of a liquidator in *re Briant Colour Printing* [1977] 1 WLR 942, another rateable occupation case. There the work-force of a company in liquidation had seized occupation of the premises and denied access to the liquidator. These facts were sufficient to hold that the company, via the liquidator, was prevented from being "the occupier". The Court of Appeal was unconvinced that there need be someone who is "occupier", but was prepared to hold that "the workforce" or its "committee" was "the occupier" if necessary.

However in *Meigh v Wickenden* the policy was of ensuring that "someone can be found who can be convicted of an offence", and the Court was happy to attach liability to the receiver as "occupier" under the Factories Act, based on his ability to control the factory. Indeed, both *Panamericana v Northern Badger* and *Lord Advocate v Aero Technologies* can be seen to be driven by a similar policy, the Canadian and Scottish Courts (respectively) finding abhorrent the notion that the companies being in receivership there could be no "occupier" to whom liability could attach.

The second issue is whether there can be more than one "occupier". This corresponds to what we said in the context of the relationship with the polluting activity about whether the defendant must have the primary "control" over the activity. Must a lender be the primary "occupier" of land, in order to be liable, or can one of several occupiers be liable ?

Both Parliament and the Courts have approached this question differently depending on the particular context. Parliament has on occasion defined the "occupier" as including "any number of persons" (Explosives Act 1875 s.108) or as being limited "the person ... entitled to possession" (Caravan Sites and Control of Development Act 1960 s.1), a term treated as meaning one person to the relief of the mortgagee in *Haymarket*).

We have already mentioned a passage from Lord Denning's judgment in *Wheat v Lacon* which makes clear that for the purposes of the Occupier's Liability Act he considered that there could be more than one "occupier". Three of his colleagues (Lords Morris, Pearson and

Pearce) agreed. And again this tied in with the ideas of "control" and "duty", so that among several occupiers, those with most "control" would have a higher "duty". Lord Morris said (at 586):

> "it may, therefore, often be that the extent of the particular control which is exercised within the sphere of joint occupation will become a pointer as to the nature and extent of the duty which reasonably devolves upon a particular occupier..."

Here again, *Lord Advocate v Aero Technologies* presents a marked contrast of approach. There Lord Sutherland could (at 136):

> "see no reason in principle why both the company and the receivers ... should not be regarded as joint occupiers ... The position may be different for the purposes of payment of rates and accordingly I find the case of *Ratford* of little assistance ..."

The Court in *re Briant* was resistant to the argument that although not the sole or primary "occupier" the liquidator was "an occupier". The finding of the Court is summarised in this passage from Buckley LJ (at 954-5):

> "The applicants contend that in the present case there were concurrent uses and that the liquidator's position was paramount, the concurrent uses of course being the use of the factory for the purpose of housing the plant and machinery, and the use of the factory for the purpose of conducting the printing business which was being carried on by the committee or by the work force. This seems to me to be inconsistent with the true state of affairs which existed during the relevant period. The liquidator was wholly excluded from the works and was denied access to the plant and machinery; the committee was in the fullest possible sense in adverse possession - or, if not the committee, then the work force. No doubt the liquidator could, by legal proceedings and after a lapse of time, have recovered possession, but while he was out of possession he was in no position to control in any manner or to any extent the factory or the plant and machinery or to make any use of them: he was powerless. In such a situation it is in my opinion impossible to describe the liquidator as having been in a paramount position..."

Similarly, we have seen how in *Ratford* the Court treated the question as being an 'either/or' one: the fact that there was a "typical receivership" was "quite consistent with the company remaining in legal possession and rateable occupation ..."

tackling the statutory context

After *Southern Water Authority v Nature Conservancy Council* the primary consideration. There are indications from that case as to what kinds of factor were considered significant as to "occupier" - in the context of the Wildlife & Countryside Act 1981.

- Section 28 referred to the liability being that of "the owner or occupier of any land which has been notified". Accordingly, Lord Mustill thought that a defendant need not have been an occupier "at the time of the notification" but could "have subsequently come into occupation of notified land" and then carried out the prohibited conduct on the land. This is another example of the need for a purchaser to conduct adequate investigations as to potential liability. It was supported by the provision that notification under section 28 created a land charge of which such a purchaser "may be presumed to have notice".

- In section 29 the Act stated that "no person" should carry out a banned act, which Lord Mustill contrasted with "owner or occupier" in section 28 and concluded (at 782) that "the category of owners and occupiers is narrower than that of persons who are carrying out proscribed operations on the land".

- Lord Mustill thought it compelling (at 783) that under the terms of the Act the "ultimate sanction" was the compulsory acquisition of the defendant's "interest", so that "occupier" could only include persons who could "be described as having an interest in the land".

- Most importantly perhaps was Lord Mustill's emphasis on "the elaborate machinery of notices, waiting periods, agreements and so forth" under the Act and "the juxtaposition with 'owner'. These were the ingredients in the ratio of the case (at 782), that "occupier" was:

> "someone who, although lacking the title of an owner,

> nevertheless stands in such a comprehensive and stable relationship with the land as to be, in company with the actual owner, someone to whom the mechanisms can sensibly be made to apply ..."

"occupier" under the EPA

What observations, then, can be made from the statutory context in which "occupier" appears in the EPA ? These seem to us to be the most important features:

- First, under the schemes there is reference throughout to "the occupier". This seems to contemplate only one occupier. However, the same could have been said of "the person responsible" in section 80, which section 81(1) makes clear is potentially plural. The mention of service of "a notice" may also support the argument that the EPA contemplates that there cannot be multiple "occupiers", though this is not at all clear.

- As to whether there need be an occupier, and so whether it is sufficient simply to identify the person who is most closely connected to the property, section 59(7)(b) seems to be conclusive. That provision allows waste clean-up operations without the service of a notice where "there is no occupier of the land".

- It is notable that there is a juxtaposition of "occupier" with "owner" in the context of statutory nuisance (s.80), but not in the case of waste (s.59). This may be suggestive of a narrower definition in the former context, where in any case "occupier" will not be needed to achieve anything which "owner" could do. There might be an argument for saying that in section 59 (unlike s.80 and indeed s.61) Parliament chose only "occupier", and therefore intended deliberately to exclude "owners", though the answer would seem to be that only 'owners who are not also occupiers' are excluded from section 59.

- Both uses of "occupier" in the EPA (ss.80 and 59) are based on statutory machinery involving the service of a notice. In this respect the situation is not unlike *Southern Water Authority v Nature Conservancy Council* itself, where the existence of a notice machinery dictated the degree of the necessary "comprehensive and stable relationship". However, the machinery in the EPA is not as "elaborate" as that in the Wildlife & Countryside Act 1981 (the EPA does not have the extended waiting periods, counter-notices etc).

- The chronological question, as with "owner, may be answerable by a plain reading of the Act. The first type of clean-up costs recovery under section 59, and that under section 80, seem to contemplate simply that the defendant is "occupier" at the time of service of the relevant notice. So, it is contemplated that an "occupier" will have to comply with the relevant notice notwithstanding that he has come into "occupation" since the polluting act took place or began.

- However, as for the second section 59 type of recovery, where emergency steps were taken by the authority, it might be argued that the relevant time is simply that of attempted recovery of the costs. As under section 61 (discussed above with regard to "owner" and chronology) the word "exercises" may suggest that "incurred" means "which are incurred" so that the relevant time is the time when the clean-up operations took place. Furthermore there is no "for the time being" in section 59(8) (cf. ss.61 & 81). Moreover, there is an interesting construction argument here, which goes as follows. Where the property has gone from having no occupier at the time of clean-up operations to having an occupier at the time of recovery, costs cannot be sought from the "occupier" (since s.59(8) only applies to an occupier where the steps were emergency steps (s.59(7)(a)) not where there was no occupier at the time of the clean-up (s.59(7)(b)). It can be said to be arbitrary, indeed perverse, to penalise a person who becomes on "occupier" after clean-up where he takes occupation from another person but not where he takes unoccupied property, and that accordingly the relevant time must be the time of the work.

- The fact that a defendant may be liable for clean-up costs notwithstanding that he came on the scene after the polluting act, is subject of course to the question of defences. Under section 80 there is a "reasonable excuse" defence. Likewise the "occupier" for the first type of costs recovery in section 59 can have the notice quashed, and for the second type has a defence, essentially of proving that he was an "innocent purchaser". All this, plus the fact that section 80 states that the "person responsible cannot be found", shows that "occupier" requires no culpability.

general observations

First, a mortgagee in possession would apparently satisfy both a *Wheat v Lacon*-type "control" test and the *Southern Water Authority v Nature Conservancy Council* "stable relationship". Thus, as suggested in *Poland v Earl Cadogan*, on taking possession a mortgagee may displace, and presumably become, the "occupier".

Second, the principle seems to be, here as in the context of "owner", that a 'purchaser' should investigate whether there is waste or a nuisance (or potential nuisance) on land, and that in acquiring the property that person may be assuming responsibility for these kinds of environmental damage. This principle ties in with *Harris v Birkenhead* and would seem to be wholly appropriate to apply to mortgagees taking possession. We return to this below.

Third, the question whether a mortgagee not in possession is an occupier could turn on whether he exerts sufficient "control" or has a sufficiently "comprehensive and stable relationship with the land". The issues as to the former have been discussed in the last chapter. As to the latter, a mortgagee not in possession can readily be seen to have a "stable" relationship with the land, indeed this includes the role of receiving notices (eg. from the Land Registry as to further charges). What seems likely is that the relationship would not be sufficiently "comprehensive".

Finally, turning to receivers, both *Meigh v Wickenden* and *Ratford* may have been removed from the scene by the anti-comparison approach in *Southern Water Authority v Nature Conservancy Council*. The former would have been the closer of the two analogies, and its strong policy reasoning (finding someone to whom to "fasten responsibility") most worrying for receivers. The latter is more distant in context (rating) but far more comforting for receivers, preferring the continuing occupation of the company in the "typical receivership". It may well be that a receiver's role is sufficiently "stable and comprehensive", or involves a sufficient degree of "control", that he could be seen as "occupier" for the purposes of the EPA.

(3) Discussion

When, then, will a lender's relationship with land be sufficient for the Courts to identify it as satisfying the trigger terms of "owner" or "occupier" ?

choices for the Courts

We have seen how the distinction between a mortgagee in possession and one not in possession may be a critical one from the point of view of whether his relationship with land is such that liability attaches under the waste and statutory nuisance provisions of the EPA.

A mortgagee in possession is, we think, likely to be deemed an "owner" for the purposes of those regimes, as acknowledged by the Courts in other contexts such as those in *Maguire* and *Haymarket*. He is also likely to be considered "occupier", material only from the point of view of section 59 where "owner" is not mentioned, since he would be in precisely the sort of "comprehensive and stable relationship with the land" to make the statutory machinery apply to him. He would also, of course, satisfy the need for "control", were a *Wheat v Lacon*-type approach taken.

The difficulty is with the lender whose relationship with the land is less intimate than that of the mortgagee in possession. This includes mortgagees not in possession, banks handling rents, and receivers. The problem is that "owner" and "occupier" in the EPA are undefined, and may be sufficiently flexible to include such persons should the judicial will dictate.

It is a simple point, but one worth re-stating, that Parliament could have excluded mortgagees not in possession from an express definition of "owner", as it did in the WRA definition. It chose not to do so in the EPA (and even in the WRA to do so for some purposes only).

The risks for lenders who handle rents are clear from the COPA and WRA meanings of "owner" as considered in the context of receivers in *Solomons v Gertzenstein* and banks in *Midland Bank v Conway*. If the concept of receipt of rents "as agent" is included then there is a straight choice between the two approaches in those cases. Of course of the two, lenders would prefer *Midland Bank v Conway*. And in terms of the 'anti-analogy principle', it is compelling that *Midland Bank v Conway* may even satisfy Lord Mustill's strict "purpose" and "context" test (for statutory nuisance under the EPA at least) being concerned specifically with an abatement notice for statutory nuisance. But in seeking to rely on the approach there, the vital question is whether the lender satisfies what was referred to there as a "special relationship". Once more the dangers of becoming too 'involved' are apparent: indeed, it may be that the sort of 'involvement' which the Court in *Midland Bank v Conway* contemplated could have triggered the lender liability in that case was that which was thought capable of having a similar role in *re a Company ex parte Copp* (see Chapter 8). The problem is that the Courts did not specify what was meant by "special relationship" in either case.

Even if a receiver does not satisfy the trigger of "owner", it seems likely that he would be likely to have a sufficiently "comprehensive and stable relationship with the land" to be deemed an "occupier" for the purposes of the machinery for waste removal or abatement notices along the lines of *Southern Water Authority v Nature Conservancy Council*. This would be so even if the 'anti-analogy principle' marginalises the approach in *Meigh v Wickenden*. Similarly, *Ratford* would not assist the receiver the rating context being the most distant of all. For the mortgagee not in possession the saving notion may be the word "comprehensive".

To both the receiver and the mortgagee not in possession it is comforting that *Wheat v Lacon* has been restricted to its context by Lord Mustill. But the fact remains that it would be perfectly open to the Courts to apply a "control"/"duty" approach in the context of the EPA. As we have said already, such an approach would fit with the analysis in the last chapter as to liability arising out of the relationship with a polluting activity. In particular the policy considerations emphasizing the ability to "control" and "prevent" from that analysis are echoed in the approach of cases like *Wheat v Lacon* and *Meigh v Wickenden*, the 'strict liability' nature of which is consistent with cases like *Alphacell*, *Pegrum* and *Ashcroft*.

Covertly at least, how the Courts treat lenders in the context of their relationship with land will depend as a question of policy as to the role of the EPA. The Courts have a choice which can be illustrated by reference to comments of two Chief Justices. On the one hand, their attitude to 'lender liability' under the EPA could be like Viscount Caldecote CJ's attitude in *Meigh v Wickenden*, when holding the receiver (rather than the company) liable under the Factories Act:

> "The occupier's responsibility under the Act does not depend

> on proof of personal blame or even knowledge of the contravention ... The Factories Act 1937 is drastic in its provisions. It is clearly framed in such a way as to make it certain that someone can be found who can be convicted of an offence in the event of a contravention..."

On the other hand, the suggestion of 'lender liability' under the EPA could be treated in a similar way to that in which Lord Parker CJ in *Midland Bank v Conway* dismissed the argument that a bank could be liable to comply with an abatement notice under the PHA ([1965] 1 WLR 1165 at 1169):

> "It is ... an artificial definition; it has nothing to do with whether the person served is capable of abating the nuisance or has the authority to abate the nuisance. It is solely to enable the local authority to find someone upon whom to serve a notice..."

questions of responsibility

We have speculated that the strict liability and "control" aspects of *Meigh v Wickenden* and *Wheat v Lacon* could become the kind of approach adopted by the Courts in the context of environmental protection, and that this would tie in with the control / policy / duty analysis from the last chapter.

However, even putting this to one side, the central theme from the EPA regimes in relation to both "owner" and "occupier" is that of a duty, or responsibility at least, to investigate. The key to seeing this lies in what we have characterised as questions of "chronology".

As we have seen, liability seems to attach to the person who is "owner" or "occupier" at the following moments: the time of service of the abatement notice (s.80), the time of service of the waste removal notice (s.59), or at the time of clean-up operations (or possibly of attempted recovery of the costs) (ss.61 & 81).

What arises from this insight is that liability can attach to a person who has become "owner" or "occupier" after the relevant polluting act took place or began. The strictness of this is supported by further illustrations from the statutory nuisance schemes: for example, that liability for breach of an abatement notice can arise where the "person responsible" cannot be found (s.80); that it is expressly contemplated that the person who is liable for abatement costs ("the person who is for the time being the owner") may be different from the "owner" whose "act or default" caused the nuisance (s.81). As for waste, the "noxious gas" clean-up costs liability attaches to the "owner for the time being" (s.61). And even the costs in connection with a waste removal notice or emergency steps (s.59), where there is protection for an "innocent purchaser", the onus is on the defendant to prove his innocence (s.59).

The intention here is obvious, that in becoming "owner" or "occupier" the defendant may be assuming responsibilities in the context of statutory nuisance or waste for what has gone on before. In other words, those who become "owner" or "occupier" are assuming environmental duties which may be both strict and retroactive.

This perspective is further supported by the fact that in the context of liability under section 61 for clean-up costs in connection with "noxious gas"-type waste, Parliament has provided a water-tight method to enable the would-be "owner" to avoid or discharge his duty to the environment. This is the defence under section 61(9), for an "owner" who can show that the surrender of a waste disposal licence for the site had been formally accepted by the waste disposal authority.

What this means is that the "owner" and "occupier" provisions of the waste and statutory nuisance regimes of the EPA may be re-cast in terms of the following responsibilities, these matters being those which the Act shows that the relevant person should have taken into account:

- On the part of a person who is considering becoming "owner" of land, a responsibility to investigate:
    - whether there is any "structural defect" on the land (s.80);
    - whether there is any existing nuisance, and if so whether the "person responsible" can be found (s.80);
    - the prospects of any future nuisance (s.80);
    - whether any nuisance was caused by a previous "owner" and/or whether any abatement notice has been served (s.81);

- whether there is any waste on the land likely to give rise to the accumulation of gas or liquid which could cause pollution of the environment or harm to human health (s.61);

- whether the appropriate waste licence surrender has been accepted by the waste regulation authority (s.61);

- On the part of a person considering becoming "occupier" of the land:

  - whether there is any existing nuisance, and if so whether the "person responsible" can be found (s.80);

  - the prospects of any future nuisance (s.80);

  - whether there is any "controlled waste" present on the land (s.59);

  - whether any waste was deposited other than under a waste management licence (s.59);

  - whether he can show that he did not deposit, knowingly cause or knowingly permit such waste to be present (s.59).

This approach is consistent with a case like *Harris v Birkenhead* where the Court held, in effect, that the local authority ought to have had in mind that in serving a compulsory purchaser order it was assuming responsibilities, thereby satisfying the trigger of "occupier" under the Occupiers Liability Act. Moreover, it echoes the 'taking the rough with the smooth' notion which is identifiable from North America, that in foreclosing a mortgagee-bank assumes environmental responsibilities (*US v Maryland Bank*), as does a receiver when accepting an appointment (*Panamericana v Northern Badger*).

When approached in this way, the "owner" and "occupier" issue turns into the question:

- When should it be the responsibility of a lender to investigate the environmental status of the land with which it is concerned?

Or, put another way:

- At what stage does the lender take sufficient benefit from the land that he must be seen also to assume responsibility for its condition ?

For our purposes, the vital issue is whether the Courts will be prepared to respond to those questions with answers like the following:

- When a mortgagee is considering taking possession.

- When a receiver is considering taking an appointment in connection with the land.

- When a prospective mortgagee is considering taking a Charge over the land.

- When a bank or receiver is considering entering into a relationship where he:

  - handles rents; or

  - can "control", or "prevent" what happens on the land; or

  - will share directly in the profits of what happens on the land.

What will worry lenders and delight environmentalists is that, looked at in this way, it could be said that each of these answers would be justified.

PART IV

LENDER SELF-PROTECTION

CHAPTER 10

SAFE LENDING

(1) Aims and risks

In Chapter 7, we identified the "dual aims" of lenders, knowing the borrower and avoiding liability, and have characterised the dilemma which they face. In short, and if the metaphor can be forgiven, the lender wants to know its borrower as intimately as possible without itself becoming infected. How can it achieve these aims?

the decision to lend

The lender's primary concern, when contemplating making a loan or continuing a facility, is a full understanding of the risks. In particular, it needs to be aware of the nature and scale of any environmental liabilities which the borrower could face. The most obvious of these are things like the following: the costs of obtaining a licence; the expenditure to be incurred in complying with its terms (notably of the concept of BATNEEC); the likely level of fine in the event of an infringement; and the scale of possible clean-up costs should it all go badly wrong.

Moreover, the lender needs to ensure that it will be kept fully abreast of future developments. It will want to review loan facilities regularly, and to be able to do so on the basis of accurate information as to how the risks have changed. It needs loan terms which enable it to monitor its exposure closely, ensuring that it is provided with information as to material events. Those events include the following: whether notices have been served on the borrower; whether a prosecution has been commenced; whether the land has been entered in the "contaminated land" register.

And, as we have said, the lender's concern is not simply commercial. It will want to ensure that its public image is not threatened by its association with, and support of, environmental recklessness.

It is clear that the lender will need to think extremely carefully about how "active" or "positive" a role it takes in its borrower's affairs. This arises from the risk of incurring liability, and is exacerbated by the uncertainty as the limit to which it can go before such liability is capable of being attached.

The UK lender does not yet have the benefit of any judicial reassurance as to whether participation in "purely financial aspects of operations", as against "operational", "production" or "disposal" activities, is safe lending (*United States v Mirabile*). Or even whether it can involve itself in "discrete financial decisions" or "specific management advice" in relation to its borrower without having to foot the pollution bill (*United States v Fleet Factors*). Nor is there any domestic equivalent of USEPA's Rule, which seeks to reassure American leaders that they can take steps both prior to and during the loan without fear of incurring liability. These 'safe lending' steps, we recall, were the following. First, prior to lending: undertaking or requiring an environmental inspection; requiring clean-up or other compliance steps. Second, during the loan: inspecting the site; monitoring the borrower's business position; requiring clean-up or other compliance steps; providing financial advice; taking steps to prevent the effects of default; preventing a diminution in value of the property.

Lenders should think especially carefully about such activities as: factoring; profit-sharing; venture-capital; handling of rents; receiving of debts; authorization of transactions; board-representation and so on. These are the types of activity which would seem to approach what was contemplated by the English Courts in cases like *re a Company ex parte Copp* and *Midland Bank v Conway*.

Nor is it clear which side of the 'power to participate' (*US v Fleet Factors*) and 'actual participation' (*Mirabile*; *Guidice*) debate an English Court would be likely to take. Accordingly, the lender may be in danger even though it has not exercised "control": it could be enough that it had the power to do so. The lender could be seen, for example, to have "permitted" or "suffered" the pollution, or to be one of the "person[s] responsible" for it.

Such liability is consistent with the 'strict liability' approach of environmental cases like *Alphacell*, *Pegrum* and *Ashcroft*, the "control" tests in cases like *Berton* and *Wheat v Lacon*, and even the concept of the "best person" to ensure compliance mentioned in *Croyalgrange*. It would translate into a "duty" on the part of the lender to ensure that pollution does not take place, where the lender had the power to prevent the pollution. It might not matter, then, that the lender has not exercised the powers which it had reserved.

Indeed, the rather strange combination of robust imposition of liability and the *Sherras v De Rutzen* characterisation de-criminalising pollution offences (see *Alphacell* and *Pegrum*) could be precisely the kind of policy recipe to enable the courts readily to contemplate lender liability.

Another dimension is that lenders should think twice before presenting their environmental awareness or expertise to their customers. The consequence of being seen, through advertising or assurances, to have assumed the role of "environmental adviser" would give a *Hedley Byrne* or *Woods v Martins Bank* route around cases like *Barnes* and *Redmond*, such that the lender could be in breach of a duty to advise or warn its customer.

We have stressed throughout the theme of 'control'. It would seem prudent for lenders to restrict the extent to which they exercise influence over their customers, or insist on the capacity to do so. But it is certainly not possible for lenders to completely distance themselves from knowledge of their customers' activities. Apart from being commercially foolish, such a course would mean that lenders would be depriving themselves of those parts of the environmental law machinery which could assist them (registers, licences, surrenders etc). Also, paradoxically, the lender's "scrutiny" could earn it not only the status of potential defendant but an effective defence to any prosecution: for example, by showing "due diligence" under section 33 of the EPA. And in distancing themselves completely, lenders could fall foul of Lord Bridge's hypothetical defendant (in *Croyalgrange*) who "had deliberately shut his eyes to the obvious or refrained from inquiry because he suspected the truth but did not want to have his suspicion confirmed".

taking security

It is also clear that the lender should be aware of the risks when contemplating taking security. We have seen the insolvency perspective in this, that a bank with an established relationship with its borrower may be at risk of a security constituting a preference (*re a Company ex parte Copp*). The important point here is that potential environmental liabilities may represent prospective or contingent liabilities for the purposes of the insolvency test.

More generally, the lender needs to be fully aware of what the security is, or may be, worth. Is there a prospect of a *Panamericana v*

Northern Badger-type situation, where a Court clean-up order might have the effect of depriving the lender of its security ? What is the true value of land anyway, when its environmental characteristics are accurately assessed ? What is the likelihood of that value decreasing as a result of environmental damage or registration as "contaminated land" ?

Importantly, the lender when taking security must be aware of the risk that when the time comes, environmental considerations may mean that it cannot enforce the security. For example, going into possession of mortgaged property may attach liabilities to the lender exceeding the debts it is owed, or it may be unable to appoint a receiver under a debenture because no-one will accept such an appointment without a full environmental indemnity from the lender. We look at these and other perils of security-enforcement in the next chapter.

Finally there is some risk that the lender's vulnerability in taking security is not simply that it may not be able to enforce its security for fear of incurring liability, but that liability may attach because of the very existence of the security, quite apart from whether it may be enforced or not.

In this respect, the issues fit into those we have already discussed, in that a crucial question may be whether the security puts the lender in a position of "control", gives it a power to prevent pollution, and can be seen to attach to it an environmental "duty".

Alternatively, looked at from the point of view of the waste and statutory nuisance regimes, the taking of the security may be the appropriate time at which the "responsibility" to investigate matters in relation to land arises. The relevant matters, we have seen are things such as: the existence of licences; whether a waste licence has been formally surrendered; whether waste on land is likely to result in "noxious gas"; whether there is "controlled waste" on the land; whether the activity on land represents a nuisance; and so on. Again, this could 'trigger' the *Wheat v Lacon*-type "control" concept or possibly the *South West Water v Nature Conservancy Council* "stable and comprehensive relationship with the land".

(2) Principles of safe lending

Trying to put all this together, we have endeavoured to come up with "ten principles of safe lending", designed to help lenders protect themselves:

1. *carry out thorough environmental investigations prior to lending: including past, present and future activities and plans*

Environmental impact assessments are already an integral part of planning law (via the 1988 Town & Country Planning (Assessment of Environmental Effects) Regulations, SI 1988 No.1199). Similarly, environmental consultants are gaining a higher profile in conveyancing, mergers & acquisitions, and lending. In the United States the environmental audit has a well-developed role in credit approval, and banks have established policies of types of environmental audit, depending on categorisation or the risk of the activity concerned: the highest risk being activities like chemical plants, radioactive material, waste disposal, etc. Those audits range from simple site visits and investigation of regulatory compliance to thorough scientific tests and surveys.

In outline, the lender is interested in the following:

- the past use of the site;
- its present use;
- plans for its future use;
- planning assessment and costs of planning consent / compliance;
- its physical condition;
- the relevant regulatory regime: relevant prohibitions; targets; trigger levels (domestic and EC);
- the appropriate licence: charges for application;
- the borrower's regulatory standing and history: applications, licences, conditions, prosecutions, surrenders, etc;
- the site's regulatory standing and history: registration, etc;
- the existence of hazardous substances at the site: its nature, location, quantity and source;

- methods of handling / disposal of such substances: including arrangements / contracts for removal, security;

- projected costs of compliance with regulations / licence conditions: eg. costs of compliance with BATNEEC;

- possible future developments as to climate and geology;

- the likely impact of licence withdrawal / suspension;

- the likely impact of an environmental accident;

- the extent to which the borrower is insured against environmental liability.

In addition lenders should devise their own questionnaire for completion by potential borrowers. Satisfactory answers should be a condition of any lending. An obligation to notify the lender of any change in the answers after lending has taken place should be imposed.

2. *investigate communications with the policing authority: registers, licences, applications and surrenders*

In conducting its investigations, it is obvious that the lender should make use of those parts of the regulatory machinery which can assist it: the registers; the detailed information required to accompany licensing applications; the terms of any licence. If a licensed activity is to continue, it is vital to ensure that there is a relevant, current permission and that its terms are being complied with to the satisfaction of the policing authority.

If the licensed activity is in the past but not the present or future, then it is vital to ensure that the relevant licence surrender has taken place, and in the case of waste that this has been formally accepted by the authority.

One avenue which may develop for lenders in due course is the possibility of direct communications with the appropriate policing authority. Lenders may find themselves able to seek comfort from the authority prior to the decision to lend, as to the nature of their borrower's activities and compliance.

They may even want to seek assurance as to their own intended role, though whether this would be given may be doubtful given the prospect of a lender later seeking to raise arguments that any assurance gave rise to a legitimate expectation, a claim in negligence or perhaps a "reasonable excuse". There may be reluctance on the part of lenders too. They may not want to encourage policing authorities to scrutinize their roles, to give them 'ideas' or fuel for any 'lender liability' action (for example presenting ready proof that the lender was aware of the risk of pollution).

It is possible, of course, that guidance may come from the relevant authorities as to how they perceive the scope of lenders' duties and potential liabilities, like USEPA's Rule in the United States.

3. make the borrower pay for, and facilitate, the investigations

One way in which the lender can seek to minimise the prospect of incurring liability through notions of "participation" or "control" arising out of its investigations is to put the onus on the borrower to obtain the relevant environmental audit and supply the relevant regulatory compliance information. This is akin perhaps to the mortgage valuation, insisted upon by a lender but required to be paid for by the borrower.

4. insist on experienced, and well-insured, environmental auditors

This is obvious. It is essential that the 'environmental auditor' used is one whose status satisfies the lender, and it is vital to ensure that there are no *Caparo v Dickman* ([1990] 2 AC 605) kind of problems as to the extent of his duty of care.

The environmental auditor will need to consider in detail the borrower's site and activities, with reference to the legal context. One of the current problems in the domestic context, is the perception that there are not (yet) environmental auditors of adequate experience and skill. That skill needs to span the scientific, legal and accountancy fields.

It is therefore vital that the environmental auditor has adequate professional indemnity insurance cover, extending to his duty to the bank who relies upon his assessment.

5. *ensure environmental security evaluation, from experienced, and well-insured, environmental surveyors/valuers*

Unlike the environmental audit, there is nothing new in insisting on an accurate valuation of the property and assets of a corporate borrower. Clearly, 'accurate' means taking into account environmental factors, including future risks.

So, where planning permission is relevant, the surveyor must address environmental questions as to why permission might be refused, or conditions which might be imposed together with their costs.

The most striking new dimension is of course the register of "contaminated land", which will directly affect the value and marketability of property. Less direct, but vitally important, are questions relating to the prospect of liability for clean-up costs, eg. whether a licence relating to a past activity has been accepted by the authority. Then there is a whole series of questions relating to assets: for example, whether plant and machinery relate to a process or method which is proscribed or obsolete.

6. *include environmental covenants and default triggers in the loan terms*

A prudent lender will want to insist on loan terms such as the following:

- representations / warranties as to: the absence of hazardous substances at the site; knowledge as to existing or potential clean-up costs liability and third party claims; any proceedings underway or contemplated relating to environmental liability; past regulatory compliance;

- covenants as to the regular reporting of regulatory compliance, and the immediate reporting of the presence of hazardous substances and knowledge of clean-up liability or third party claims or any proceedings, and of any suspension of any licence or notice served;

- the lender's right to demand information relating to environmental / regulatory compliance;

- provision that all clean-up costs and compliance costs to be borne by the borrower;

- an indemnity regarding any costs or liability incurred by the lender regarding any environmental breach;

- provision making clear that the lender's investigations are simply part of its loan underwriting activities;

- provision making clear that the lender is not controlling or managing the borrower's operations or advising it as to its financial position, environmental programme or liability;

- the duty to provide information from Board meetings;

- a term stating that the lender's offer is conditional upon regulatory compliance;

- a covenant relating to adequate environmental liability insurance;

- provision for accelerated demand or repayment upon an environmental breach.

7. *insist on regular information to allow environmental monitoring during the lending*

The nature of the environmental information which will be important to monitor during the loan term, particularly if that term is long, is the same as the information relevant prior to lending (above).

The crucial thing is to include adequate terms in the loan agreement (above), and for the lender to rely not only on information supplied by the borrower but to make its own investigations on periodic reviews of the loan facility.

Such monitoring should be introduced for old loans which involve environmental risk. The timing for introducing new requirements will be the lender's regular review of a facility.

8. *avoid "participation" and "control"*

As we have said, the lender should be aware of the risks connected with the following:

- having a representative on the borrower's board;
- direct participation in the company's affairs;
- the right of veto as to change of directors, etc;
- receipt of rents;
- factoring agreements;
- venture capital.

Moreover, a lender should make it clear, in loan terms but also correspondence, that investigations and monitoring are not intended to influence, control, or advise the borrower

9. include suitable terms in security documentation

Debenture terms may be very important, particularly in relation to the 'agency' role of a receiver and manager, and whether to give (or take) an indemnity in respect of environmental liability. We will return to this in the next chapter.

Mortgage terms could contain terms as referred to above. They could also seek to deflect the argument that, prior to enforcement at least, the security holder does not exercise control or have a comprehensive and stable relationship.

10. keep good records of what is done and why

This is an obvious point. Record-keeping is an activity at which the banks are generally good but in the context will, we think, need to be particularly good.

CHAPTER 11

SAFE DEBT-COLLECTION

Here there is a single overriding principle: 'look before you leap'. Prior to any decision as to enforcing a security, taking receipt of rents, going into possession, appointing a receiver, accepting an appointment as a receiver, and so on, the lender should conduct an environmental assessment. Lenders will be understandably keen to avoid enforcing security and then finding that the liabilities taken on exceed the debt or expenses.

Here again, in addition to the factors which relate to the borrower's potential liabilities, are the issues which concern how the environmental risks might translate into direct liability for the lender. The lender will need an accurate assessment of the liabilities of the borrower, itself and any person whom it has appointed as agent or to whom it has given an indemnity.

Many of the activities which constitute debt-collection will be the best examples of exercising the "control" contemplated in the caselaw and discussed in Chapters 8 and 9 above. And if the English Courts choose to come down on the *Mirabile/Guidice* side of "control", that actual participation rather than the power to participate (*US v Fleet Factors*) is required to trigger any lender liability, then steps taken in debt-collection are likely to be highly significant.

Moreover, there is no "secured creditor exemption" in UK (or EC) law, despite lobbying from the banking community. It could therefore be said that English Law is potentially even more far-reaching from the point of view of lenders than CERCLA in the US. And even if a CERCLA-type exemption were developed in English law, there would be the problems of "participation in management" which would underline rather than resolve the lender's dilemma.

Nor, again, is there guidance as contained in USEPA's Rule, which assures American lenders that they can take the following steps: taking title or possession of the site (if done primarily to protect the lender's security interest and if followed by reasonable steps to divest itself of the property expeditiously); maintaining business activities after foreclosure (again, if done to protect the security interest); and taking steps to prepare the site for sale.

We have seen already the potential perils of handling rents: *Solomons* where the receiver was liable for breach of statutory duty, and even *Midland Bank v Conway* where the bank would have been liable for disrepair had there been a "special relationship".

Similarly, we have mentioned that were the *re Sarflax* approach the correct one regarding persons who collect assets and distribute proceeds, then receivers/managers in particular face allegations of direct criminality for "carrying on" businesses which cause pollution. This is all the more so where the receiver chooses to allow a company's operations to continue. There the strictness of the *Meigh v Wickenden*-type approach would serve to fasten lender liability on the receiver, consistent with the *Alphacell/Ashcroft* principles and requiring no negligence or knowledge on the part of receiver or manager. What is more, debenture-holders need be aware of the possible implications of *Standard Chartered Bank v Walker*-type "interference with the receivership", even where the receiver is expressly agent of the company.

There is then the clearest-cut risk-taker, the mortgagee who chooses to take possession. We have seen hints of the implications of that decision in the context of both "owner" (*Maguire v Leigh-on-Sea; Westminster CC v Haymarket*) and "occupier" (*Poland v Earl Cadogan*).

Each of these examples is capable of satisfying the notions of "control" which we have discussed. This then, is where cases like *Meigh v Wickenden* and *Westminster CC v Haymarket* join *Wheat v Lacon*, *Alphacell*, and *Berton*.

Moreover, in the context of waste and nuisance, the debt-collector (particularly where enforcing security) can readily be seen to be given by the law the "responsibility" to investigate the existence of a licence or its formal surrender, the presence of "controlled waste", the risk of "noxious gas", the existence of a nuisance, and so on. That responsibility would be akin to the "due diligence" component of the "innocent purchaser" defence under CERCLA. And put in *Southern Water Authority v Nature Conservancy Council* terms, the "responsibility" arises from the person's "comprehensive and stable relationship with the land" such that the notice machinery can properly apply to him.

Such 'duty' language would of course correspond to the notion of 'taking the rough with the smooth' emphasised in *United States v Maryland Bank* and echoed in cases like *Panamericana v Northern Badger* and *Lord Advocate v Aero Technologies*.

In short, the lender who comes to collect debts and enforce security needs to conduct a thorough 'environmental assessment' of the potential value and risks attendant on his intended conduct before any enforcement steps are taken. Liquidators, receivers and secured creditors alike need be aware that the 'trump card' of a Court order for clean-up may be played by the policing authority, reducing or extinguishing the value of assets available for everyone else, as was achieved by the Canadian ERCB in *Panamericana v Northern Badger*.

The lender may think that the simplest course is to appoint a liquidator, so that he takes the responsibility. However at some stage the lender must elect whether to enforce its security. If it releases 'contaminated' security it will then become an unsecured creditor. The liquidator will be the agent of the company, and is unlikely to incur personal responsibility. The expenses of a 'clean-up' will be an expense in the liquidation and will take priority over unsecured debts. The advantage of liquidation to the lender faced with an insolvent polluter is that liquidation may limit the lender's liability. However it cannot limit any liability which the lender has already incurred.

The steps when assessing debt-collecting or security-enforcement as to land are very similar to those suggested in the context of 'safe lending' in the last chapter and we will not repeat them. We re-emphasize though the necessity that the auditor, surveyor, indeed lawyer involved in assisting the lender in its decision should have both adequate experience and professional indemnity cover.

Finally, when it comes to the appointment of receivers, there may well develop a 'battle of the forms' with both appointer and receiver seeking to insist on an indemnity to protect its position as to possible environmental liabilities. How this is resolved is likely to depend on practical, commercial and insurance-related considerations. But someone, whether the appointer or the receiver or both, will want to assess the receiver's potential liabilities very carefully, and will watch developments after his appointment with some anxiety.

APPENDIX A:

EXTRACT FROM ENVIRONMENTAL PROTECTION ACT 1990

NOTE: This extract is intended only as an outline.
It contains only some of the main features of the
EPA schemes as to air pollution; waste on land;
and statutory nuisance

PART I

INTEGRATED POLLUTION CONTROL AND AIR POLLUTION CONTROL BY LOCAL AUTHORITIES

1.—(1) The following provisions have effect for the interpretation of this Part.

(2)-(6) …

(7) The 'enforcing authority', in relation to England and Wales, is the chief inspector or the local authority by whom, under section 4 below, the functions conferred or imposed by this Part otherwise than on the Secretary of State are for the time being exercisable in relation respectively to releases of substances into the environment or into the air; and 'local enforcing authority' means any such local authority.

(8)-(13) …

2.—(1) The Secretary of State may, by regulations, prescribe any description of process as a process for the carrying on of which after a prescribed date an authorisation is required under section 6 below.

(2)-(7) …

3.—(1) The Secretary of State may make regulations under subsection (2) or (4) below establishing standards, objectives or requirements in relation to particular prescribed processes or particular substances.

(2)-(8) …

4.—(1) This section determines the authority by whom the functions conferred or imposed by this Part otherwise than on the Secretary of State are exercisable and the purposes for which they are exercisable.

(2) Those functions, in their application to prescribed processes designated for central control, shall be functions of the chief inspector appointed for England and Wales by the Secretary of State under section 16 below and, in relation to Scotland, of the chief inspector so appointed for Scotland or of the river purification authority, as determined under regulations made under section 5(1) below, and shall be exercisable for the purpose of preventing or minimising pollution of the environment due to the release of substances into any environmental medium.

(3) Subject to subsection (4) below, those functions, in their application to prescribed processes designated for local control, shall be functions of —

(a) in the case of a prescribed process carried on (or to be carried on) by means of mobile plant, the local authority in whose area the person carrying on the process has his principal place of business; and

(b) in any other cases, the local authority in whose area the prescribed processes are (or are to be) carried on;

and the functions applicable to such processes shall be exercisable for the purpose of preventing or minimising pollution of the environment due to the release of substances into the air (but not into any other environmental medium).

(4)-(12) …

…

6.—(1) No person shall carry on a prescribed process after the date prescribed or determined for that description of process by or under regulations under section 2(1) above (but subject to any transitional provision made by the regulations) except under an authorisation granted by the enforcing authority and in accordance with the conditions to which it is subject.

(2)-(8) …

7.—(1) There shall be included in an authorisation—

(a) subject to paragraph (b) below, such specific conditions as the enforcing authority considers appropriate, when taken with the general condition implied by subsection (4) below, for achieving the objectives specified in subsection (2) below;

(b) such conditions as are specified in directions given by the Secretary of State under subsection (3) below; and

(c) such other conditions (if any) as appear to the enforcing authority to be appropriate;

but no conditions shall be imposed for the purpose only of securing the health of persons at work (within the meaning of Part 1 of the Health and Safety at Work etc. Act 1974).

(2) Those objectives are—

(a) ensuring that, in carrying on a prescribed process, the best available techniques not entailing excessive cost will be used—

(i) for preventing the release of substances prescribed for any environmental medium into that medium or, where that is not practicable by such means, for reducing the release of such substances to a minimum and for rendering harmless any such substances which are so released; and

(ii) for rendering harmless any other substances which might cause harm if released into any environmental medium;

(b) compliance with any directions by the Secretary of State given for the implementation of any obligations of the United Kingdom under the Community Treaties or international law relating to environmental protection;

(c) compliance with any limits or requirements and achievement of any quality standards or quality objectives prescribed by the Secretary of State under any of the relevant enactments;

(d) compliance with any requirements applicable to the grant of authorisations specified by or under a plan made by the Secretary of State under section 3(5) above.

(3) …

(4) Subject to subsections (5) and (6) below, there is implied in every authorisation a general condition that, in carrying on the process to which the authorisation applies, the person carrying it on must use the best available techniques not entailing excessive cost—

(a) for preventing the release of substances prescribed for any environmental medium into that medium or, where that is not practicable by such means, for reducing the release of such substances to a minimum and for rendering harmless any such substances which are so released; and

(b) for rendering harmless any other substances which might cause harm if released into any environmental medium.

(5) …

(6) The obligation implied by virtue of subsection (4) above shall not apply in relation to any aspect of the process in question which is regulated by a condition imposed under subsection (1) above.

(7) The objectives referred to in subsection (2) above shall, where the process—

(a) is one designated for central control; and

(b) is likely to involve the release of substances into more than one environmental medium;

include the objective of ensuring that the best available techniques not entailing excessive cost will be used for minimising the pollution which may be caused to the environment taken as a whole by the releases having regard to the best practicable environmental option available as respects the substances which may be released.

(8) An authorisation for carrying on a prescribed process may, without prejudice to the generality of subsection (1) above, include conditions—

(a) imposing limits on the amount or composition of any substance produced by or utilised in the process in any period; and

(b) requiring advance notification of any proposed change in the manner of carrying on the process.

(9)...

(10) References to the best available techniques not entailing excessive cost, in relation to a process, include (in addition to references to any technical means and technology) references to the number, qualifications, training and supervision of persons employed in the process and the design, construction, lay-out and maintenance of the buildings in which it is carried on.

(11)...

(12) In subsection (2) above "the relevant enactments" are any enactments or instruments contained in or made for the time being under—

(a) section 2 of the Clean Air Act 1968;
(b) section 2 of the European Communities Act 1972;
(c) Part I of the Health and Safety at Work etc. Act 1974;
(d) Parts II, III or IV of the Control of Pollution Act 1974;
(e) Part III of the Water Act 1989; and
(f) section 3 of this Act

...

9.—(1) An authorisation for the carrying on of any prescribed process may be transferred by the holder to a person who proposes to carry on the process in the holder's place.

(2)-(3) ...

10.—(1) The enforcing authority may at any time, subject to the requirements of section 7 above, and, in cases to which they apply, the requirements of Part II of Schedule 1 to this Act, vary an authorisation and shall do so if it appears to the authority at that time that that section requires conditions to be included which are different from the subsisting conditions.

(2)-(8) ...

11.—(1) A person carrying on a prescribed process under an authorisation who wishes to make a relevant change in the process may at any time—

(a) notify the enforcing authority in the prescribed form of that fact, and

(b) request the enforcing authority to make a determination, in relation to the proposed change, of the matters mentioned in subsection (2) below;

and a person making a request under paragraph (b) above shall furnish the enforcing authority with such information as may be prescribed or as the authority may by notice require.

(2) On receiving a request under subsection (1) above the enforcing authority shall determine—

(a) whether the proposed change would involve a breach of any condition of the authorisation;

(b) if it would not involve such a breach, whether the authority would be likely to vary the conditions of the authorisation as a result of the change;

(c) if it would involve such a breach, whether the authority would consider varying the conditions of the authorisation so that the change may be made, and

(d) whether the change would involve a substantial change in the manner in which the process is being carried on;

and the enforcing authority shall notify the holder of the authorisation of its determination of those matters.

(3)-(11) …

12.—(1) The enforcing authority may at any time revoke an authorisation by notice in writing to the person holding the authorisation.

(2)-(5) …

13.—(1) If the enforcing authority is of the opinion that the person carrying on a prescribed process under an authorisation is contravening any condition of the authorisation, or is likely to contravene any such condition, the authority may serve on him a notice ("an enforcement notice").

(2) An enforcement notice shall—

(a) state that the authority is of the said opinion;

(b) specify the matters constituting the contravention or the matters making it likely that the contravention will arise, as the case may be;

(c) specify the steps that must be taken to remedy the contravention or to remedy the matters making it likely that the contravention will arise, as the case may be; and

(d) specify the period within which those steps must be taken

(3) …

14.—(1) If the enforcing authority is of the opinion, as respects the carrying on of a prescribed process under an authorisation, that the continuing to carry it on, or the continuing to carry it on in a particular manner, involves an imminent risk of serious pollution of the environment the authority shall serve a notice ("a prohibition notice") on the person carrying on the process.

(2) A prohibition notice may be served whether or not the manner of carrying on the process in question contravenes a condition of the authorisation and may relate to any aspects of the process, whether regulated by the conditions of the authorisation or not.

(3) A prohibition notice shall—

(a) state the authority's opinion;

(b) specify the risk involved in the process;

(c) specify the steps that must be taken to remove it and the period within which they must be taken; and

(d) direct that the authorisation shall, until the notice is withdrawn, wholly or to the extent specified in the notice cease to have effect to authorise the carrying on of the process;

and where the direction applies to part only of the process it may impose conditions to be observed in carrying on the part which is authorised to be carried on.

(4)-(5) ...

15.—(1) The following persons, namely:—

(a) a person who has been refused the grant of an authorisation under section 6 above;

(b) a person who is aggrieved by the conditions attached, under any provision of this Part, to his authorisation;

(c) a person who has been refused a variation of an authorisation on an application under section 11 above;

(d) a person whose authorisation has been revoked under section 12 above;

may appeal against the decision of the enforcing authority to the Secretary of State (except where the decision implements a direction of his).

(2) A person on whom a variation notice, an enforcement notice or a prohibition notice is served may appeal against the notice to the Secretary of State.

(3)-(10) ...

16.—(1) The Secretary of State may appoint as inspectors (under whatever title he may determine) such persons having suitable qualifications as he thinks necessary for carrying this Part into effect in relation to prescribed processes designated for central control or for the time being transferred under section 4(4) above to central control, and may terminate any appointment made under this subsection.

(2)-(5) …

(6) Any local authority may appoint as inspectors (under whatever title the authority may determine) such persons having suitable qualifications as the authority think necessary for carrying this Part into effect in the authority's area in relation to prescribed processes designated for local control (and not so transferred), and may terminate any appointment made under this subsection.

(7)-(8) …

17.—(1) An inspector may, on production (if so required) of his authority, exercise any of the powers in subsection (3) below for the purposes of the discharge of the functions of the enforcing authority.

(2) Those powers, so far as exercisable in relation to premises, are exercisable in relation:—

(a) to premises on which a prescribed process is, or is believed (on reasonable grounds) to be, carried on; and

(b) to premises on which a prescribed process has been carried on (whether or not the process was a prescribed process when it was carried on) the condition of which is believed (on reasonable grounds) to be such as to give rise to a risk of serious pollution of the environment.

(3) The powers of an inspector referred to above are—

(a) at any reasonable time (or, in a situation in which in his opinion there is an immediate risk of serious pollution of the environment, at any time) to enter premises which he has reason to believe it is necessary for him to enter;

(b) …

(c) to make such examination and investigation as may in any circumstances be necessary;

(d)-(l) …

(4)-(10) …

18.—(1) Where, in the case of any article or substance found by him on any premises which he has power to enter, an inspector has reasonable cause to believe that, in the circumstances in which he finds it, the article or substance is a cause of imminent danger of serious harm he may seize it and cause it to be rendered harmless (whether by destruction or otherwise).

(2)-(3) …

…

20.—(1) It shall be the duty of each enforcing authority, as respects prescribed processes for which it is the enforcing authority, to maintain, in accordance with regulations made by the Secretary of State, a register containing prescribed particulars of or relating to—

(a) applications for authorisations made to that authority;

(b) the authorisations which have been granted by that authority or in respect of which the authority has functions under this Part;

(c) variation notices, enforcement notices and prohibition notices issued by that authority;

(d) revocations of authorisations effected by that authority;

(e) appeals under section 15 above;

(f) convictions for such offences under section 23 (1) below as may be prescribed;

(g) information obtained or furnished in pursuance of the conditions of authorisations or under any provision of this Part;

(h) directions given to the authority under any provision of this Part by the Secretary of State; and

(i) such other matters relating to the carrying on of prescribed processes or any pollution of the environment caused thereby as may be prescribed;

…

(2)-(10) …

…

23.—(1) It is an offence for a person—

(a) to contravene section 6(1) above;

(b) …

(c) to fail to comply with or contravene any requirement or prohibition imposed by an enforcement notice or a prohibition notice;

(d)-(k) …

(l) to fail to comply with an order made by a court under section 26 below.

(2) A person guilty of an offence under paragraph (a), (c) or (1) of subsection (1) above shall be liable;

(a) on summary conviction, to a fine not exceeding £20,000;

(b) on conviction on indictment, to a fine or to imprisonment for a term not exceeding two years, or to both

(3)-(5) …

24.—If the enforcing authority is of the opinion that proceedings for an offence under section 23(1) (c) above would afford an ineffectual remedy against a person who has failed to comply with the requirements of an enforcement notice or a prohibition notice, the authority may take proceedings in the High Court or, in Scotland, in any court of competent jurisdiction for the purpose of securing compliance with the notice.

25.—(1) In any proceedings for an offence under section 23(1) (a) above consisting in a failure to comply with the general condition implied in every authorisation by section 7(4) above, it shall be for the accused to prove that there was no better available technique not entailing excessive cost than was in fact used to satisfy the condition.

(2) …

26.—(1) Where a person is convicted of an offence under section 23(1) (a) or (c) above in respect of any matters which appear to the court to be matters which it is in his power to remedy, the court may, in addition to or instead of imposing any punishment, order him, within such time as may be fixed by the order, to take such steps as may be specified in the order for remedying those matters.

(2)-(3) …

27.—(1) Where the commission of an offence under section 23 (1) (a) or (c) above causes any harm which it is possible to remedy, the chief inspector or, in Scotland, a river purification authority may, subject to subsection (2) below -

(a) arrange for any reasonable steps to be taken towards remedying the harm; and

(b) recover the cost of taking those steps from any person convicted of that offence.

(2) …

…

PART II

WASTE ON LAND

...

30.—(1) For the purposes of this Part the following authorities are, subject to section 31 below, waste regulation authorities, namely—

(a) for any non-metropolitan county in England, the county council;

(b) for Greater London, the authority constituted as the London Waste Regulation Authority.

(c) for the metropolitan county of Greater Manchester, the authority constituted as the Greater Manchester Waste Disposal Authority;

(d) for the metropolitan county of Merseyside, the authority constituted as the Merseyside Waste Disposal Authority;

(e) for any district in any other metropolitan county in England, the council of the district;

(f) for any district in Wales, the council of the district;

(g) in Scotland, an islands or district council;

and the authorities mentioned in paragraph (c) and (d) above shall for the purposes of their functions as waste regulation authorities be known as the Greater Manchester Waste Regulation Authority and the Merseyside Waste Regulation Authority respectively.

(2)-(8) ...

...

33.—(1) Subject to subsection (2) and (3) below and, in relation to Scotland, to section 54 below, a person shall not—

(a) deposit controlled waste, or knowingly cause or knowingly permit controlled waste to be deposited in or on any land unless a waste management licence authorising the deposit is in force and the deposit is in accordance with the licence;

(b) treat, keep or dispose of controlled waste, or knowingly cause or knowingly permit controlled waste to be treated, kept or disposed of —

(i) in or on any land, or

(ii) by means of any mobile plant

except under and in accordance with a waste management licence;

(c) treat, keep or dispose of controlled waste in a manner likely to cause pollution of the environment or harm to human health.

(2)-(5) …

(6) A person who contravenes subsection (1) above or any condition of a waste management licence commits an offence.

(7) It shall be a defence for a person charged with an offence under this section to prove—

(a) that he took all reasonable precautions and exercised all due diligence to avoid the commission of the offence; or

(b) that he acted under instructions from his employer and neither knew nor had reason to suppose that the acts done by him constituted a contravention of subsection (1) above; or

(c) that the acts alleged to constitute the contravention were done in an emergency in order to avoid danger to the public and that, as soon as reasonably practicable after they were done, particulars of them were furnished to the waste regulation authority in whose area the treatment or disposal of the waste took place.

(8) Except in a case falling within subsection (9) below, a person who commits an offence under this section shall be liable—

(a) on summary conviction, to imprisonment for a term not exceeding six months or a fine not exceeding £20,000 or both; and

(b) on conviction on indictment, to imprisonment for a term not exceeding two years or a fine or both.

(9) A person who commits an offence under this section in relation to special waste shall be liable—

(a) on summary conviction, to imprisonment for a term not exceeding six months or a fine not exceeding £20,000 or both;

(b) on conviction on indictment, to imprisonment for a term not exceeding five years or a fine or both.

34.—(1) Subject to subsection (2) below, it shall be the duty of any person who imports, produces, carries, keeps, treats or disposes of controlled waste, or as a broker, has control of such waste, to take all such measures applicable to him in that capacity as are reasonable in the circumstances—

(a) to prevent any contravention by any other person of section 33 above;

(b) to prevent the escape of the waste from his control or that of any other person; and

(c) on the transfer of the waste, to secure

(i) that the transfer is only to an authorised person or to a person for authorised transport purposes; and

(ii) that there is transferred such a written description of the waste as will enable other persons to avoid a contravention of that section and to comply with the duty under this subsection as respects the escape of waste.

(2)-(5) …

(6) Any person who fails to comply with the duty imposed by subsection (1) above or with any requirement imposed under subsection (5) above shall be liable—

(a) on summary conviction, to a fine not exceeding the statutory maximum; and

(b) on conviction on indictment, to a fine.

(7) The Secretary of State shall, after consultation with such persons or bodies as appear to him representative of the interests concerned, prepare and issue a code of practice for the purpose of providing to persons practical guidance on how to discharge the duty imposed on them by subsection (1) above.

(8)-(9) …

(10) A code of practice issued under subsection (7) above shall be admissible in evidence and if any provision of such a code appears to the court to be relevant to any question arising in the proceedings it shall be taken into account in determining that question.

(11) …

35.—(1) A waste management licence is a licence granted by a waste regulation authority authorising the treatment, keeping or disposal of any specified description of controlled waste in or on specified land or the treatment or disposal of any specified description of controlled waste by means of specified mobile plant.

(2) A licence shall be granted to the following person, that is to say—

(a) in the case of a licence relating to the treatment, keeping or disposal of waste in or on land, to the person who is in occupation of the land; and

(b) in the case of a licence relating to the treatment or disposal of waste by means of mobile plant, to the person who operates the plant.

(3) A licence shall be granted on such terms and subject to such conditions as appear to the waste regulation authority to be appropriate and the conditions may relate—

(a) to the activities which the licence authorises, and

(b) to the precautions to be taken and works to be carried out in connection with or in consequence of those activities;

and accordingly requirements may be imposed in the licence which are to be complied with before the activities which the licence authorises have begun or after the activities which the licence authorises have ceased

(4)-(8) ….

(9) A licence may not be surrendered by the holder except in accordance with section 39 below.

(10) A licence is not transferable by the holder but the waste regulation authority may transfer it to another person under section 40 below.

(11) A licence shall continue in force until it is revoked entirely by the waste regulation authority under section 38 below or it is surrendered or its surrender is accepted under section 39 below.

(12) …

36.—(1)-(2) …

(3) Subject to subsection (2) above and subsection (4) below, a waste regulation authority to which an application for a licence has been duly made shall not reject the application if it is satisfied that the applicant is a fit and proper person unless it is satisfied that its rejection is necessary for the purpose of preventing—

(a) pollution of the environment;

(b) harm to human health; or

(c) serious detriment to the amenities of the locality;

but paragraph (c) above is inapplicable where planning permission is in force in relation to the use to which the land will be put under the licence.

(4)-(10) …

37.—(1) While a licence issued by a waste regulation authority is in force, the authority may, subject to regulations under section 35(6) above and to subsection (3) below,—

(a) on its own initiative, modify the conditions of the licence to any extent which, in the opinion of the authority, is desirable and is unlikely to require unreasonable expense on the part of the holder; and

(b) on the application of the licence holder accompanied by the prescribed fee payable under section 41 below, modify the conditions of his licence to the extent requested in the application.

(2)-(6) ...

38.—(1) Where a licence granted by a waste regulation authority is in force and it appears to the authority—

(a) that the holder of the licence has ceased to be a fit and proper person by reason of his having been convicted of a relevant offence; or

(b) that the continuation of the activities authorised by the licence would cause pollution of the environment or harm to human health or would be seriously detrimental to the amenities of the locality affected; and

(c) that the pollution, harm or detriment cannot be avoided by modifying the conditions of the licence;

the authority may exercise, as it thinks fit, either of the powers conferred by subsections (3) and (4) below.

(2) ...

(3) The authority may, under this subsection, revoke the licence so far as it authorises the carrying on of the activities specified in the licence or such of them as the authority specifies in revoking the licence.

(4) The authority may, under this subsection, revoke the licence entirely.

(5) ...

(6) Where a licence granted by a waste regulation authority is in force and it appears to the authority -

(a) that the holder of the licence has ceased to be a fit and proper person by reason of the management of the activities authorised by the licence having ceased to be in the hands of a technically competent person, or

(b) that serious pollution of the environment or serious harm to human health has resulted from, or is about to be caused by, the activities to which the licence relates or the happening or threatened happening of an event affecting those activities; and

(c) that the continuing to carry on those activities, or any of those activities, in the circumstances will continue, or as the case may be, cause serious pollution of the environment or serious harm to human health;

the authority may suspend the licence so far as it authorises the carrying on of the activities specified in the licence or such of them as the authority specifies in suspending the licence.

(7)-(8) …

(9) Where a licence is suspended under subsection (6) above, the authority, in suspending it or at any time while it is suspended, may require the holder of the licence to take such measures to deal with or avert the pollution or harm as the authority considers necessary.

(10) A person who, without reasonable excuse, fails to comply with any requirement imposed under subsection (9) above otherwise than in relation to special waste shall be liable—

(a) on summary conviction, to a fine of an amount not exceeding the statutory maximum; and

(b) on conviction on indictment, to imprisonment for a term not exceeding two years or a fine or both.

(11) A person who, without reasonable excuse, fails to comply with any requirement imposed under subsection (9) above in relation to special waste shall be liable—

(a) on summary conviction, to imprisonment for a term not exceeding six months or a fine not exceeding the statutory maximum or both; and

(b) on conviction on indictment, to imprisonment for a term not exceeding five years or a fine or both.

(12) …

39.—(1) A licence may be surrendered by its holder to the authority which granted it but, in the case of a site licence, only if the authority accepts the surrender.

(2)-(5) …

(6) If the authority is satisfied that the condition of the land is unlikely to cause the pollution or harm mentioned in subsection (5) above, the authority shall, subject to subsection (7) below, accept the surrender of the licence; but otherwise the authority shall refuse to accept it.

(7)-(8) …

(9) Where the surrender of a licence is accepted under this section the authority shall issue to the applicant, with the notice of its determination, a certificate (a "certificate of completion") stating that it is satisfied as mentioned in subsection (6) above and, on the issue of that certificate, the licence shall cease to have effect.

(10)-(11) …

40.—(1) …

(2) Where the holder of a licence desires that the licence be transferred to another person ("the proposed transferee") the licence holder and the proposed transferee shall jointly make an application to the waste regulation authority which granted the licence for a transfer of it.

(3)-(6) ...

...

42.—(1) While a licence is in force it shall be the duty of the waste regulation authority which granted the licence to take the steps needed—

(a) for the purpose of ensuring that the activities authorised by the licence do not cause pollution of the environment or harm to human health or become seriously detrimental to the amenities of the locality affected by the activities; and

(b) for the purpose of ensuring that the conditions of the licence are complied with.

(2) ...

(3) For the purpose of performing the duty imposed on it by subsection (1) above, any officer of the authority authorised in writing for the purpose by the authority may, if it appears to him that by reason of an emergency it is necessary to do so, carry out work on the land or in relation to plant or equipment on the land to which the licence relates or, as the case may be, in relation to the mobile plant to which the licence relates.

(4) Where a waste regulation authority incurs any expenditure by virtue of subsection (3) above, the authority may recover the amount of the expenditure from the holder of the licence or, if the licence has been surrendered, from the former holder of it, except where the holder or former holder of the licence shows that there was no emergency requiring any work or except such of the expenditure as he shows was unnecessary.

(5) Where it appears to a waste regulation authority that a condition of a licence granted by it is not being complied with, then, without prejudice to any proceedings under section 33(6) above, the authority may -

(a) require the licence holder to comply with the condition within a specified time; and

(b) if in the opinion of the authority the licence holder has not complied with the condition within that time, exercise any of the powers specified in subsection (6) below.

(6) The powers which become exercisable in the event mentioned in subsection 5(b) above are the following -

(a) to revoke the licence so far as it authorises the carrying on of the activities specified in the licence or such of them as the authority specifies in revoking the licence;

(b) to revoke the licence entirely; and

(c) to suspend the licence so far as it authorises the carrying on of the activities specified in the licence or, as the case may be, the activities specified by the authority in suspending the licence.

(7)-(8) …

43.—(1) Where, except in pursuance of a direction given by the Secretary of State,—

(a) an application for a licence or a modification of the conditions of a licence is rejected;

(b) a licence is granted subject to conditions;

(c) the conditions of a licence are modified;

(d) a licence is suspended;

(e) a licence is revoked under section 38 or 42 above;

(f) an application to surrender a licence is rejected; or

(g) an application for the transfer of a licence is rejected;

then, except in the case of an application for a transfer, the applicant for the licence or, as the case may be, the holder or former holder of it may appeal from the decision to the Secretary of State and, in the case of an application for a transfer, the proposed transferee may do so.

(2)-(8) …

…

59.—(1) If any controlled waste is deposited in or on any land in the area of a waste regulation authority or waste collection authority in contravention of section 33(1) above, the authority may, by notice served on him, require the occupier to do either or both of the following, that is—

(a) to remove the waste from the land within a specified period not less than a period of twenty one days beginning with the service of the notice;

(b) to take within such a period specified steps with a view to eliminating or reducing the consequences of the deposit of the waste.

(2) A person on whom any requirements are imposed under subsection (1) above may, within the period of twenty one days mentioned in that subsection, appeal against

the requirement to a magistrates' court, or in Scotland, to the sheriff by way of summary application.

(3) On any appeal under subsection (2) above the court shall quash the requirement if it is satisfied that -

(a) the appellant neither deposited nor knowingly caused nor knowingly permitted the deposit of the waste; or

(b) there is a material defect in the notice;

and in any other case shall either modify the requirement or dismiss the appeal.

(4) ....

(5) If a person on whom a requirement imposed under subsection (1) above fails, without reasonable excuse, to comply with the requirement he shall be liable, on summary conviction, to a fine not exceeding level 5 on the standard scale and to a further fine of an amount equal to one tenth of level 5 on the standard scale for each day on which the failure continues after conviction of the offence and before the authority has begun to exercise its powers under subsection (6) below.

(6) Where a person on whom a requirement has been imposed under subsection (1) above by an authority fails to comply with the requirement the authority may do what that person was required to do and may recover from him any expenses reasonably incurred by the authority in doing it.

(7) If it appears to a waste regulation authority or waste collection authority that waste has been deposited in or on any land in contravention of section 33(1) above and that—

(a) in order to remove or prevent pollution of land, water or air or harm to human health it is necessary that the waste be forthwith removed or other steps taken to eliminate or reduce the consequences of the deposit or both; or

(b) there is no occupier of the land; or

(c) the occupier neither made nor knowingly permitted the deposit of the waste;

the authority may remove the waste from the land or take other steps to eliminate or reduce the consequences of the deposit or, as the case may require, to remove the waste and take those steps.

(8) Where an authority exercises any of the powers conferred on it by subsection (7) above it shall be entitled to recover the cost incurred by it in removing the waste or taking the steps or both and in disposing of the waste—

(a) in a case falling within subsection 7(a) above from the occupier of the land unless he proves that he neither made nor knowingly caused nor knowingly permitted the deposit of the waste;

(b) in any case, from any person who deposited or knowingly caused or knowingly permitted the deposit of any of the waste;

except such of the cost as the occupier or that person shows was incurred unnecessarily.

(9) …

…

61.—(1) Except as respects land in relation to which a site licence is in force, it shall be the duty of every waste regulation authority to cause its area to be inspected from time to time to detect whether any land is in such a condition, by reason of the relevant matters affecting the land, that it may cause pollution of the environment or harm to human health.

(2) The matters affecting land relevant for the purposes of this section are the concentration or accumulation in, and emission or discharge from, the land of noxious gases or noxious liquids caused by deposits of controlled waste in the land.

(3)-(6) …

(7) Where, on an inspection by a waste regulation authority of any land under this section, it appears to the authority that the condition of the land is, by reason of the relevant matters affecting the land, such that pollution of the environment or harm to human health is likely to be caused it shall be the duty of the authority to do such works and take such other steps (whether on the land affected or on adjacent land) as appear to the authority to be reasonable to avoid such pollution or harm.

(8) Where an authority exercises in relation to waste on any land the duty imposed by subsection (7) above, the authority shall, except in a case falling within subsection (9) below, be entitled to recover the cost or part of the cost incurred in doing so from the person who is for the time being the owner of the land, except such of the cost as that person shows was incurred unreasonably.

(9) Subsection (8) above does not apply in a case where the authority accepted the surrender under section 39 above of the waste management licence which authorised the activities in the course of which the waste was deposited.

(10) In deciding whether to recover the cost and, if so, how much to recover of the cost which it is entitled to recover under subsection (8) above, the authority shall have regard to any hardship which the recovery may cause to the owner of the land.

(11) …

…

64.—(1) Subject to sections 65 and 66 below, it shall be the duty of each waste regulation authority to maintain a register containing prescribed particulars of or relating to—

(a) current or recently current licences ('licenses') granted by the authority;

(b) current or recently current applications to the authority for licences;

(c) applications made to the authority under section 37 above for the modification of licences;

(d) notices issued by the authority under section 37 above effecting the modification of licences;

(e) notices issued by the authority under section 38 above effecting the revocation or suspension of licences or imposing requirements on the holders of licences;

(f) appeals under section 43 above relating to decisions of the authority;

(g) certificates of completion issued by the authority under section 39(9) above;

(h) notices issued by the authority imposing requirements on the holders of licenses under section 42(5) above;

(i) convictions of the holders of licences granted by the authority for any offence under this Part (whether in relation to a licence so granted or not);

(j) the occasions on which the authority has discharged any function under section 42 or 61 above;

(k) directions given to the authority under any provision of this Part by the Secretary of State;

(l) in Scotland, resolutions made by the authority under section 54 above;

(m) such matters relating to the treatment, keeping or disposal of waste in the area of the authority or any pollution of the environment caused thereby as may be prescribed;

and any other document or information required to be kept in the register under any provision of this Act.

(2)-(8) …

…

68.—(1) …

(2) The Secretary of State may appoint as inspectors (under whatever title he may determine) such persons having suitable qualifications as he thinks necessary for assisting him in discharging his functions under this Part, and may terminate any appointment made under this subsection.

(3)-(5) …

69.—(1) An inspector may, on production (if so required) of his authority, exercise any of the powers specified in subsection (3) below for the purpose of—

(a) discharging any functions conferred or imposed by or under this Part on the Secretary of State or, as the case may be, a waste regulation authority or on the inspector;

(b) determining whether, and if so in what manner, such a function should be discharged; or

(c) determining whether any provision of this Part or of an instrument under it is being complied with.

(2) Those powers are exercisable in relation to—

(a) land in or on which, or vessels in or by means of which, controlled waste is being or has been deposited, treated, kept or disposed of;

(b) land in or on which, or vessels in or by means of which, controlled waste is (on reasonable grounds) believed to be being, or to have been, deposited, treated, kept or disposed of;

(c) land which is or is (on reasonable grounds) believed to be affected by the deposit, treatment, keeping or disposal of controlled waste on other land;

and in this section "premises" means any such land or any such vessel.

(3) The powers of an inspector referred to above are—

(a) at any reasonable time (or, in a situation in which in his opinion there is an immediate risk of serious pollution of the environment or serious harm to human health, at any time) to enter premises which he has reason to believe it is necessary for him to enter;

(b) ...

(c) to make such examination and investigation as may in any circumstances be necessary;

(d)-(k) ...

(4)-(8) ...

(9) Any person who—

(a) fails, without reasonable excuse, to comply with any requirement imposed under this section;

(b) prevents any other person from appearing before or from answering any question to which an inspector may by virtue of subsection (3) above require an answer; or

(c) intentionally obstructs an inspector in the exercise or performance of his powers or duties;

shall be liable, on summary conviction, to a fine not exceeding level 5 on the standard scale.

(10)-(11) ...

70.—(1) Where, in the case of any article or substance found by him on any premises which he has power to enter, an inspector has reasonable cause to believe that, in the circumstances in which he finds it, the article or substance is a cause of imminent danger of serious pollution of the environment or serious harm to human health, he may seize it and cause it to be rendered harmless (whether by destruction or otherwise).

(2)-(4) ...

...

73.—(1)-(5) ...

(6) Where any damage is caused by waste which has been deposited in or on land, any person who deposited it, or knowingly caused or knowingly permitted it to be deposited, in either case so as to commit an offence under section 33(1) or 63(2) above, is liable for the damage except where the damage—

(a) was due wholly to the fault of the person who suffered it; or

(b) was suffered by a person who voluntarily accepted the risk of the damage being caused;

but without prejudice to any liability arising otherwise than under this subsection.

(7) The matters which may be proved by way of defence under section 33(7) above may be proved also by way of defence to an action brought under subsection (6) above.

(8) In subsection (6) above—

"damage" includes the death of, or injury to, any person (including any disease and any impairment of physical or mental condition); and

"fault" has the same meaning as in the Law Reform (Contributory Negligence) Act 1945.

(9) ...

74.—(1) The following provisions apply for the purposes of the discharge by a waste regulation authority of any function under this Part which requires the authority to determine whether a person is or is not a fit and proper person to hold a waste management licence.

(2) ...

(3) Subject to subsection (4) below, a person shall be treated as not being a fit and proper person if it appears to the authority—

(a)-(b) …

(c) that the person who holds or is to hold the licence has not made and either has no intention of making or is in no position to make financial provision adequate to discharge the obligations arising from the licence.

(4)-(7) …

…

PART III

STATUTORY NUISANCES AND CLEAN AIR

79.—(1) Subject to subsections (2) to (6) below, the following matters constitute "statutory nuisances" for the purpose of this Part, that is to say—

(a) any premises in such a state as to be prejudicial to health or a nuisance;

(b) smoke emitted from premises so as to be prejudicial to health or a nuisance;

(c) fumes or gases emitted from premises so as to be prejudicial to health or a nuisance;

(d) any dust, steam, smell or other effluvia arising on industrial, trade or business premises and being prejudicial to health or a nuisance;

(e) any accumulation or deposit which is prejudicial to health or a nuisance;

(f) any animal kept in such a place or manner as to be prejudicial to health or a nuisance;

(g) noise emitted from premises so as to be prejudicial to health or a nuisance;

(h) any other matter declared by any enactment to be a statutory nuisance;

and it shall be the duty of every local authority to cause its area to be inspected from time to time to detect any statutory nuisances which ought to be dealt with under section 80 below and, where a complaint of a statutory nuisance is made to it by a person living within its area, to take such steps as are reasonably practicable to investigate the complaint.

(2)-(6) …

(7) In this Part—

…

"person responsible", in relation to a statutory nuisance, means the person to whose act, default or sufferance the nuisance is attributable;

...

(8) ...

(9) In this Part "best practicable means" is to be interpreted by reference to the following provisions—

(a) "practicable" means reasonably practicable having regard among other things to local conditions and circumstances, to the current state of technical knowledge and to the financial implications;

(b) the means to be employed include the design, installation, maintenance and manner and periods of operation of plant and machinery, and the design, construction and maintenance of buildings and structures.

(c) the test is to apply only so far as compatible with any duty imposed by law;

(d) the test is to apply only so far as compatible with safety and safe working conditions, and with the exigencies of any emergency or unforeseeable circumstances.

and, in circumstances where a code of practice under section 71 of the Control of Pollution Act 1974 (noise minimisation) is applicable, regard shall also be had to guidance given in it.

(10)-(12) ...

80.—(1) Where a local authority is satisfied that a statutory nuisance exists, or is likely to occur or recur, in the area of the authority, the local authority shall serve a notice ("an abatement notice") imposing all or any of the following requirements—

(a) requiring the abatement of the nuisance or prohibiting or restricting its occurrence or recurrence;

(b) requiring the execution of such works, and the taking of such other steps, as may be necessary for any of those purposes,

and the notice shall specify the time or times within which the requirements of the notice are to be complied with.

(2) The abatement notice shall be served—

(a) except in a case falling within paragraph (b) or (c) below, on the person responsible for the nuisance;

(b) where the nuisance arises from any defect of a structural character, on the owner of the premises;

(c) where the person responsible for the nuisance cannot be found or the nuisance has not yet occurred, on the owner or occupier of the premises.

(3) The person served with the notice may appeal against the notice to a magistrates' court within the period of twenty one days beginning with the date on which he was served with the notice.

(4) If a person on whom an abatement notice is served, without reasonable excuse, contravenes or fails to comply with any requirement or prohibition imposed by the notice, he shall be guilty of an offence.

(5) Except in a case falling within subsection (6) below, a person who commits an offence under subsection (4) above shall be liable on summary conviction to a fine not exceeding level 5 on the standard scale together with a further fine of an amount equal to one tenth of that level for each day on which the offence continues after the conviction.

(6) A person who commits an offence under subsection (4) above on industrial, trade or business premises shall be liable on summary conviction to a fine not exceeding £20,000.

(7) Subject to subsection (8) below, in any proceedings for an offence under subsection (4) above in respect of a statutory nuisance it shall be a defence to prove that the best practicable means were used to prevent, or to counteract the effects of, the nuisance.

(8) The defence under subsection (7) above is not available—

(a) in the case of a nuisance falling within paragraph (a), (d), (e), (f) or (g) of section 79(1) above except where the nuisance arises on industrial, trade or business premises;

(b) in the case of a nuisance falling within paragraph (b) of section 79(1) above except where the smoke is emitted from a chimney; and

(c) in the case of a nuisance falling within paragraph (c) or (h) of section 79(1) above.

(9)-(10) …

81.—(1) Where more than one person is responsible for a statutory nuisance section 80 above shall apply to each of those persons whether or not what any one of them is responsible for would by itself amount to a nuisance.

(2) …

(3) Where an abatement notice has not been complied with the local authority may, whether or not they take proceedings for an offence under section 80(4) above, abate the nuisance and do whatever may be necessary in execution of the notice.

(4) Any expenses reasonably incurred by a local authority in abating, or preventing the recurrence of, a statutory nuisance under subsection (3) above may be recovered by them from the person by whose act or default the nuisance was caused and, if that person is the owner of the premises, from any person who is for the time being the owner thereof; and the court may apportion the expenses between persons by whose acts or defaults the nuisance is caused in such manner as the court consider fair and reasonable.

(5) If a local authority is of the opinion that proceedings for an offence under section 80(4) above would afford an inadequate remedy in the case of any statutory nuisance, they may, subject to subsection (6) below, take proceedings in the High Court for the purpose of securing the abatement, prohibition or restriction of the nuisance, and the proceedings shall be maintainable notwithstanding the local authority have suffered no damage from the nuisance.

(6)-(7) …

82.—(1) A magistrates' court may act under this section on a complaint made by any person on the ground that he is aggrieved by the existence of a statutory nuisance.

(2) If the magistrates' court is satisfied that the alleged nuisance exists, or that although abated it is likely to recur on the same premises, the court shall make an order for either or both of the following purposes -

(a) requiring the defendant to abate the nuisance within a time specified in the order, and to execute any works necessary for that purpose;

(b) prohibiting a recurrence of the nuisance, and requiring the defendant within a time specified in the order, to execute any works necessary to prevent the recurrence;

and may also impose on the defendant a fine not exceeding level 5 on the standard scale.

(3) …

(4) Proceedings for an order under subsection (2) above shall be brought -

(a) except in a case falling within paragraph (b) or (c) below, against the person responsible for the nuisance;

(b) where the nuisance arises from any defect of a structural character, against the owner of the premises;

(c) where the person responsible for the nuisance cannot be found, against the owner or occupier of the premises.

(5) Where more than one person is responsible for a statutory nuisance, subsections (1) to (4) above shall apply to each of those persons whether or not what any one of them is responsible for would by itself amount to a nuisance.

(6)-(7) …

(8) A person who, without reasonable excuse, contravenes any requirement or prohibition imposed by an order under subsection (2) above shall be guilty of an offence and liable on summary conviction to a fine not exceeding level 5 on the standard scale together with a further fine of an amount equal to one tenth of that level for each day on which the offence continues after the conviction.

(9) Subject to subsection (10) below, in any proceedings for an offence under subsection (8) above in respect of a statutory nuisance it shall be a defence to prove that the best practicable means were used to prevent, or to counteract the effects of, the nuisance.

(10) The defence under subsection (9) above is not available—

(a) in the case of a nuisance falling within paragraph (a), (d), (e), (f) or (g) of section 79(1) above except where the nuisance arises on industrial, trade or business premises;

(b) in the case of a nuisance falling within paragraph (b) of section 79(1) above except where the smoke is emitted from a chimney.

(c) in the case of a nuisance falling within paragraph (c) or (h) of section 79(1) above; and

(d) in the case of a nuisance which is such as to render the premises unfit for human habitation.

(11)-(13) ...

...

PART VIII

MISCELLANEOUS

143.—(1) For the purposes of the registers to be maintained under this section, the Secretary of State may, by regulations—

(a) specify contaminative uses of land;

(b) prescribe the form of the registers and the particulars to be included in them; and

(c) make such other provision as appears to him to be appropriate in connection with the maintenance of the registers.

(2) It shall be the duty of a local authority, as respects land in its area subject to contamination, to maintain, in accordance with the regulations, a register in the prescribed form and containing the prescribed particulars.

(3) The duty imposed by subsection (2) above on a local authority is a duty to compile and maintain the register from the information available to the authority from time to time.

(4)-(5) …

(6) In this section—

"contaminative use" means any use of land which may cause it to be contaminated with noxious substances;

"land subject to contamination" means land which is being or has been put to a contaminative use;

…

…

PART IX

GENERAL

156.—(1) The Secretary of State may by regulations provide that the provisions to which this section applies shall have effect with such modifications as may be prescribed for the purpose of enabling Her Majesty's Government in the United Kingdom—

(a) to give effect to any Community obligation or exercise any related right; or

(b) to give effect to any obligation or exercise any related right under any international agreement to which the United Kingdom is for the time being a party.

(2) This section applies to the following provisions of this Act—

(a) Part I;

(b) Part II;

(c) Part VI; and

(d) Part VIII, sections 140, 141 or 142;

and the provisions of the Radioactive Substances Act 1960.

(3) In this section—

"modifications" includes additions, alterations and omissions;

"prescribed" means prescribed in regulations under this section; and

"related right", in relation to an obligation, includes any derogation or other right to make more onerous provisions available in respect of that obligation.

(4) …

157.—(1) Where an offence under any provision of this Act committed by a body corporate is proved to have been committed with the consent or connivance of, or to have been attributable to any neglect on the part of, any director, manager, secretary or other similar officer of the body corporate or a person who was purporting to act in any such capacity, he as well as the body corporate shall be guilty of that offence and shall be liable to be proceeded against and punished accordingly.

(2) Where the affairs of a body corporate are managed by its members, subsection (1) above shall apply in relation to the acts or defaults of a member in connection with his functions of management as if he were a director of the body corporate.

158.—Where the commission by any person of an offence under Part I, II, IV, or VI, or section 140,141 or 142 above is due to the act or default of some other person, that other person may be charged with and convicted of the offence by virtue of this section whether or not proceedings for the offence are taken against the first-mentioned person.

...

SCHEDULE 3

STATUTORY NUISANCES: SUPPLEMENTARY PROVISIONS

...

2.—(1) Subject to sub-paragraph (2) below, any person authorised by a local authority may, on production (if so required) of his authority, enter any premises at any reasonable time—

(a) for the purpose of ascertaining whether or not a statutory nuisance exists; or

(b) for the purpose of taking any action, or executing any work, authorised or required by Part III.

(2)-(7) ...

...

APPENDIX B;

EXTRACT FROM WATER RESOURCES ACT 1991

NOTE: This extract is intended only as an outline.
It contains only some of the main features
of the WRA scheme as to water pollution.

PART III

CONTROL OF POLLUTION OF WATER RESOURCES

CHAPTER I

QUALITY OBJECTIVES

82.—(1) The Secretary of State may, in relation to any description of controlled waters (being a description applying to some or all of the waters of a particular class or of two or more different classes), by regulations prescribe a system of classifying the quality of those waters according to criteria specified in the regulations.

(2) …

83.—(1) For the purpose of maintaining and improving the quality of controlled waters the Secretary of State may, by serving a notice on the Authority specifying—

(a) one or more of the classifications for the time being prescribed under section 82 above; and

(b) in relation to each specified classification, a date,

establish the water quality objectives for any waters which are, or are included in, waters of a description prescribed for the purposes of that section.

(2)-(6) …

…

CHAPTER II

POLLUTION OFFENCES

85.—(1) A person contravenes this section if he causes or knowingly permits any poisonous, noxious or polluting matter or any solid waste matter to enter any controlled waters.

(2) A person contravenes this section if he causes or knowingly permits any matter, other than trade effluent or sewage effluent, to enter controlled waters by being discharged from a drain or sewer in contravention of a prohibition imposed under section 86 below.

(3) A person contravenes this section if he causes or knowingly permits any trade effluent or sewage effluent to be discharged—

(a) into any controlled waters; or

(b) from land in England and Wales, through a pipe, into the sea outside the seaward limits of controlled waters.

(4) A person contravenes this section if he causes or knowingly permits any trade effluent or sewage effluent to be discharged, in contravention of any prohibition imposed under section 86 below, from a building or from any fixed plant—

(a) on to or into any land; or

(b) into any waters of a lake or pond which are not inland freshwaters.

(5) A person contravenes this section if he causes or knowingly permits any matter whatever to enter any inland freshwaters so as to tend (either directly or in combination with other matter which he or another person causes or permits to enter those waters) to impede the proper flow of the waters in a manner leading, or likely to lead, to a substantial aggravation of -

(a) pollution due to other causes; or

(b) the consequences of such pollution.

(6) Subject to the following provisions of this Chapter, a person who contravenes this section or the conditions of any consent given under this Chapter for the purposes of this section shall be guilty of an offence and liable—

(a) on summary conviction, to imprisonment for a term not exceeding three months or to a fine not exceeding £20,000 or to both;

(b) on conviction on indictment, to imprisonment for a term not exceeding two years or to a fine or to both.

86.—(1) For the purposes of section 85 above a discharge of any effluent or other matter is, in relation to any person, in contravention of a prohibition imposed under this section if, subject to the following provisions of this section -

(a) the Authority has given that person notice prohibiting him from making or, as the case may be, continuing the discharge; or

(b) the Authority has given that person notice prohibiting him from making or, as the case may be, continuing the discharge unless specified conditions are observed, and those conditions are not observed.

(2) For the purposes of section 85 above a discharge of any effluent or other matter is also in contravention of a prohibition imposed under this section if the effluent or matter discharged—

(a) contains a prescribed substance or a prescribed concentration of such a substance; or

(b) derives from a prescribed process or from a process involving the use of prescribed substances or the use of such substances in quantities which exceed the prescribed amounts.

(3)-(6) …

88.—(1) Subject to the following provisions of this section, a person shall not be guilty of an offence under section 85 above in respect of the entry of any matter into any waters or any discharge if the entry occurs or the discharge is made under and in accordance with, or as a result of any act or omission under and in accordance with—

(a) a consent given under this Chapter or under Part II of the Control of Pollution Act 1974 (which makes corresponding provision for Scotland);

(b) an authorisation for a prescribed process designated for central control granted under Part I of the Environmental Protection Act 1990;

(c) a waste management or disposal licence;

(d) a licence granted under Part II of the Food and Environment Protection Act 1985;

(e) section 163 below or section 165 of the Water Industry Act 1991 (discharges for works purposes);

(f) any local statutory provision or statutory order which expressly confers power to discharge effluent into water; or

(g) any prescribed enactment.

(2) Schedule 10 of this Act shall have effect, subject to section 91 below, with respect to the making of applications for consents under this Chapter for the purposes of subsection (1)(a) above and with respect to the giving, revocation and modification of such consents.

(3)-(4) …

…

91.—(1) This section applies where the Authority, otherwise than in pursuance of a direction of the Secretary of State—

(a) on an application for a consent under this Chapter for the purposes of section 88(1)(a) above, has refused a consent for any discharges;

(b) in giving a discharge consent, has made that consent subject to conditions;

(c) has revoked a discharge consent, modified the conditions of any such consent or provided that any such consent which was unconditional shall be subject to conditions;

(d) has, for the purposes of paragraph 7(1) or (2) of Schedule 10 to this Act, specified a period in relation to a discharge consent without the agreement of the person who proposes to make, or makes, discharges in pursuance of that consent;

(e) has refused a consent for the purposes of section 89(4)(a) above for any deposit; or

(f) has refused a consent for the purposes of section 90 above for the doing of anything by any person or, in giving any such consent, made that consent subject to conditions.

(2) The person, if any, who applied for a consent in question, or any person whose deposits, discharges or other conduct is or would be authorised by the consent may appeal against the decision to the Secretary of State.

(3)-(8) …

CHAPTER III

POWERS TO PREVENT AND CONTROL POLLUTION

92.—(1) The Secretary of State may by regulations make provision—

(a) for prohibiting a person from having custody or control of any poisonous, noxious or polluting matter unless prescribed works and prescribed precautions and other steps have been carried out or taken for the purpose of preventing or controlling the entry of the matter into any controlled waters;

(b) for requiring a person who already has custody or control of, or makes use of, any such matter to carry out such works for that purpose and to take such precautions and other steps for that purpose as may be prescribed.

(2) Without prejudice to the generality of the power conferred by subsection (1) above, regulations under that subsection may—

(a) confer power on the Authority—

(i) to determine for the purposes of the regulations the circumstances in which a person is required to carry out works or to take any precautions or other steps; and

(ii) by notice to that person, to impose the requirement and to specify or describe the works, precautions or other steps which that person is required to carry out or take;

(b)-(c) …

…

CHAPTER IV

SUPPLEMENTAL PROVISIONS WITH RESPECT TO WATER POLLUTION

…

100.—Except in so far as this Part expressly otherwise provides and subject to the provisions of section 18 of the Interpretation Act 1978 (which relates to offences under two or more laws), nothing in this Part—

(a) confers a right of action in any civil proceedings (other than proceedings for the recovery of a fine) in respect of any contravention of this Part or any subordinate legislation, consent or other instrument made, given or issued under this Part;

(b) derogates from any right of action or other remedy (whether civil or criminal) in proceedings instituted otherwise than under this Part; or

(c) affects any restriction imposed by or under any other enactment, whether public, local or private.

…

PART VII

LAND AND WORKS POWERS

CHAPTER I

POWERS OF THE AUTHORITY

…

161.—(1) Subject to subsection (2) below, where it appears to the Authority that any poisonous, noxious or polluting matter or any solid waste matter is likely to enter, or to be or to have been present in, any controlled waters, the Authority shall be entitled to carry out the following works and operations, that is to say—

(a) in a case where the matter appears likely to enter any controlled waters, works and operations for the purpose of preventing it from doing so; or

(b) in a case where the matter appears to be or to have been present in any controlled waters, works and operations for the purpose—

(i) of removing or disposing of the matter;

(ii) of remedying or mitigating any pollution caused by its presence in the waters; or

(iii) so far as it is reasonably practicable to do so, of restoring the waters, including any flora and fauna dependent on the aquatic environment of the waters, to their state immediately before the matter became present in the waters.

(2) Nothing in subsection (1) above shall entitle the Authority to impede or prevent the making of any discharge in pursuance of a consent given under Chapter II of Part III of this Act.

(3) Where the Authority carries out any such works or operations as are mentioned in subsection (1) above, it shall, subject to subsection (4) below, be entitled to recover the expenses reasonably incurred in doing so from any person who, as the case may be—

(a) caused or knowingly permitted the matter in question to be present at the place from which it was likely, in the opinion of the Authority, to enter any controlled waters; or

(b) caused or knowingly permitted the matter in question to be present in any controlled waters.

(4)-(6) …

…

CHAPTER II

POWERS OF ENTRY

169.—(1) Any person designated in writing for the purpose by either of the Ministers or by the Authority may—

(a) enter any premises or vessel for the purpose of ascertaining whether any provision of an enactment to which this section applies, of any subordinate legislation or other instrument made by virtue of any such enactment or of any byelaws made by the Authority is being or has been contravened;

(b) …

(2) …

(3) This section applies to any enactment contained in this Act and to any other enactment under or for the purposes of which the Authority carries out functions.

…

PART VIII

INFORMATION PROVISIONS

...

190.—(1) It shall be the duty of the Authority to maintain, in accordance with regulations made by the Secretary of State, registers containing prescribed particulars of—

(a) any notices of water quality objectives or other notices served under section 83 above;

(b) applications made for consents under Chapter II of Part III of this Act;

(c) consents given under that Chapter and the conditions to which the consents are subject;

(d) certificates issued under paragraph 1(7) of Schedule 10 to this Act;

(e) the following, that is to say—

(i) samples of water or effluent taken by the Authority for the purposes of any of the water pollution provisions of this Act;

(ii) information produced by analyses of those samples;

(iii) such information with respect to samples of water or effluent taken by any other person, and the analyses of those samples, as is acquired by the Authority from any person under arrangements made by the Authority for the purposes of any of those provisions; and

(iv) the steps taken in consequence of any such information as is mentioned in any of sub-paragraphs (i) to (iii) above;

and

(f) any matter about which particulars are required to be kept in any register under section 20 of the Environmental Protection Act 1990 (particulars about authorisations for prescribed processes etc.) by the chief inspector under Part I of that Act.

(2)-(3) ...

PART IX

MISCELLANEOUS AND SUPPLEMENTAL

...

217.—(1) Where a body corporate is guilty of an offence under this Act and that offence is proved to have been committed with the consent or connivance of, or to be attributable to any neglect on the part of, any director, manager, secretary or other similar officer of the body corporate or any person who was purporting to act in any such capacity, then he, as well as the body corporate, shall be guilty of that offence and shall be liable to be proceeded against and punished accordingly.

(2) Where the affairs of a body corporate are managed by its members, subsection (1) above shall apply in relation to the acts and defaults of a member in connection with his functions of management as if he were a director of the body corporate.

(3) Without prejudice to subsections (1) and (2) above, where the commission by any person of an offence under the water pollution provisions of this Act is due to the act or default of some other person, that other person may be charged with and convicted of the offence whether or not proceedings for the offence are taken against the first mentioned person.

...

221.—(1) In this Act, except in so far as the content otherwise requires—

...

"owner" in relation to any premises, means the person who—

(a) is for the time being receiving the rack-rent of the premises, whether on his own account or as agent or trustee for another person; or

(b) would receive the rack-rent if the premises were let at a rack-rent,

but for the purposes of Schedule 2 to this Act, Chapter II of Part II of this Act and the related water resources provisions does not include a mortgagee not in possession, and cognate expressions shall be construed accordingly;

...

(2)-(9) ...

...

INDEX

United Kingdom Environmental Law Association (UKELA)

UKELA is a registered charity in a company limited by guarantee. It has currently over a thousand members from a wide range of interests including lawyers in private practice, industry, the public sector, academic and also non-lawyers.

The association aims to promote the enhancement and conservation of the environment and in particular to advance the education of the public in all matters relating to the development, teaching, application and practice of law. It holds an annual conference, issues a quarterly bulletin 'Environmental Law' and holds regular meetings.

Anyone interested in joining UKELA should contact the honorary secretary, Stephen Lloyd, at Bates Wells & Braithwaite, 61 Charterhouse Street, London EC1M 6HA.

Telephone: 071 251 1122
Facsimile: 071 251 2061